TEXAS WILD

TEXAS WILD

*The Land, Plants, and Animals
of the Lone Star State*

BY RICHARD PHELAN
PHOTOGRAPHS BY JIM BONES

A SUNRISE BOOK | E. P. DUTTON & CO., INC. | NEW YORK

Library of Congress Cataloging in Publication Data
Phelan, Richard.
  Texas wild.
  "A Sunrise book."
  Includes bibliographical references and index.
    1. Natural history—Texas.   I. Bones, Jim.
II. Title.
QH105.T4P45   1976   500.9'764   75-40490

ISBN: 0-87690-218-2

Published simultaneously in Canada by
Clarke, Irwin & Company Limited, Toronto and Vancouver

Design by Al Cetta. Line drawings by Dorothea von Elbe.

To Winnie Kennedy

CONTENTS

ACKNOWLEDGMENTS

My thanks to:

Alexander and Thais Boeringa

Fred Bullard

Bob Burleson

Howard Dodgen

Mary Beth Fleischer

Jim and Becky Garner

Mary Beth Hansell

Marshall Johnston

Kent and Lucy Keeth

Chester Kielman

Alan Macdougall

J. C. Martin

Gordon and Vody Mills

William and Virginia Ming

Robbie Morris

Warren Pulich

David and Judy Riskind

Bob Sims

John Smith

John Spinks

Al Springs

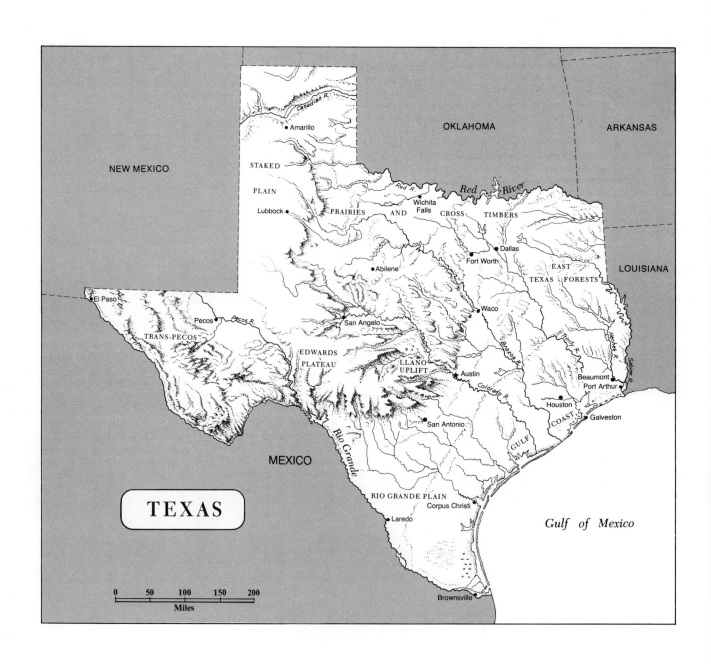

NEW MEXICO

OKLAHOMA

ARKANSAS

Canadian R.

• Amarillo

STAKED

PLAIN

Red R.

Red River

PRAIRIES

AND

CROSS

TIMBERS

Wichita
Falls

Lubbock •

• Abilene

Dallas

Fort Worth

EAST

TEXAS   FORESTS

LOUISIANA

El Paso

Pecos •

Pecos R.

TRANS-PECOS

San Angelo •

Waco

EDWARDS

PLATEAU

LLANO
UPLIFT

Austin

Colorado R.

Brazos R.

Trinity R.

Neches R.

Sabine R.

Beaumont
Port Arthur

Houston

MEXICO

Rio Grande

San Antonio •

GULF

COAST

Galveston

RIO GRANDE PLAIN

• Laredo

Corpus Christi

Gulf   of   Mexico

TEXAS

Brownsville

0   50   100   150   200
Miles

PREFACE

Beyond the heavy industry and the freeways, the natural world of Texas survives. For most of us our contact with it is somewhat distant. We see it chiefly from our cars, and wish we knew more about it.

I wrote this book to satisfy that desire. My own interest in the natural world is mild, affectionate, nontechnical, even intermittent. There are times when I just can't get around to it. *Texas Wild* is for people in roughly the same situation. It deals with the nature that you see as you drive across Texas in a car, and also with what you see if you get out, perhaps with binoculars, and walk across a pasture, along a back road, or into one of our state or national parks.

You will find within our boundaries, because of the accidents of history, an amazing variety of land forms and climates. No other state has so many. Texas takes in wet southeastern woodlands and dry southwestern deserts. The Great Plains reach in from the north. Our Trans-Pecos mountains are part of the Rockies. The waters of the Gulf of Mexico slap against a long shoreline that runs down to a *tierra caliente* like that of Mexico.

So much variety sounds chaotic but turns out to be orderly and precise. The natural divisions of Texas were traced and their boundaries mapped by nineteenth-century geologists, who also, in most cases, gave them their names. These divisions—the Edwards Plateau, the Grand Prairie, the Llano Uplift, and so on—are called physiographic regions. (*Physiography* is just *physical geography* squeezed into one word.)

You can tell when you pass from one physiographic region to the next. The shape of the hills, the force of the wind, the birds on the telephone lines are different, and so, often, are the trees and weeds and wildflowers, and the animals in their dens. In a time of sameness, when man-made Texas looks like man-made New Jersey, nature gives us the only variety we have.

These natural divisions serve handily as chapter divisions for this book. Handily, but not invariably; I have put the Piney Woods and the adjoining Post Oaks together in one chapter, and no less than five different

[11]

farming and ranching regions, all veined by various forks of the Brazos River, together in another.

The book's first chapter deals with the westernmost Trans-Pecos region. The next chapters proceed eastward through the Edwards Plateau and the Llano Uplift, then north to the Staked Plain. From there the chapters follow a roughly clockwise pattern around to the south, ending with the Rio Grande Plain.

Whatever seemed most interesting as I traveled through each region, or as I scanned the enormous amounts of material in archives and libraries, is in this book. Most of the places described are accessible to the public, and the plants, birds, and animals mentioned are those one is most likely to see. But here and there I write about rarities that could use a little sympathy and a little help.

This is no all-purpose volume. No book about Texas could be, at less than *Encyclopaedia Britannica* length. If your special interest is butterflies or lizards or Pre-Cambrian rocks, you will still need field guides and checklists. One of the things this book sets out to do is encourage you to read other books about Texas. The chapter notes at the end mention some that I have particularly liked.

DICK PHELAN
McGregor, Texas

TEXAS WILD

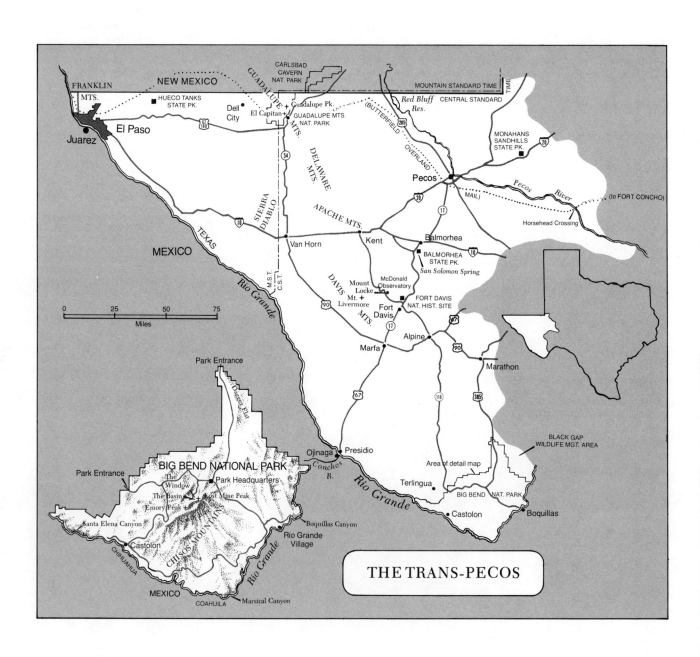

THE TRANS-PECOS

1 | THE TRANS-PECOS

"Now we're in God's country," said a friend of mine once, as we crossed the Pecos River westbound. I thought so too, but for a different reason. He was born in Trans-Pecos Texas. To him it is home. For me, it's God's country because man has changed it less, occupied it less, than any other part of the state. It keeps something of Texas's old-time wildness and freedom.

It is big, empty country with few roads, few people, and little water. Its broad stretches of desert—all part of the Chihuahuan Desert—are broken by mountains. There are some thirty named mountain ranges in all, most of them rocky and dry. A few of the biggest ones—the Chisos, Davis, and Guadalupe Mountains—rise into cool altitudes and have pine forests and springs.

Most of the year the Trans-Pecos air is impeccably clear. McDonald Observatory, in the Davis Mountains, has two of the world's major telescopes. Unlike the observatories near Tucson and Los Angeles, it has no problem with the glow of city lights. El Paso, 175 airline miles away, is the nearest city.

With its greasewood, flash floods, and scanty rain, the Trans-Pecos is part of the Southwest, the kind of country that Arizona and New Mexico are made of. And the Pecos River, which saws off a great chunk of western Texas, is not a true boundary for the region. The river cuts out the Monahans sand dunes, which should be included, and leaves in the Stockton Plateau, which shouldn't be. But the name Trans-Pecos is long-established and handy, and no one minds that it isn't entirely accurate.

From horseback to airship, it has been hard on many kinds of travel. In the 1930s the big Navy dirigibles Akron and Macon were tossed about dangerously by violent updrafts from the hot desert floor when they flew over the Trans-Pecos. Sometimes they had to halt in midair and wait, or make detours. Now the powerful thermal currents lift gliders. Marfa, Texas, is one of the sailplane capitals of the country.

No one has ever liked the Pecos River much. It flows mostly through barren country, and its water is smelly with minerals and mud. Early travelers drank it only because they had to. Most of them crossed it at the same place, a point called Horsehead Crossing, chosen because it was crossable and was on the way to the next water hole westward. Comanche Indians, returning north from their autumn raids in Mexico, would drive herds of stolen horses long distances without water. When they reached this crossing, many of the thirst-crazed horses drank too much of the mineral-charged water and died. Their skulls, bleaching on the bank, gave the place its name. Horsehead Crossing is now unused, but history lovers know where it is and sometimes visit it. Forty-Niners used it on their way to California. The Goodnight-Loving cattle trail crossed the Pecos there, and so did the Butterfield Overland Mail.

From Horsehead Crossing, the Comanche raiders sometimes headed northwest, to what we now call the Monahans Sandhills. This stretch of dunes runs for one hundred miles and reaches into five counties. Monahans Sandhills State Park is just a tiny piece of the whole. A ten-minute slog through its sand takes you beyond the tourist litter and footprints into a clean, simple, lively world. For the dunes are not a desert.

There is good water under the sand, and lots of it. Here and there, windmills lift it out. At the park's campsites, mockingbirds and thrashers perch on the oozing faucets and stand on their heads to drink from them.

It's odd to see willows in these dry sands, small but healthy. The famous little Havard oaks, rarely more than three feet high, send roots down as much as ninety feet and bear heavy crops of big acorns that make the sandhills a good place for fattening hogs. The mesquite trees are somewhat bigger than the oaks. There are grasses and wildflowers.

The dunes, broiler-hot on summer days, are breezy and cool at night, and beautiful by moonlight. Being relatively free of insects, they make a good place to camp.

These sands once covered the floor of a Permian sea. It drained and dried away, and left the dunes. Most people seem to prefer the big sixty-foot dunes of pure photogenic sand, but the smaller ones, bearing the little oaks, or sunflowers, or yucca, or grasses, offer more to observe.

There is a race of small grasshoppers precisely the color of the sand. Foxes, coyotes, rabbits, and skunks live in the dunes, and so did the Lobo wolf until the early settlers killed it off. Hawks hunt in the air above. One morning at sunrise I saw a pair of scaled quail and their six small chicks running over a dune, stitching its surface with their tiny tracks.

The day's events are written in the sand, and then erased. Even large insects leave tracks. A spot of wet sand no bigger than your thumbnail is some small animal's urine. You can follow a bird's tracks over a dune, from the place where it landed to the place where, with a spring that pushed back the sand, it took to the air.

Try spitting down the steep lee slope of a dune. Scatter shots are best. Each droplet of saliva becomes a ball of liquid coated with sand, and rolls like a marble to the bottom. Even drops no bigger than a pinhead, just big enough to see, will do this.

In a few places, as at Willow Springs (northwest of the park) water makes pools at the surface. The Indians knew this, and the Spaniards learned from them. In the days of wagon trains, Willow Springs was a vital water stop. A wagon train was massacred there, probably in 1883. Apparently nobody missed the victims at the time. They simply disappeared, and reentered history in 1901, when the ruins of forty burned wagons, ox yokes, human bones, and family possessions were dug out of the sand.

Many Trans-Pecos mountain ranges are fault-block mountains—big chunks of the earth's crust that have come loose and tilted, just as a piece of concrete sidewalk may tilt and settle in the ground, with one end buried and the other sticking up above the surface. Fault-block mountains thus have a steep escarpment on one side and a long, gentle slope on the other.

The mountains have been there a long time, flaking away, dissolving in rain. Once they were much higher, and deep valleys lay between them. As material eroded from them it filled the valleys. Now hot, sandy desert plains and basins stretch from one range of mountains to the next. The peaks themselves are lower, worn down, and the bases of the mountains are buried from one to three thousand feet deep in their own detritus.

This arrangement has created *bolsones*, stretches of desert entirely surrounded by mountains so that no water can flow out. *Bolson* in Spanish means big purse—something that holds what is put into it. Rainwater streams down the mountain sides, leaching salts and other minerals out of the rocks and washing sand and gravel for miles out onto the desert floor—toward the lowest point of the *bolson*, of course—and the water and salts collect there, making a shallow lake.

The lake soon evaporates, leaving the salts and minerals behind. Most of the salt is the kind we season food with. With each rain more salt is washed in. The low point is thus a salt flat in dry weather and a salt lake after rain.

The Spanish name for a salt flat is *playa*. The big *playa* just west of the Guadalupe Mountains is crossed by Highway 180, which has ditches on both sides. Sometimes they are filled with clear water. I dipped a mouthful once, experimentally, but decided not to swallow it. It was many times saltier than the sea.

Not much grows in a salt flat, but a few things do. Such plants are called halophytes, which means salt-growers. Wolfberry, sea purslane, and salt grass, for example, grow large in dunes along the Gulf of Mexico, but small in the Trans-Pecos salt flats, where they have plenty of salt but not enough rain.[1]

There were once more *bolsones* in the Trans-Pecos than there are now. Long ago the Rio Grande and the Pecos cut through them and gave them drainage, and their salt flats washed downstream into the sea. One of the best remaining *bolsones* runs north from Van Horn (on Interstate 10) to Guadalupe National Park. It is a long desert valley walled in by the Delaware Mountains on the east and the Sierra Diablo—classic fault-block mountains—on the west. The low point of the basin, white with salt, is some thirty-five miles north of Van Horn on the little Highway 54, which runs along just below the grim Diablo escarpment.

The plant you can't miss in the Trans-Pecos is creosote bush. It covers, or anyway occupies, thousands of square miles. It is almost, but not quite, tough enough to grow in salt flats. Creosote bushes stand well apart from each other, spaced out like trees in an orchard, with mostly bare ground showing between them. They stand three to five feet high: tough, greenish-brown shrubs, drab-looking even when their tiny yellow flowers are in bloom.

Two things make the ground bare between creosote bushes. One is that few other plants can grow in the alkaline soil and drought that creosote bushes like. The other is that the roots of the bushes excrete a toxin into the soil which kills some plants that try to grow up around them.

Indians and pioneers made medicines and glue out of creosote bushes. Nowadays the plant's gift to man is useless but very pleasant: after a rain, creosote bushes give off a pungent, spicy smell that suggests dryness even though water is what releases it into the air. Virtually every resident of El Paso and Juarez is familiar with this post-rain smell, but relatively few know that it drifts into the cities from thousands of acres of wet creosote bushes in the surrounding desert.

El Paso was founded and still exists because it *is* a pass. Here the Rio Grande breaks through mountains—the Juarez Mountains in Mexico, the Franklins in Texas. The break offered Spain's priests and soldiers the easiest route between Mexico City and Santa Fé. El Paso del Norte was the full name of the little settlement in Spanish times, and it did lie near the northern limits of the empire.

Vineyards once grew on the river banks, watered from the Rio Grande. The wine made from them was called "Pass wine" and was considered good. A few acres of land at the old mission of Ysleta, now within El Paso's city limits, have been in continuous cultivation since 1682.

Railroads, highways, and airlines converge to thread through this notch in the mountains. The road through El Paso goes on west and crosses the Continental Divide at the lowest elevation of any transcontinental highway route, and has the least snow in winter.

El Paso is a large city, the only one in the Trans-Pecos, and it is expanding in a desert. (Juarez, across the river, is an even bigger one.) Its steady, ever-worsening problem is water. The city uses huge amounts of it and yet may not (there are some small exceptions) take water from the Rio Grande. Nor may it draw water from underground wells in Mexico or New Mexico, both of which are just beyond the city limits.

Fortunately the Hueco Bolson, a desert area just east of El Paso, is underlain by a vast aquifer. It just isn't vast enough. Some of the water is drinkable, some brackish, some salty, and all of it lies hundreds of feet beneath a surface of creosote bush and sand.

El Paso's wells extend for many miles into this desert, and the city is pumping water out of the ground almost twice as fast as nature is putting it back. Some day the entire area, including Juarez, across the river, will run dry. Everyone knows this, but there is no movement to cut down on the growth of either city.

Instead there are plans to import water from far away, to recycle water, to purify salt water, to get courts to award the water of the Rio Grande to El Paso instead of to the farmers who use it now for irrigation.

Meanwhile El Paso keeps growing, with an annual rainfall of less than nine inches and an annual evaporation rate of more than nine feet. This means that a lake, if there were such a thing in El Paso, would gain nine inches of water in a year from rain falling on its surface and lose nine feet from evaporation into the dry and thirsty air. That air is why the mouths of newcomers to El Paso feel dry for days after they arrive.

Thirty miles or so east of El Paso is a beautiful, almost magical water supply, the Hueco Tanks. The tanks, however, are scaled to the small demands of earlier centuries, not to the huge consumption of the present. The tanks are natural cisterns, hidden in immense, beautiful piles of granitelike rocks.

Throughout human history (and prehistory, for that matter) the rocks have sheltered these pools of cold, pure rain water in the midst of a desert. Cowboys, Indians, Forty-Niners, badmen, all have gratefully drunk the water.

Rain runs down the boulders and collects in irregular basins hollowed out of the rocks themselves. Some of them hold only a few cupfuls of water, some are huge. Deeply protected from wind and sun, the bigger pools last from one rainy season to the next. They are still a drinking place for wildlife. In its time, the Butterfield Overland Mail (St. Louis to San Francisco) made an overnight stop at the tanks.

The rocks form shelters where people have camped for thousands of years, and on the walls is one of Texas's great collections of Indian rock paintings. Some have been damaged by time and rain, others by people with spray paint. The Hueco Tanks are now being developed as a Texas State Park, which will offer a mild protection for the pictographs but greatly increase the number of visitors.

Some desert animals don't have to drink. They *manufacture* most of the water they need in their own bodies, by a metabolic process, and also get small amounts from their food. One of these well-equipped creatures is the kangaroo rat.

Strangers on Trans-Pecos highways, driving at night, sometimes don't believe what they glimpse in their headlight beams: tiny kangaroos, not much bigger than mice, hopping across the pavement just a shade too fast to be clearly seen. They are of course not tiny kangaroos but kangaroo rats, coming out of their burrows at night to feed on grass seed—too much grass seed, some ranchers think.

They are not marsupials, of course, but mammals. They can swing their long tails to change direction in mid-hop, and thus escape predators, including man. They never drink water, even after a rain when they could. There are three Trans-Pecos species. One of them, the Ord Kangaroo Rat, is partial to sand and is found both in the Trans-Pecos and on Padre Island. It burrows deep enough into the sand to reach a comfortable underground temperature, plugs its burrow to keep heat or cold out, and spends the daylight hours in privacy and safety, probably asleep.

Kangaroo rats are hard to catch, and some of them bite. Their flesh, says one authority, is "white, tender, and delicious as chicken." Since the living animal weighs only a few ounces, it would take a lot of work to catch, dress, and cook a kangaroo-rat dinner, even for one man camping alone.

Travelers may or may not see kangaroo rats. They are certainly going to see cactus. Perhaps the Rio Grande Plain has even more of it than the Trans-Pecos. But here the plants are highly visible, not hidden in brush. And visible along with them are other thorny plants—sotols, yuccas, agaves—which visitors often confuse with each other and with the cacti. A good handbook will help anyone learn to tell one species from another.

Cacti originated in the Western Hemisphere. But travelers have taken them round the world, and they now grow on every continent. I once ate a prickly-pear fruit in Morocco, peeled for me by a ragged, grim young Arab who held it out on the blade of his evil-looking knife, dripping a thin red juice. He made a sort of living that way, from a pushcart.

The two best habitats of cacti are along the Tropic of Cancer in Mexico and the Tropic of Capricorn in Paraguay and Brazil. There they are more plentiful, in both numbers and species, than anywhere else. But Texas does quite well, especially in its western half.[2]

Most cacti are so cactuslike that nobody doubts for a moment what they are. About others it's hard to be sure. A cholla, for example, looks like a cactus struggling to take the form of a small tree; but it is a cactus too. Rather few people nowadays have been jumped at by a jumping cholla. I was lucky enough to have this minor but mystifying experience.

Hiking near the river in Big Bend National Park, I would have sworn I hadn't touched a single cactus plant. Much of my attention was given just to avoiding them. But I felt a scratch, looked down, and found a surprisingly big chunk of cholla attached to the back of my trousers at knee level. Of course it had not jumped through the air, or been fired at me by the plant it came from. The outer segments of jumping cholla are so loosely attached to the plant, and their thorns are so cleverly barbed, that a piece will come loose and ride away on a man's clothes without his knowing he has brushed against it. And the chances are good that it will take root and grow on the spot where he throws it down.

The night-blooming cereus is a cactus, and grows in the Trans-Pecos. But it is rare, inconspicuous, and hard to find. Its flower, the most beautiful of all cactus flowers (which is saying a lot), opens at sunset and closes at daybreak, and can be smelled downwind for a quarter of a mile.[3] The vision-inducing peyote is also a cactus, and grows in places along the Rio Grande from the Big Bend almost down to the sea.

Can a thirsty man get a good drink from a barrel cactus? Tradition says yes, and so do some books by cactus experts. More than one botanist friend of mine says no. All you get, they say, is a slimy, chewy substance, which is what a cactus turns its stored water into and which, on being chewed, yields up a few drops of liquid from each mouthful. I have no intention of cutting the top off a seventy-five-year-old barrel cactus to find out who is right.

All cacti are good at hoarding water when there is any to collect, and all have waxy skins that keep most of it from evaporating. They all have bright, beautiful flowers and edible fruits—some tastier than others. And cacti are credited with various tricks for defending themselves against the hot sun. I keep running across the claim that prickly-pear pads, especially in the desert, grow mostly edgewise to the noonday sun, to lessen their exposure to its heat. I have looked at many a prickly pear, and can never see that this is true.

On the other hand it is obvious that the thick, interlocking thorns on most barrel and pincushion cacti do help cool the surface of the plant with moving bars of shade, just like the shade of a gardener's lath house.

The ocotillo, which might be a cactus, is not. The plant is made en-

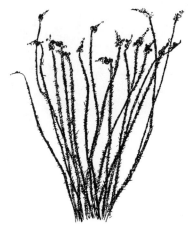

tirely of long, slender, crooked, thorny wands which flare upward from the ground, sometimes for fifteen or twenty feet. It is cactus-colored (dull green) and has thorns and pretty flowers. But it is not a succulent, as all cacti are, and it bears leaves, as no cactus does. They are small leaves, and they don't grow by the season but appear after a rain. When the weather gets dry again the leaves drop off, and the plant looks dead. Texas has only one species of ocotillo. Mexico has seven, and people there still set the plants in rows and even weave them together to make a living, lacerating fence that nothing much bigger than a mouse would try to get through.

Agaves, yuccas, and sotols all grow among the Trans-Pecos cactus fields, and in people's yards over much of Texas. Again, a handbook and some experience are needed if the novice is going to learn which is which. All three species make a cluster of heavy, thorny, blade-like leaves near the ground and then send up tall stalks which bloom. They all have edible parts and produce juices which can be turned into liquids that make men drunk—sotol, mescal, pulque, tequila. All yield fibers that make mats, baskets, and ropes. And all produce saponin, which Indians and poor Mexicans have used for centuries as soap.

But then there are differences. Agaves belong to the amaryllis family. They grow for years and years without blooming at all. Then one spring they send up a tall stem, it blooms, and subsequently the whole plant dies. Century plants are the best-known agaves, and you can find them in Big Bend National Park. But the commonest is the drab little lechugilla, which covers miles of rocky hillsides in the Trans-Pecos and makes walking tricky. Lechugilla leaves suggest bunches of green bananas growing close to the ground, but with a thorn on the end of each one. Here and there among the host of the living you'll see a dead stalk rising from a dead clump of leaves—a plant that has bloomed and died.

Sotols and yuccas are both members of the lily family, and resemble each other more than either one resembles an agave. They bloom every year, not just once in their lives. Sotol has a sugary mass at its center which cattle will eat, but someone has to chop the plant open so they can get past the dagger-like leaves. Indians used to roast this to make a food called *mescal*. Old mescal pits (where the roasting was done) are still identifiable in the Trans-Pecos. There is one on the saddle just below Guadalupe Peak.

Yucca (Spanish dagger or Spanish bayonet) is the one most people can recognize, though they may give this name to sotols and agaves too. Yuccas come in many species of different shapes and sizes, and the thorns on the tip of each leaf are among the hardest in nature. They are handy for sewing or for puncturing rattlesnake bites, and it's possible, with some species, to break off a thorn so that a long strand of fiber peels away with it down the yucca leaf, and you have both needle and thread in one piece.

Guadalupe Mountains National Park is so new that for several years it's going to be pleasantly plain, lacking an elaborate visitor center, lacking campgrounds where people can plug into lights and water. Most of the Guadalupe range is in New Mexico. Only the part which extends into Texas has been made into a national park.

The Guadalupes are limestone mountains, laid down as a reef about 200 million years ago when the area lay under a Permian sea. It is the best-preserved fossil reef on the planet, a superb museum of Permian marine life. Fossil plants and animals are embedded even in the highest peaks, now nearly 9,000 feet above sea level.

The present crude campground and ranger station (a wooden shack) are high on the mountain's flank, near the old stage stop called Pine Spring. Below lie miles of desert. Above are the mountain heights, with trails leading up, and fifty-five miles of rough hiking trails in the higher country.

The trip that everybody wants to make (and many do) is up Guadalupe Peak, the highest point in Texas. It is not a hard climb. Any good walker can make it, provided he goes at an appropriate pace.

Comfortable shoes, a canteen of water, and a sandwich are all the equipment needed. A camera is nice too, for the view from the peak reaches northward far into New Mexico and southeastward to the Davis Mountains, eighty miles away.

Below Guadalupe Peak are salt flats, large ones, the low point of a huge *bolson* that lies in both Texas and New Mexico. To the south, traffic slides silently up and down the steep grades of U.S. 180 like beads along a wire. And precisely on the highest point in Texas (8,751 feet) is what many people, including me, consider an offensive piece of litter.

It is a shiny metal pyramid about five feet high, anchored there by American Airlines in praise of its early, low-flying pilots who managed to get past the Guadalupes without crashing into them. (Other pilots have not been so lucky. The Guadalupes are full of old plane wrecks.) The few people who live in the country below have a kind of affection for the commemorative pyramid because it reflects the sun at various times of day and can be seen for miles as a glittering point of light.

Except for this marker, there was not a scrap of litter on Guadalupe Peak when I climbed it. The people who take the trouble to get up there apparently care enough about the place to leave it clean. Wildflowers bloomed among the rocks, and coarse, lush grasses were flourishing after summer thunderstorms. The air had a delicacy and freshness that I thought I might be imagining, but I wasn't. Others noticed it too.

El Capitan is the imposing rock face that travelers see from fifty miles out on highways approaching the park. Many people think *it* is Guadalupe Peak, but the higher peak lies inconspicuously just behind El Capitan, to the north. A staggeringly huge chunk of bare biscuit-colored limestone, El Capitan rises for thousands of feet, two thousand of which are vertical, above the desert. It can be climbed, but you don't make a frontal attack. You go most of the way up the Guadalupe Peak trail and then approach El Capitan from behind—from the mountain mass out of which it juts like a headland. It's a good idea to get some information from the park rangers before trying the climb.

The forests in the high Guadalupes are far from dense, for the soil is rocky and dry. Hikers must take water on their backs—a gallon a day per person. The main trees are Ponderosa pines and Douglas firs. Merriam elk once lived in the Guadalupes, but were killed off soon after white settlers came with cattle and rifles. The present animals are American elk, established in 1928 with a small herd brought from Colorado.

They are worth seeing, though not easy to see. A big white-tailed deer weighs two hundred pounds; a big elk seven hundred. You can try waiting for them to come and drink at twilight at a place called the Bowl. You can, that is, if there is water in the Bowl. Often the high country is totally dry, and the wild animals come down at night to drink from various springs which break out of the limestone two or three thousand feet below the summits: Smith Spring, Pine Spring, Guadalupe Spring, etc.

A few black bears and mountain lions remain in the Guadalupes. Bobcats, ringtails, coyotes, and turkeys are common. Porcupines may gnaw the salty straps of your backpack when you are camped. And Texas's only chipmunks live in these mountains and perhaps in the nearby Sierra Diablo. (Those little signs in Texas gardens that say "Caution—Chipmunk Crossing" may charm some people but are totally inaccurate.) The Guadalupe chipmunks are shy, quite unlikely to take food from your hand as chipmunks do in the Colorado Rockies.

Smith Spring is a pretty place that even the most sedentary can walk to. In a canyon hung midway between the dry desert and the dry peaks, the little stream supports wildflowers, dragonflies, ferns, and shade trees. The walk back from Smith Spring is best toward sundown, when birds are watering at the pond near the trail and the distant mountains to the south are emerging from the daytime glare and turning eight or ten shades of blue.

The park's pride, and its carefully protected showplace, is big McKittrick Canyon. It is several miles long and several thousand feet deep, and enclosed by fawn-colored cliffs full of caves and pinnacles. The trail keeps to the bottom for two miles or so before it starts to climb.

Here plants from several life zones are sociably mingled: pines and firs from above, yucca and cactus from the desert below, walnut and big-tooth maple which really belong in temperate forests hundreds of miles to the east. The little stream in the canyon helps make all this possible. In isolation from the rest of the world, a number of species have developed which grow nowhere else—a honeysuckle, a mint, and a columbine, for example.

The Texas madrone also grows in McKittrick Canyon, and near the Pine Spring campground. Here and there in the Trans-Pecos, in exactly the right conditions, this strange and beautiful tree hangs on. Its trunk and limbs are red—cherry-red, or orange-red, or sometimes the lavender-purple of cream that has been poured over blackberries. With red limbs, shiny green leaves, white blossoms, and edible red berries, the madrone seems to have escaped from some gentle enchanted forest.

A few people are so taken with madrone trees that they dig a small one up, unaware that the trees will not live outside their present range. They are in fact an endangered species, because young madrone seedlings no longer survive in the wild—no one is yet sure why. Some botanists think that the present heavy populations of deer and goats eat every young sprout while it is tender, and never give it a chance to become a tree. Whatever the reason, there is a possibility that when the present mature trees are gone there will be no more.

Between mountain ranges, where the country is treeless and open and grows the browse plants that they prefer, herds of pronghorn survive—smaller than they used to be, but protected by landowners who sell the rights to hunt them.

They are usually called antelope, or pronghorn antelope. They are, however, only very distant relations to the antelopes, all of which are native to Africa or Asia. The pronghorn is the only living member of its biological family. In anatomy it falls somewhere between deer and cattle but looks more like a deer. Open plains are its home, where it can see for miles and run like the wind—faster than any other mammal in North America.

Pronghorns have a fatal curiosity, though. They tend to approach and investigate any moving object. For many thousands of years this proce-dure was safe, because the pronghorn could outrun anything that proved dangerous. It can't outrun bullets, though, and now for a century hunters have attracted pronghorns by waving a handkerchief to bring the animals into range. Nonhunters can do the same, just to get a look at them.

They are pretty animals, mostly fawn-colored and white, with black horns. The females' little horns are rarely pronged. Both sexes have a broad white rump, with hairs that can be made to stand up and look even whiter. People once believed that pronghorns signaled to each other

across great distances with these white flashes, though nobody knew what messages were sent. It seems more likely, though, that the white patch is just something easy to see and follow when a pronghorn is running at thirty to forty-five miles per hour and having to divide its attention between the rough ground underfoot and the other animals running close ahead.

For all their gentle beauty, the Davis Mountains are in one sense inhospitable. Virtually every foot of them is privately owned, and the ranchers have had so many bad experiences with vandals and game thieves that they rarely give permission to camp or hike.

Among the few places where campers may legitimately spend the night is Davis Mountains State Park. There the soil is rich with potato-chip crumbs and soft-drink dregs, and the campsites are made almost uninhabitable by a huge overpopulation of ants.

But the Davis Mountains should be seen, experienced somehow. They have the best forests of all the Trans-Pecos mountains. They rise high enough to wring rain out of the desert air—nearly twice as much as the surrounding plains get. Their fissured and broken volcanic rocks absorb water and give it up again as hundreds of small springs and streams. The scenery is magnificent, especially the long lava escarpments. And the sweet summer climate, five thousand feet or more above the sea, is the best in Texas.

Through friends, I met someone who let me make a ten-mile hike through a beautiful canyon and into the uplands. Along the highways I found big rock hills which can be climbed in an hour or less. They contain many more birds, grasses, and wildflowers than a distant view of them suggests.

The whole region is volcanic, the biggest area of igneous rocks in the state. No volcanic vents—that is, the holes where the lava came out of the earth—have ever been found within it. They are probably buried under the lava that flowed out of them, and then hardened, and then weathered into soil.

These mountains, with their coolness, water, and rich grass, have been a refuge and oasis for all the people who ever crossed the dry Trans-Pecos. The beautiful Limpia Canyon and Wild Rose Pass, where Highway 17 now runs, were used by Indians, Spaniards, and the U.S. Cavalry.

Fort Davis, near the canyon, was founded in 1854 as a cavalry station. It was perhaps the handsomest frontier fort ever built in Texas, and it stood in the most beautiful setting. Some of it still stands, stabilized and restored, as the Fort Davis National Historic Site.

The unrestored ruins and the parade ground are perhaps more evocative of the past than the rebuilt buildings, which look modern. Hiking trails link the fort to the state park just two or three miles away. They follow high ridges and the views are good.

A seventy-eight-mile scenic loop winds through the mountains, with Mount Livermore, the highest peak (8,381 feet), roughly in its center and visible from points along the way. The road passes some prairie country at the mountains' edge where pronghorns graze and run.

And it passes the Rock Pile, a famous jumble of boulders that from a distance looks easy to climb. Once near, you find that each rock in the pile is as big as a freight engine, smooth, and lacking in footholds. But people who pick and balance their way into the upper reaches of the Rock Pile find small pools of water in the rocks, warmed by the sun and alive with many tiny animal forms. Birds bathe and butterflies drink. Little plants grow in cracks. A whole series of tiny wild communities hangs up there, unsuspected by the picnickers below.

McDonald Observatory welcomes visitors in the daytime. The mountaintop settlement of astronomers and technicians has a vaguely foreign flavor, probably coming from its multiple levels and its perch so far above the normal world. No amateur astronomer ever learns much astronomy from the public tour of a great observatory. But the huge McDonald instruments are there to be marveled at, and the views from the mountain top are good.

Botanists can do better. The whole range of Davis Mountains' vegetation, from the valley grasses to Mount Locke's pines, oaks, and wildflowers, lies in the sixteen miles between Fort Davis and the observatory. One notable thing is the *absence* of creosote bushes. The only two large Trans-Pecos areas without them are the fertile Davis Mountains and the sand dunes around Monahans.

At the northern edge of the Davis range lies the appealing little town of Balmorhea. It exists because of the huge San Solomon Spring nearby, which fills a vast swimming pool in Balmorhea State Park, then makes a lake, and finally waters thousands of acres of cotton. The town has irrigation ditches along its main street shaded by the magnificent cottonwood trees that nearly always grow beside water in the West. On hot summer days, some tourists wade in the irrigation ditches, under the trees.

Many a man and animal has died of thirst in the Trans-Pecos. Yet in places this arid land produces fortunes in water. The spring at Balmorhea flows 26 million gallons a day. To the east, at Fort Stockton, Comanche Spring watered six thousand acres of farmland as early as 1877.[4] It is now greatly depleted because people have drilled wells into the aquifer which supplies it, and pumped water out.

Most of the Texas tributaries of the Rio Grande and the Pecos are mere dry washes except in flash-flood season. But the two rivers themselves for thousands of years brought unfailing water from the Rocky Mountains to the Texas desert. The valley of the Rio Grande both above and below El Paso is a narrow strip of rich irrigated farmland, some of it in Mexico. Red Bluff Reservoir, made by a dam on the Pecos, now supplies several irrigation districts.

In 1948 a rancher near Dell City, drilling a small well, hit an unsuspected and incredible water supply. It now produces 750 million gallons a day, and has turned 44,000 acres of Trans-Pecos desert into farmland. No one knows how long this bonanza will last. But given man's current habit of taking water out of the ground far faster than nature puts it back, we can suppose that it won't last many decades.

Besides flowing water both above ground and below, the Trans-Pecos has natural cisterns—always in rough, rocky country—where rainwater collects and keeps clean and cool through the dry seasons.

They are called *tinajas*, their Spanish name, and they occur in mountain canyons and in the dry arroyos that lead to the Rio Grande. When men traveled on foot and on horse, they followed careful routes from river to *tinaja* to spring, in order to stay alive. Getting lost meant dying of thirst.

Today the two big rivers are dammed and tamed and in places pumped dry, and the great springs feed irrigation ditches. But a few shepherds and backpackers still go to the old *tinajas*, which are hidden away in remote country and quite unchanged. There they brush back a floating leaf or two and drink the water, as men have done for centuries.

The little ranch town of Marathon lies in a remarkable area called the Marathon Basin, an area which geologists call a window. Here almost the entire geological history of Texas lies visible at the surface, the rocks of each period so neatly exposed they are like textbook illustrations. A number of universities send their geology students to the Marathon Basin in the summers, to live there and study in the field.

This "window" is different from the one in the Grand Canyon, where the Colorado River has cut down vertically through billions of years of rock strata, one on top of the other. In the Marathon Basin, the strata lie side by side for twenty or thirty miles, with the oldest toward the center of the basin and the youngest on the outer edges. They got that way because pressure from below, probably an intrusion of magma, made a bulge in the surface of the earth and forced all the strata of rocks to bend upward.

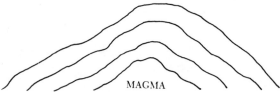

MAGMA

Then erosion cut the top off the bulge and exposed, side by side, the rock layers that had originally been put down one above the other. The softer layers have eroded faster than the hard ones, making the basin floor uneven—a series of hard-rock ridges and soft-rock valleys or flats.

Highway 385 leads south from Marathon, passing through some twenty miles of the Marathon Basin before it enters that showpiece of the Trans-Pecos, Big Bend National Park.

There is always a pleasant climate somewhere in Big Bend National Park. In winter you can camp by the Rio Grande and in that southern desert find what amounts to a mild, sunny autumn. In summer you go into the Chisos Mountains, at around five thousand feet, and wear a jacket after sundown.

For all its recent development and its streams of tourists, most of the park remains wild and empty. The majority of visitors go only where their cars will take them. This leaves hundreds of square miles of desert, whole mountain ranges, and complex canyon systems largely undisturbed—a nice thing for wild animals and wilderness lovers.

Some of the hiking trails are well-built and popular, and admittedly they lead to the most famous spots. Others are remote, made long ago by ranch hands or smugglers and now neglected, and rewarding in their own way for those who like to leave the beaten track.

The variety of land forms within the park is huge. You can drown in the river, die of thrist in the desert, or perish in the mountains of rattlesnake bite or a climbing accident. Actually very few people die in any of these ways in the Big Bend. The figures show that the greatest threat to visitors is traffic accidents. But there *are* five separate life zones, and the possibilities of these varied misadventures are there.

First there is a watery strip along the Rio Grande, with willows, cottonwoods, beavers, and catfish. Then the desert flats begin—not really flat but sloping upward toward the mountains. The various flats are different in character, some specializing in creosote bushes, others in rocks, and one (called Dagger Flat) in giant yuccas which bloom magnificently in spring.

In the foothills are rough desert grasslands, now recovering a little from the overgrazing they suffered in pre-Park days.[5] At about 4,500 feet the woodlands begin, chiefly piñon pines, junipers, and oaks. They range on up to the peaks, except that in a few protected spots a fifth life zone is found—the Transition Zone, with the trees of the high Rockies: Ponderosa pine, Douglas fir, and (in one place only) the Arizona cypress.

These bits of the Transition Zone occur on north-facing slopes and in high, narrow, shady canyons, the coolest places in the park. Probably they are surviving pockets from the Ice Age, when glaciers lay across the northern United States and the whole Trans-Pecos was chilly enough to grow forests of pine and fir. Then the Ice Cap melted, the world warmed up, and the Big Bend grew too hot for trees of the Rocky Mountain type except in its highest, coolest places.

To the visitor the park looks primitive, untouched, even perhaps untouchable. It seems too vast and harsh to be affected much by man. But its ecology was drastically changed between 1890 and 1940, when it became a national park. Forests were cut from the Chisos Mountains to fuel the quicksilver mines of Terlingua and Study Butte, two mining centers which are now ghost towns outside the park's boundaries. Ranchers killed as many golden eagles and lobo wolves as possible, trying to exterminate them. (The eagles, in the 1930s, were hunted very successfully from small airplanes by men with shotguns.)

The Mexican rubber plant was all but wiped out during the first World War, when the country needed a lot of rubber in a hurry. The rich toboso grass on Tornillo Flat was cut for hay and overgrazed, and has never recovered. The Big Bend looks wild and cruel, and it is. But the area's ecology is geared to the little rain that falls, and highly vulnerable to exploitation.[6] It has been heavily damaged.

The beautiful Chisos Mountains are the center of everything. All roads lead into them and end in a high natural hollow called the Basin, where visitors congregate.

The Chisos Mountains are volcanic, built by eruptions in the Cenozoic era. They rise out of older sedimentary limestones and shales. Trails lead up from the Basin to places of extraordinary beauty. Best of all is the South Rim, a high lava cliff which offers a hundred-mile view into Mexico. From it the Rio Grande can be seen here and there below, winding through bits of open country. It is about fifteen miles away and five thousand feet lower down.

Many people ride rented horses to the South Rim, a thirteen-mile round trip, and return saddle-sore and sunburned, perhaps wishing they had walked and worn more clothes. The Chisos sun, I found one August day, will stencil your undershirt on your back in thirty minutes.

A detour from the South Rim trail leads up Emory Peak, the highest point in the park. The climb is not difficult. I once spent a few hours up there, alone except for the company of twenty or thirty thousand ladybugs. They covered bushes, cacti, rocks, grass. I suppose they had come to the peaks to escape the midday heat of the country below. Years later, a friend told me he once found a similar convention of ladybugs on a mountain in California.

Other trails from the Basin campground lead up to Lost Mine Peak and down to the Window, the big notch where water drains out of the Basin after rain. The Window is the only opening through which Basin visitors can see out into the world. What they see, far below, is a lunar landscape of rocky, unpeopled hills.

Every dozen years or so the Trans-Pecos gets lengthy summer rains instead of isolated thunderstorms, and this sets it to producing flowers. One such year was 1966. The Rio Grande was thirteen feet above its normal level in Big Bend National Park and a stretch of mountainside had slumped down—from rain!—onto the South Rim trail.

I was there in September. It still rained at intervals, and the peaks rose into a cloud deck. The mountains had turned from brown to green. Grasses grew tall and healthy, and a great variety of wildflowers had risen out of the rocks and were in brilliant bloom. Daisies, morning glories, Mexican poppies stood high in roadside ditches and little woodland flowers bloomed in the forests. Even permanent residents of the park were amazed at the show of flowers.

The Rio Grande makes three big canyons in the park, cutting through a separate mountain range for each of them. The river was there first, flowering across the places where the mountains were later to be. As they slowly rose out of the earth, the Rio Grande (then nameless) wore its channel through them and sawed them in two.

The flowing water, with its abrasive load of sand and rocks, can cut through a mountain range as surely as a buzz saw can cut a log, except that the job takes millions of years. The canyons are now from 1,200 to 1,700 feet deep, with the river still grinding along in their bottoms, wearing them deeper. One of them, Santa Elena Canyon, is in places only twenty-five feet wide at water level, with vertical walls going up to a narrow strip of sky.

Canoeists and raftsmen float through each canyon separately, skipping the long desert stretches in between. Skill is needed. Santa Elena has a quarter-mile portage where a section of the canyon wall on the Mexican side has fallen into the river. Despite a warning sign, a canoeist occasionally fails to put ashore in time, gets carried into the boulders that the river roars through, and has to abandon his wrecked craft.

Seen from the South Rim, Mexico, beyond the Rio Grande, looks uninhabited. But people do live among those bony mountains, and some of them cross into the park—illegally—to harvest tones of a wild plant called *candelilla*. It looks like a clump of green, leafless rods. By a simple process the Mexicans render a rich wax from this plant, and it has considerable commercial value. Industry uses it in shoe polishes, phonograph records, and chewing gum.

No one is supposed to harm a plant in a national park. But the Mexicans are poor, the park is large and has many remote canyons, and the temptation is strong. For decades, the National Park Service rangers have fought a wry, long-running battle with the Mexicans.

When they find a "wax camp" they chase the Mexicans back across the river, destroy the crude rendering vat, and perhaps confiscate some blocks of wax, which are solid and hard. But the Mexicans are persistent, they need money, and the battle is never really won. They keep coming back.

One ranger told me of a night years ago when men from a wax camp crept into the big Boquillas campground near the river and stealthily removed the battery water from all the tourists' cars. They needed the acid for rendering their wax. There was mass puzzlement the next morning when thirty tourists found, one after another, that their cars wouldn't start.

Most tourists visit the Big Bend merely because it is a national park, something to be visited; or because they want a place to park their campers. People with a livelier curiosity than most tourists have can find many remarkable things.

The Colima Warbler, for example, is a plain little bird, but it draws knowledgeable bird watchers to the park for a compelling reason: it breeds in the Chisos Mountains and nowhere else in the United States. In winter it moves to Mexico. Hummingbirds favor the Chisos Mountains, too. A greater variety of species can be found there than in most parts of Texas. And people who would like to see a golden eagle have a good chance of glimpsing one over the Big Bend. The airborne shotguns of the 1930s failed to get them all.

Our biggest bluebonnet grows in the park: the Chisos Bluebonnet, with purple-blue flowers twice as big as those of the Texas Bluebonnet, which is the state flower. Along the Rio Grande one finds the screwbean mesquite, a smallish tree whose pods make a spiral of almost mathematical precision, like the threads of a screw. If one of these pods were metal it could be screwed into a board. In the great desert flats between the mountain ranges are the tracks and fossilized remains of dinosaurs and other extinct reptiles from the Jurassic.

But bigger and better than any single treasure that the park offers is the park itself. It covers more than a thousand square miles. From its rims and mountaintops you see an enormous stony world that reaches on and on, far beyond the park boundaries, before it curves away out of sight over the horizon. The sky is unbelievably clean, the air sweet, the silence that of prehistory. It tells visitors how brief and small their lives are, and makes them grateful.

East of the park, the Black Gap Wildlife Management Area occupies a rocky region where only eight inches of rain fall in the average year. Here the Texas Parks and Wildlife Department is trying to reestablish desert bighorn sheep in Texas.

The last of the native bighorns died out in the 1950s, victims of hunting and of diseases caught from domestic sheep. The new stock, brought from Arizona, is watched over in a six hundred-acre holding pasture. Some of the young have been set free in the mountains to show whether they can survive in a truly wild state. Since the management area covers 100,000 acres of rugged country with few roads and trails, no one knows as yet how well the young bighorns are doing.

Mule deer live in the Black Gap area too, as they do in many Trans-Pecos mountains. They may not be killed in either of the two national parks, but about four hundred are "harvested" from Black Gap each year in a public hunt.

Mule deer are somewhat larger than white-tailed deer and have notably big ears. Seeing an antlerless female in my truck headlights one night, I thought for a moment she *was* a mule, or perhaps a burro. Mule deer are accomplished jumpers. They can clear seven-foot fences with ease, leap twenty feet on flat ground and thirty when running downhill. In the rough country they favor, they can use this skill. (White-tailed deer are found in brushy country all over Texas; mule deer only in the Trans-Pecos and certain areas of the Panhandle.)

Hunters like mule deer because of their size, and also because they are slightly uncommon. There is a little additional status in killing one. In the official language of the Parks and Wildlife Department, "the demand for mule deer hunting in the Trans-Pecos region currently exceeds the supply of this resource." There is also a problem of fawn survival; too many of them die. As a result the mule deer, like the whitewing dove, has an uncertain future in Texas.

Beyond Black Gap, the Rio Grande, flowing northeast, enters a series of canyons which, lumped together, are called the Lower Canyons. They are roughly 1,200 feet deep and run on for seventy-five miles, making up one of the wildest and most beautiful natural regions left in either the United States or Mexico.[7] (One side of the river is Texas, the other Coahuila.)

The canyon rims are desert. But in the bottom the Rio Grande supports shade trees, wildflowers, catfish, and singing birds. Springs of pure warm water, probably heated by molten rock beneath the surface, flow out of the canyon walls and into the river. One of them fills a luxurious natural bathtub, big enough for ten or twelve bathers, with water at 85 degrees.[8]

There are grassy banks to camp on and many wild animals and birds. Hiking is impossible; you have to travel by water. The canyon walls often rise directly from the river, leaving no ground to walk on.

The Lower Canyons are a wild paradise for those who meet no misfortune. Big fish are available in the river and the water from the springs doesn't need to be purified. The rapids are few and easily portaged. One paddles downstream, looking up at majestic rock formations and unreachable caves.

But a smashed canoe or an injured person can instantly create what some outdoorsmen like to call "a survival situation." It may be that no one else will come down the river for weeks. The only way to get equipment or an injured man out of the canyons is to keep going to the end.

An able-bodied man can climb out almost anywhere, but then faces a hike of twenty to fifty miles across waterless, roadless desert cut by canyons, as well as the possibility of getting lost.

I floated through the Lower Canyons with a group of twenty. Nothing went wrong. We saw five species of hawks and a golden eagle. We found a young mountain lion dead in the river. Muddy banks showed the tracks of deer, raccoons, coyotes, and bobcats, and there were beaver slides here and there. One evening we dined on fillets of catfish, caught from the river. We explored side canyons, climbed to the rim, and met on the Coahuila side six young Mexicans who hoped to become wetbacks.

In five days we experienced a variety of April winds and weathers, and no trouble at all. But we were ready for almost any emergency, if one came, and we numbered so many men and so many rafts and canoes that our margin of safety was wide. It is the very small groups—two people in a single canoe, for example—that are most vulnerable.

On the western side of Big Bend National Park, running northwest up the Rio Grande for about 175 miles, lies rough, untraveled country, lightly specked with old Spanish settlements and the ruins of frontier forts. A beautifully engineered highway, called the River Road, runs from the park to the town of Presidio. Beyond that are steadily worsening roads and tiny villages beside the river. Finally even these play out.

For thirty years, beginning in 1852, Presidio was a way-station on the Chihuahua Trail, that amazingly crooked trade route linking the old Texas port of Indianola with the mining capital of Chihuahua, then bigger than any town in Texas and a ravenous consumer of American goods.

The trail was crooked because it had to avoid mountains and canyons and strike water holes fairly often. At Presidio, wagons could ford the Rio Grande. The final stretch across the desert to Chihuahua could be covered in about four days. A train now makes it in four hours.

Ojinaga, across the river from Presidio, is where thousands of Americans have boarded the Chihuahua al Pacifico Railway for a two-day trip across the Chihuahuan Desert and the Sierra Madre Occidental to the Gulf of California.

Sixty miles above Presidio, among harsh mountains and dry canyons, is Texas's highest waterfall, Capote Falls. It is only about two hundred feet high, and the stream which makes it, Capote Creek, can be stepped across. But the little waterfall is beautiful, as yet unspoiled and unlittered (the final two-mile walk discourages many), and it nourishes columbines and maidenhair ferns in the midst of desert. Many people go there as a sort of pilgrimage. Few venture into the difficult country farther up the Rio Grande.

From Ojinaga and Presidio, all the way upriver to El Paso, the Rio Grande is often a dry ditch. Its water is now collected in Elephant Butte Reservoir, in New Mexico, and used for irrigation. At Ojinaga a big river, the Conchos, comes in from Mexico, and the Rio Grande is in business again.

It is mostly Conchos water that fills the canyons of Big Bend National Park and makes them navigable by canoe. It does the same for the Lower Canyons. Recently Mexico dammed the Conchos to make a lake in the Chihuahuan Desert, and thus now controls much of the water that in the past filled the river from the Big Bend to the Gulf of Mexico.

The U.S. Army's famous and inconclusive experiment with camels, begun in the 1850s, involved two major tests of the animals in the Trans-Pecos. The Camel Corps headquarters was in greener country, near Kerrville, and the camels were marched from there to Fort Stockton. Then they went over complicated zigzag routes between Fort Stockton and the Rio Grande.

The camels carried feed and water for the horses and mules which went along for comparison, but got none of it themselves. They did without water between water holes, sometimes for several days, and lived off bitter desert shrubs like greasewood and bitterweed that the other livestock wouldn't eat.

Their unshod feet held up well on the sharp rocks. One camel, bitten by a rattlesnake, showed no ill effects. The second expedition got into serious trouble, almost running out of water with no idea of where the next water hole might be. Only water which the camels carried saved the lives of the suffering, half-crazed men and mules. The camels suffered too, but they did without until the expedition found water.

On the whole the camels performed well, carrying far bigger loads than horses and mules could and faring better than they did in the harsh Southwest environment.[9] It was men who failed, through their contempt for the camels and their mismanagement of them. (A few enlightened men and officers were involved in the experiment, but not enough.) The Civil War wrecked the Corps and scattered the camels, and when it was over the era of railroad building began.

The camels had created a sensation in Texas, attracting crowds and frightening horses. A woman knitted a pair of socks from camel hair and sent them to President Franklin Pierce. Some camels escaped into the Southwestern deserts and survived there quite well until people shot them. After the breakup of the Camel Corps, some were worked to death hauling salt in Nevada.

A few Turks, Egyptians, and Syrians had been brought to Texas along with the animals to teach camel-handling to the Americans. Some of these men finished out their lives in the United States, leaving various marks behind. One died at Quartzsite, Arizona, in 1903, after many years as a wandering prospector in the Sonoran Desert. A small monument stands at Quartzsite in his memory. Another camel driver drifted into Mexico and married a Yaqui Indian. One of his sons, Plutarco Elias Calles, became President of Mexico in 1924.

Oddly enough, camels lived in Texas about 50 million years ago, the ancient ancestors of those which returned in the 1850s. For camels are not native to Africa and Asia. They evolved in the New World and made their way to the other continents, perhaps by way of Alaska and Siberia. Their nearest relatives now in the Americas are the llamas of the Andes. Many fossil remains of camels have been found in Texas.

So the 120 camels brought to Texas in the 1850s were actually returning home. Their visit, however, was short. They could have survived in the wild but people would not let them.

A little traveling show turned up in San Antonio in 1910. With it was an old she-camel who bore the U.S. Army brand. She was probably one of many calves born long ago at Camp Verde, near Kerrville, the headquarters of the camel experiment. Newspapers ran stories about her for a few days. Then the little circus left town with the old beast, and the Army's Camel Corps settled quietly into history.

2 | THE EDWARDS PLATEAU

The Edwards Plateau is dominated by silence and space. None of the big cities of Texas is found there. Most counties have just one town, the county seat. The region covers 31,000 square miles, nearly all of it ranch-land, and has the best year-round climate in Texas. Summer nights are dry and cool, with a steady breeze from the south. Winters are sunny and mild.

In Indian times, only about 120 years ago, the plateau was chiefly grass-land. Then ranching came, and enough grass was soon eaten and trampled to give woody plants a start. The plateau is now scrubby savan-nah—patches of grass scattered among stands of cedar, oak, and mes-quite. The trees are small. Mixed with them are various shrubs and many kinds of cactus. The rather austere landscape rolls on for hundreds of miles, dominated by an outsize sky.

The plateau, fifteen hundred to three thousand feet above sea level, is a big slab of limestone up to ten thousand feet thick. The deep cuts that have been made in this rock for Interstate 10, especially in the hills around Junction, are mere scratches on its surface. This limestone was put down as ocean sediments in Cretaceous time when all of the region lay under a warm sea.

It was a shallow sea—only six hundred feet deep, with big marine reptiles swimming in it—yet it built up sediments on its bottom nearly two miles thick. The process took millions of years. The ocean floor kept sinking as the weight of the sediments accumulated, while the sea above it remained shallow.

The Edwards limestone, unlike that of the Blackland Prairie (Chapter 5), has not decomposed into a rich, deep soil. On the contrary, it has hardly made any soil at all. Scarcity of rain is one reason, and lack of appropriate plants another. As you drive through any highway cut—its walls will be white or cream-colored rock—glance at its upper edge. There you will see a fringe of grass and weeds, their roots fixed in an inch or two of thin brown dirt. Below that is solid limestone. Admittedly, rain has washed some of the soil away from the edge of a cut. If you dig in the middle of a pasture, you may find soil about six inches deep, rocky and thin. Yet it supports all the life there is on the Edwards Plateau, which is quite a lot. Only here and there, where soil has washed down into flats, is it deep enough for plowing, or for prairie-dog holes.

There is considerable plowing and farming around Eldorado and Fredericksburg. For the rest, the Edwards Plateau is ranchland. Cattle raisers no longer consider themselves socially superior to sheep and goat raisers. Most ranchers now grow all three, having learned that it's more profitable to do so.

In 1900, before the railroad network was complete, a curiosity called the Frisco Trailway was built from Sonora to Menard to Brady, a distance of one hundred miles, where it ended at a railhead. It was a fenced lane, 250 yards wide, designed for cattle drives. There were entrances and exits, just as there are on freeways, and rest stops—holding pens beside streams where the cattle could drink. It worked reasonably well, keeping the cattle being driven to market from mixing with those in the ranches the trail passed through, and was used until 1930.

Dry though it is, the Edwards Plateau is a great collector of underground water and generator of springs and streams. From the high country around Eldorado, rivers flow away in many directions. They run north to join the Colorado and south to join the Rio Grande. Others pour across the Balcones Escarpment—that is, through what is called the Hill Country—and out onto the Rio Grande Plain. They are among the most beautiful streams in Texas—cold and clear, fed by springs, winding through canyons and supporting tall stands of pecan trees, sycamores, and cypresses: the Frio, the Guadalupe, the Nueces, the Sabinal.

A few miles south of Junction, on privately owned land, an underground reservoir leaks through hundreds of holes in a hillside and gives a major boost to the flow of the South Llano River. This is the place long known as Seven Hundred Springs (and in beer commercials as Eleven Hundred), a major oasis of ferns, mosses, and noisy, tumbling water.

North of Del Rio the Devil's River flows down to the Rio Grande. Lying as it does in out-of-the-way ranch country, it is a stream that relatively few Texans have seen. For much of its length it is dry except after rain. But a few miles below the village of Juno, fed by springs, it becomes a tree-bordered river winding among rocky desert hills. Isolation has kept it clean. In the 1960s, some government agency announced that the Devil's River contained the last pure surface water left in Texas. It was still safe to lie on a slab of rock there and drink directly from the stream.

Real desert begins a little way west of the Devil's River and stretches

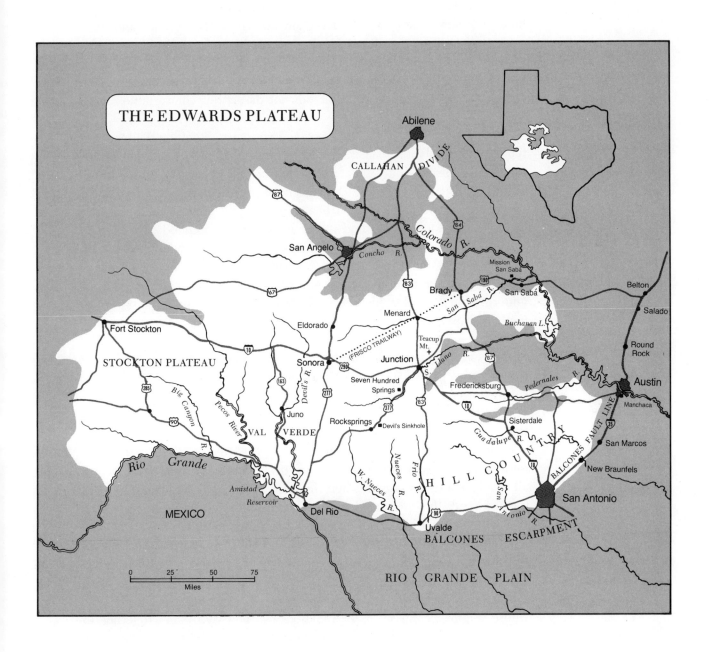

on across the Stockton Plateau toward Marathon. The Stockton Plateau is merely that part of the Edwards Plateau which lies west of the Pecos. U.S. 90 runs through it for some 150 miles.

It is not lack of rain that makes this country desert, though little rain falls. It is lack of soil. Much of the surface is rocks—big ones and little ones, the result of the slow breaking up of the rocky hillsides and plateaus. Farther west, Alpine and Marfa get about the same amount of rain—eight to fifteen inches a year. But the earth there is coated with a good volcanic soil; and that country is not desert but comfortable ranchland.

What grows among the rocks of the southern Stockton Plateau are typical desert plants—yuccas, sotols, agaves, plus cacti and the various tough, dry shrubs that make up chaparral. They are thinly scattered, with plenty of rocky ground showing between them. All are adapted in one way or another to survive heat and drought. There are no shade-loving plants such as you find in the East Texas woodlands; there is no shade.[1] There are no parasitic plants, no clinging or twining vines, no saprophytes taking their food from dead or decaying material. Everything stands alone in the sun, conserving water in succulent pads or underground roots. Or, like the creosote bush, getting along with a minimum of water and collecting that through a shallow, far-reaching root system.

This dry country looks pretty much the same throughout the year: spines, thorns, rocks. There are no autumn colors or falling leaves, and no spring flowers. It doesn't rain here in the spring.

The thunderstorm season runs from June to September. Then fragile, tiny wildflowers appear, close to the surface of the ground. Their way of adapting to the desert is to spend most of the year as seeds. When the rains start they suddenly germinate, grow, bloom, and bear fresh seeds, all in a few summer weeks. Then the rains stop, the little plants die, and the new seeds they produced wait in the ground ten months or so for next year's thunderstorms. It is a curious way to live, roughly equivalent to a human being's sleeping for sixty years and then staying awake for five. But it is the only way these frail plants have managed to survive in the desert.

It is a desert crossed by two big streams, the Pecos and the Rio Grande, whose origins lie far away in the Rockies. The two come together in western Val Verde County. Along both rivers near their junctions are scores of rock shelters, the kind of shallow caves that prehistoric men liked to live in. Over a long span of time, probably several thousand years, the people who lived in the Val Verde cave shelters produced the biggest and most varied collections of cave paintings ever found in Texas. Many of them are still there.

The area of painted caves is huge. Along the Rio Grande it extends twenty-five miles upstream and downstream from the Pecos's mouth. It runs for forty miles up the Pecos itself. This suggests that the Val Verde shelters were a major population center, the Houston or Dallas of their day. Actually, at any given time the number of people living there was probably small and only a few of the shelters were occupied.

Some of the cave-floor middens are ten feet deep. Excavated, they reveal a people who lived quietly along these two big streams, in a comfortable climate, killing deer, harvesting wild plants, and painting and repainting the smooth stone walls of their dwellings with all the images of their world and many from their imaginations.

In the bigger shelters, the walls are painted to a height of ten feet and for a distance of one hundred feet. (The caves are shallow, little more than overhanging ledges, and they run for a considerable distance along the river banks.) The biggest human figures are larger than life—eight feet tall. They have no faces, sometimes no heads, and nothing to indicate whether they are men or women.

Deer, feathers, insects, plants, eels appear on the walls. Many figures are hard to identify, and some are merely ornamental designs. Pictures of mountain lions, the largest of them sixteen feet long, suggest that the painters either worshipped mountain lions or feared them excessively.[2] The colors used in all the pictures are black and white, orange and yellow, and two shades of red—all made from ocher, white clay, or carbon.

Hundreds of square yards of the paintings were hopelessly faded with age before archaeologists began to study them. When the Amistad Reservoir filled with water recently, a number of the shelters were flooded. Others are now easy to reach by motorboat and have been painted over by visitors with aerosol spray cans. Fortunately the paintings were well studied and recorded in the 1930s, long before paved roads and tourism came to the area.

Except for the rivers (the first things to be named in a new country) place names on the Edwards Plateau are rarely Spanish. They are usually Anglo-Saxon: Junction, Teacup, Rocksprings, Fort McKavett. The Spaniards never settled this country because the Comanches and Apaches wouldn't let them. They tried; they believed there were gold and silver along the Llano and San Sabá rivers. In 1757 they founded the Mission San Sabá near the present town of Menard.

A presidio, intended as protection for the mission, lay three miles away on the opposite side of the San Sabá River. Of the three hundred persons in it, more than half were women and children—soldiers' families.

The Comanches attacked the mission early one morning in March, 1758.[3] Two thousand Indians appeared outside the compound, mounted and armed and painted. The three priests came out to greet the Indians and there were professions of friendship. But while some of the Indians claimed they were just paying a friendly visit, others were raiding the mission kitchen, killing cattle, and plundering the church. In a terrible day and night ten persons, including two of the priests, were tortured, murdered, and mutilated. The others escaped in various ways, by night, to spread the news and fear over Texas. The presidio had been no help at all. Even the people of long-established and far-away San Antonio feared for months that the Comanches would attack them next.

The Comanche aim, probably, was to discourage the Spanish and Apaches from joining up against them. If so, they achieved their purpose. The San Sabá mission was never reestablished. Spain maintained the little presidio, always vulnerable and afraid, for ten years after the massacre, then abandoned it too. Some old foundations remain on the banks of the San Sabá, a mile or so upstream from Menard. They are among the few traces of Spanish settlement on the Edwards Plateau.

The San Sabá massacre established one of Texas's most durable legends, that of the lost San Sabá mine. Supposedly the Spaniards found gold near the mission, and when they were driven out left a great fortune behind. Some claim the treasure is a mine, others say it is a pile of gold and silver bullion cached in a cave.

Probably no such treasure ever existed. But thousands of persons have believed it did and have spent parts of their lives and all of their money looking for it. They have bought curious maps from strangers, dug holes, made measurements, and searched the land for signs and markers.

One of the keenest San Sabá mine-hunters was James Bowie, the Alamo hero for whom the Bowie knife was named. Sometimes, in fact, the treasure is called the Lost Bowie Mine, because Bowie is supposed actually to have seen it—some Apaches, he said, showed it to him.

Not many men, nowadays, actually get out and tramp the banks of the San Sabá in search of the legendary hoard. Most of the handed-down stories and imaginative maps of a hundred years ago have been pretty well checked out. But a few men do still study old documents in Texan and Mexican archives, trying to piece together a set of clues that will lead them to the treasure.

A century after the San Sabá fiasco, in 1852 the Americans built Fort McKavett a few miles up the river from the Spanish ruins. Fort McKavett itself is now a ruin, but an impressive one, on a hillside not far from the little green stream. Some of its white stone buildings are still standing, some are restored, some mere broken walls and windows. It was a large post, dedicated to fighting Comanches, with enough soldiers to require a thirty-acre kitchen garden of melons, tomatoes, squashes, pumpkins, and sweet potatoes. No such crops are grown there now. The old fort is partly a village with a post office and tavern, partly a state park. But there remain from frontier times a feeling of isolation and a smell of wood smoke. The 1850s seem only a decade or so in the past.

You may spend your life in Texas and never see one of the state's most beautiful wild animals, the ringtail, though there are plenty of them. If you do, it will probably be in a flashlight beam or a car's headlights, for ringtails are wholly nocturnal. Their eyeshine, in electric light, is sometimes a burning red, like embers, and sometimes pale yellow. Their eyes are large, for seeing in the dark, outlined as if with black mascara and set in a white face mask. Their furry tails are longer than their bodies and have eight black rings on a background of white. The body fur runs in color from gray to a golden yellow and the pelts are small—ringtails weigh only two or three pounds.

Their common name is ringtail *cat,* but they are not part of the cat family, although they look a little like cats and have their speed and grace. Actually they are cousins of the raccoon and the coatamundi. They like rocky places—crevices, ledges, old rock walls that are coming apart—and thus the Edwards Plateau suits them well.[4] They must also have plentiful water handy, and as stock tanks have multiplied in the Trans-Pecos (which has had unlimited rocks all along) the ringtails are becoming more common there.

They can climb trees and vertical rocks, using their claws, and can easily walk tight-wire atop barbed-wire fences, balancing with their tails. Their diet includes rats, mice, lizards, berries, acorns, baby rabbits, many insects, and a few birds. People who try to keep them as pets find they like bananas and hamburger but won't eat canned dog food. They are unhappy as pets, anyway—they hide all day in whatever box or den is provided and try all night to escape. Kept in a house, they wreck it. They climb anything they can get their claws into, including curtains and papered walls, and are as curious and mischievous as raccoons. They are better off left in the wild, glimpsed just occasionally by campers and nighttime travelers.

In World War II, the Office of Price Administration put ceilings on the prices of wild animal furs, but overlooked ringtail pelts. This, it turned out, was because the administrators in Washington did not know that, far away in the Southwest, ringtails even existed. The price of pelts quickly climbed from two dollars to ten.

Trapping furs is now a dying occupation in Texas. What most people do is hunt, and the prime game animal is the white-tailed deer. The Edwards Plateau is *the* deer-hunting country of the state. Its huge pastures, growing many kinds of brush, are good habitat for deer. They live among the ranchers' livestock, water at windmill tanks, and, like the cattle, have commercial value.

Ranchers make substantial amounts of money from deer leases. People converge on the Edwards Plateau from all directions and from hundreds of miles away when the deer season begins, in November, and spend generously on food, lodging, liquor, and ammunition. Cold-storage plants specialize in dressing deer for hunters who don't want (or don't know how) to dress their own, drying some of the venison into jerky and freezing the rest. From the businessman's point of view, deer are a major natural resource on the Edwards Plateau.

But hunting them is not just for tourists. The local people get as excited in the deer season as they do in the high-school football season. Everybody wants to kill a buck with a fine set of antlers and more points than anyone else's. Towns offer prizes to the youngest child who kills his own deer. A few hunters, mistaken for deer, get shot, and a few, unaccustomed to exercise, have heart attacks in the pastures.

Deer like to feed around dawn and dusk, and to bed down comfortably, hidden in brush, in the middle of the day and through the night. That's why you see them along highways at twilight. They jump the fences and eat the tasty plants that grow in the ditches—plants domestic livestock can't reach. Sometimes a deer makes a bad jump and fails to get his hind legs over the fence. He (or more likely she, for does are smaller than bucks) often hangs there until he dies. Except for rifles, the man-made devices that kill the most deer are fences and automobiles.

The speed and agility of deer make people suppose that they range over vast territories, but biologists who have tagged deer, released them, and watched them for years, found that they tend to spend their whole lives in a small area—in a single square mile, for example. Apparently they like to be familiar with their territory.

They will sometimes travel hundreds of miles to get back to their beloved native ground. Game management men have moved deer about in Texas a good deal, trapping them where they are plentiful and releasing them where they're scarce. One buck, released near Sheffield in the Trans-Pecos, travelled 350 miles back to the Aransas National Wildlife Refuge, where he had originally been trapped and tagged, and was trapped there again two years later.

You cannot tell the age of a buck from the number of points on his antlers. The male fawn's first set of antlers is a pair of simple spikes. In the years after that, the size of his antlers is determined by many factors, including what he gets to eat. One buck, tagged and kept track of, grew either eight-point or ten-point antlers every year for five years.

Sometimes, a doe grows antlers, but this is rare. Healthy does—what game-management men call prime animals—bear twin fawns more frequently than not, triplets fairly often, and quadruplets once in a while.

Deer are not always shy. They can be vicious, especially to each other, and they can kill rattlesnakes by chopping them up with their sharp front hooves. A woman I know says that a deer killed her brother, an able-bodied man. He had rescued the animal as an orphaned fawn and raised it in a fenced yard. It was gentle and harmless for several years, and then one day without warning it attacked him so fiercely with both hooves and antlers that he died of his wounds the next day.

Since the white man began to meddle ecologically in Texas, the state's deer populations have swung many times from far too many in a few places to almost none everywhere. Before 1903, when it became illegal to kill does in the state, deer hunting was entirely unregulated. Market hunters shot deer all year long and sold the meat in cities. Hide hunters left thousands of skinned carcasses to the vultures. Sheep ranchers bought dogs to kill wolves, and the dogs killed deer as well. Soon there were very few deer.

There have been drought years when one-third of all deer on the Edwards Plateau died of starvation or disease. These huge die-offs seem catastrophic, but deer breed rapidly and make quick recoveries. At other times and places in Texas, deer have become too plentiful and created a serious problem as they jumped fences and ate crops and kitchen gardens, even in towns.

Gradually, over the past sixty years, biologists have worked out principles of deer-herd management.[5] The principles are not always followed, because some landowners dislike deer—they eat plants that might otherwise feed livestock. The deer are not the ranchers' property, anyway. They belong to the state.

Some ranchers are beginning to realize that deer add to the value of land. It makes sense to figure them in as "animal units" in the economy of a ranch. (A cow is the basic animal unit. Six deer eat as much as one cow, so six deer make an animal unit. So do eight goats, seven sheep, or twenty-five jackrabbits, though few ranchers count jackrabbits.) The rancher knows from experience how many animal units a pasture can feed without being damaged, and he stocks his land accordingly.

The Edwards Plateau doesn't grow the biggest deer in Texas. It doesn't even grow them as big as it used to. Weight records, mounted deer heads, and the memories of old people all confirm the change. Just why it occurred has been much discussed. Some blame inbreeding or mineral deficiencies. Some say the correct ratio of bucks to does has been destroyed by the hunting of bucks only. There are even people who claim that the deer on the Edwards Plateau are a separate species, inherently smaller than deer in most other parts of the state.

Experiments have proved all these theories wrong. Edwards Plateau deer mated to deer from other regions produce offspring, proving that they are the same species. Big bucks brought in from elsewhere make no difference; the fawns they father on the Edwards Plateau grow no bigger than the other deer there.

What does make a difference is food. Competition for it in this ranch country is intense. Cows eat the grass, sheep eat the forbs, and goats eat the browse. (Forbs include weeds and wildflowers—"any herb that is not grass or grasslike." Browse is the tender, edible parts of trees and bushes —buds, shoots, young leaves, berries, acorns.)

Deer like browse best. It is their natural food. But goats are browsers too; and there are millions of goats on the Edwards Plateau. Not finding enough browse, the deer have to eat whatever they find that's edible, and they wind up slightly malnourished. Deer have been taken from the Edwards Plateau and moved to ranges where they could get more of their favorite foods. They soon averaged thirty-two pounds more in weight than their brothers and sisters who remained on the plateau.

Thin soil; thin rain. Ranch women of the plateau will phone their relatives in the next county to say excitedly that they had a nice little shower, and did y'all get any? The year's grass, and the year's profits, may depend on such bits of luck. It can be argued, and has been, that the harsh conditions of this region have forced many of the eastern trees to adapt in order to survive here; to become, or almost to become, new species.[6]

The live oak is never the big brooding, spreading tree that it is on the Gulf Coast. It is small and upright and tends to grow in clumps called mottes. The persimmon tree becomes the smaller Mexican (or Texas) persimmon, with round, juicy black fruits that have been used to make hair dye. They are edible but not much in demand. Buckeyes, mulberries, and hackberries on the Edwards Plateau are all somewhat different from their East Texas relatives.

Then there is mountain laurel, a specialty of the Edwards Plateau, with its aromatic flowers and its annual crop of pretty poisonous beans. Actually it is not a laurel but a legume, related to locusts and mesquites. The beans, called mescal beans, that come out of its tough brown pods are bright red and big enough to hide your little fingernail. Tradition says that one of them will make you drunk, two will make you sick, and three will kill you, and a recent handbook on plant poisons bears this out. The poisons in mescal beans are alkaloids, and it is likely that they don't cause drunkenness so much as hallucinations and convulsions. But it is safe to sniff the big clusters of early-spring flowers if you like their medicinal smell. And safe to wear the beans as beads if you want to. Excavations have shown that prehistoric Indians did.

The mountain laurel is plentiful. The Texas snowbell is not. On a ranch in Edwards County, visited at intervals by botanists, four of these little trees grow. They are the last specimens known to exist (except for a few seedlings in a laboratory in Austin). The Texas snowbell never grew anywhere but on the Edwards Plateau. Nibbled almost to extermination by goats, it may not be there much longer.

Of cedar there is more than anyone has ever wanted. It is thinnest in the north, but in the counties along the Balcones Escarpment it covers millions of acres of white rocky hillsides. Not even goats will eat it.

Actually the tree is a juniper, *Juniperus ashei*. But it has entered our culture as cedar—cedar brake, cedar chopper, cedar post—and can't be changed. It thrives on heat and drought. In the thickest brakes the trees grow so close together that their branches interlock all the way to the ground, leaving no room for grass or anything else—the cedar is all there is.

Luckily it has some uses. It makes excellent charcoal, and from 1880 to about 1919 a stretch along the Guadalupe River was known as Charcoal City. It was not a city at all but a thinly settled region where people lived in tents, chopped cedar, turned it into charcoal, and hauled it to San Antonio and sold it.[7]

They were called "charcoal burners." They were of many ethnic backgrounds, but most were Anglo-Saxons from the hills of the Ozarks or from Tennessee. They liked working for themselves and living outdoors. They considered "tight houses" unhealthy—if they lived in something firmer than a tent, it had to have plenty of openings and cracks to let in fresh air. And maybe they were right, for they were remarkably vigorous, tough, soft-spoken, well-behaved people whose hands and faces were usually black from charcoal. In their tents among the cedar brakes they raised large, healthy families.

Burned in the open air, cedar becomes soft white ash. The charcoal burners arranged green cedar logs in big close-packed mounds, covered these with cedar bark and dirt to keep almost all air out, and let the mass smolder for four days. The result was a load of charcoal which, stuffed into tow sacks, was ready for sale in town.

Charcoal was not used then for cooking steaks and hamburgers. It was often used as a filter to make unpalatable water taste clean and pure, as if it had come from a spring. (The procedure still works, of course. To purify heavily contaminated water, boil it for ten minutes to kill germs. Then filter it slowly through charcoal from your campfire to make it taste and smell good.)

But what almost every family used charcoal for, in the time before electricity, was heating flatirons for ironing clothes. The high, steady, smokeless heat of charcoal was ideal for the job. Blacksmiths burned it in their forges. Tinsmiths heated soldering irons with it. Ground to powder and mixed with honey, charcoal made a medicine for stomach trouble. Fed to chickens along with their feed, it kept them healthy, or so people thought.

The charcoal burners got their cedar free, in return for clearing the land it grew on for the farmers or ranchers who owned it. With an axe, a rake, a shovel, and a wagon with mules, they were in business. Charcoal City, full of rough clearings and smoking kilns, stretched along the Guadalupe across two counties, from Sisterdale to New Braunfels.

But new technology reduced the demand for charcoal, and the charcoal burners moved on to other ways of life. Many of them became cedar choppers. This is the second distinct subculture that mountain cedar has produced, and it still survives and covers a much larger area than Charcoal City ever did.[8] Cedar choppers clear land in return for the trees they cut, and they sell the cedar for fence posts. Cedar posts, which are said to outlast iron, have been in steady demand in Texas since 1875, when barbed wire was invented.

Chopping cedar all day is hard, rough work, but it seems to be a satisfactory life for those who can do it. The greatest danger is rattlesnake bites. Rattlesnakes like the dry, loose, rocky land that cedar grows on.

The cedar also attracts a small bird, the golden-cheeked warbler, which is generally said to nest nowhere in the world except on the Edwards Plateau. This is not strictly true. Golden-cheeks nest in various places on the Grand Prairie which *resemble* the Edwards Plateau. The most notable of these is Meridian State Park.

Golden-cheeks winter in southern Mexico and Central America, and come to Texas in March to raise their young. Mature cedar trees—those eighty to two hundred years old—produce soft strips of bark which the birds use in building their nests. (The younger trees don't have much bark of any kind.) The warblers use other materials too—cobwebs to bind the nest together, and soft, downy substances for linings. But the basic structure of their nests is always bark from the old mountain cedars.

Bird lovers hunt through the cedar country hoping to glimpse a golden-cheeked warbler. It is not impossible. The males are very active, always hunting for insects, and with their white breasts, black backs, and yellow cheeks they are easy to see. The females tend to stay out of sight among the leaves. The warblers' song (a hurried "tweeah, tweeah, tweesy," according to Peterson) is one of those small woodland sounds that seem to have no definite source, that seem to come from everywhere and nowhere.

The problem in seeing golden-cheeks is not their shyness but their rarity. Not many of the ancient cedars remain to supply their nest material, and those that do are being cut down steadily as land is cleared and

Sundown on an uplifted fossil reef exposed in the Sierra Diablo, from Victorio Canyon rim northwest of Van Horn. (The Trans-Pecos)

The Rio Grande and volcanic cliffs from "Big Hill" on the River Road
between Presidio and Lajitas. (The Trans-Pecos)

Rock nettle flowers in cliffs above Tornillo Creek
near the Rio Grande. (The Trans-Pecos)

RIGHT: Lava and volcanic ash in the low badlands northwest of Cerro Castellan. (The Trans-Pecos)

Desert surface near the Rio Grande by the hot springs above Boquillas. (The Trans-Pecos)

OVERLEAF: South rim of the Chisos Mountains. (The Trans-Pecos)

A high desert brushland in the Chisos Mountains
east of Panther Peak. (The Trans-Pecos)

Agave, prickly pear, and brush in the Chisos Mountains Basin. (The Trans-Pecos)

Tamarisk and boulders near the mouth
of Santa Elena Canyon. (The Trans-Pecos)

Cypress roots in the Frio River south
of Leakey. (The Edwards Plateau)

Buckeye, cedar elm, live oak, and Spanish oak northeast
of Dripping Springs. (The Edwards Plateau)

LEFT: Willows and switchgrass by Bull Creek Falls west
of Austin. (The Edwards Plateau)

RIGHT: Golden waves of coreopsis west of Oak Hill.
(The Edwards Plateau)

Buttonbush and creek stones southeast of Bee Caves.
(The Edwards Plateau)

An ice storm between Dripping Springs and Oak Hill.
(The Edwards Plateau)

housing developments spread. Even when some of their habitat is left, the birds abandon it if human beings move too close. They are not adaptable, like blue jays or grackles. They are programmed to do things in a certain way. The nests they build today are precisely like nests removed from trees eighty years ago and kept in scientific collections. They are made of the same materials and put together in the same way.

Various groups are trying to help the birds, the best way being to secure some cedar-covered land for them and then let them alone. The Travis Audubon Society has acquired a section of land as a refuge, but does not publicize its location. If it did, the crush of bird watchers hoping to see these rare little creatures would drive them away. The golden-cheek is classified as rare by the Bureau of Sports Fisheries and Wildlife. In 1968 a survey indicated that there are only about fifteen thousand of them left. They are likely to become an endangered species soon, and (if present trends continue) to vanish for good from the Edwards Plateau and from the world early in the twenty-first century.

The Balcones Escarpment is not the high cliff that its name suggests. It is, rather, a band of rocky canyon country five to twenty miles wide, the ragged, raveled edge of the Edwards Plateau. It's a transition zone where the plateau lets down to plains country on the south and east. It runs for hundreds of miles, from Del Rio on the Rio Grande to San Antonio, then northeast to Austin and beyond. This is the Texas Hill Country, a region of dude ranches and real ranches; of clear, winding streams; of caves; of thousands of small springs and a few so large that when they bubble to the surface through geologic faults they make rivers.

Balcones means "balconies" in Spanish. Not the kind movie theatres have, but the kind on which young ladies used to be serenaded in Spain. Presumably some early explorer looked up at the hills from the Rio Grande Plain and thought their high ledges resembled balconies. Or maybe he was on the heights, gazing southward across the plain, and decided that the view from up there was like the view from a balcony.

Making the escarpment took millions of years. A simplified version of what happened is this: the Edwards Plateau is made of one kind of rock and the plains to the south and east of it of several other kinds. The two regions are rather insecurely joined, geologically speaking. A great crack, or geological fault, formed across Texas along the weak joint, like a crack running across a plate. The Edwards Plateau remained firmly in place, and the coastal plain sank, in places as much as a thousand feet. This left a cliff or escarpment between the two. Then the cliff slowly crumbled and washed onto the plain below, and rivers flowing off the Edwards Plateau cut canyons into its edge.

The actual events were more complicated. There was not just one geological fault but many—big ones and small ones, occurring over a long period. They lie roughly parallel to one another, and they add up to what is called the Balcones Fault *Zone.* The coastal plain settled so slowly that erosion was able to keep the various lines of cleavage worn down. Thus there were never really sharp cliffs along the faults but always slopes and canyons which merely got bigger and deeper as the low country sank lower still.

From Austin to San Antonio, the Balcones Escarpment faces the Blackland Prairie and the change is abrupt. Rocky hills drop down to rich, smooth farmland along a fairly even line. The town of San Marcos, for example, is partly on the escarpment and partly on the plain. In Austin you can see the firm line of the Balcones hills in the western part of the city.

But from San Antonio to Del Rio, the high country and the low are interlocked. Limestone ridges extend from the Edwards Plateau onto the Rio Grande Plain, like rocky headlands running out to sea. (At various times in the past, they have been exactly that.) The major streams have made deep, narrow canyons in which the plains country reaches far upstream into the Edwards Plateau. You can stand on high, dry ridges which support only a few goats and look down into well-watered canyons with groves of pecans and sycamores. Or perhaps dense thickets of chaparral instead, for the Rio Grande brush has moved into many of the canyon bottoms.

The well-loved cypress trees of the Hill Country occur only along the streams. They are the common bald cypress, the same that grow hundreds of miles away in the swamps of East Texas and Louisiana. In the Hill Country they occupy the river banks instead of standing directly in the water, and they lack the buttresslike "knees" which help keep the swamp cypresses upright in soft mud. And they are fussy—they shun both the high, dry parts of the Edwards Plateau and the hot Rio Grande Plain. They stick to the middle stretches of the rivers, the parts which wind through the Balcones valleys and canyons. They seem like somber, clannish visitors to this region, dignified strangers from another life zone.

Travelers in the Hill Country are sometimes puzzled by trees which seem to be covered in a coarse gray fur. The stuff is ball moss, a relative of the Spanish moss that decorates the Gulf Coast. These mosses are not parasites but epiphytes, plants which may grow on another plant but take no nourishment from it. They get their food from particles in the air, dust, and rain, and sometimes demonstrate their nonparasitic nature by growing on fence wires and telephone lines. Ball moss sends no roots into the thing it grows on. It just clings. A small specimen may be no larger than a golf ball; a big one is the size of a baby's head.

A dead oak tree may become a ball-moss extravaganza—completely covered, to the tips of the smallest twigs. Many people conclude from this that ball moss eventually kills the trees it occupies, but it doesn't. A tree grows outward twelve to eighteen inches a year, and on this outermost growth its canopy of leaves is spread to the sun. Ball moss, obliged to live frugally and spread slowly on what it can get from the air, can't keep up with such rapid growth. It takes over a whole tree only after the tree has died from some other cause.

You can climb the Balcones Escarpment in an hour or so by car, starting in brush country on the plain, winding up an ever-narrowing canyon, and emerging, probably, onto a bleak stretch of goat-growing country under a vast hard sky. Or you can drive the Hill Country lengthwise, switching from one ranch road to another. For years a road-testing company has used one of the routes. It sends strings of numbered cars at high speeds through the dips and curves, in and out of canyons, and later measures the wear on tires and other parts. Each car in the fleet has a heavy metal framework at its front end, to protect it when it hits a deer.

Many Hill Country hills resemble the stairstep pyramids of Mexico. Strangers wonder if these huge quasi-architectural forms were somehow man-made. They were not. The steps on such hillsides may be six or ten feet high. The hills were laid down in layers which alternate limestone with a much softer rock called marl. The limestone now resists erosion while the layers of marl wash easily away.[9] The result is not the usual curving hillside but a series of enormous regular steps.

On some hills the strata of marl are only a few inches thick. They weather into soil in which grass and bushes grow, making long horizontal bands of vegetation on otherwise bare rocky hillsides. These strips look as if some insane and exacting gardener had laid them out with a string.

The white dusty Hill Country roads, winding through pastures under live-oak trees, are chemically kin to the white shell roads of the Gulf Coast. But the Hill Country shells are fossils, older by a hundred million years than the real shells on the Gulf. It is not uncommon to climb a hill and find it flat on top and covered with oyster beds of stone.

The walls of the Balcones canyons are unreachable even by goats, and thus now are the last refuges of certain plants nearing extinction. There, in crevices and on tiny ledges, the last living specimens of the canyon mock orange grow. The plant is normally a small tree, with sweet-smelling white flowers in the spring. But canyon walls are a difficult location. The final, or perhaps semifinal, specimens of mock orange are merely bushes.

Photographed from a plane at twenty thousand feet, the Hill Country looks like a piece of lacework. It is, in fact, the crumbling edge of the Edwards Plateau. Here and there big springs pour out of cracks in the rock and continue on the surface as rivers. These springs have powerfully influenced the history of Texas. It could be argued that the route of Interstate 35 between San Antonio and Waco was determined in Cretaceous time when the weakness of the Balcones Fault Zone was being formed. The highway links a series of cities and towns that were founded beside large springs, all surfacing along the faults. Before the cities were built, the springs were where Indians camped or maintained villages.

The series begins near the Rio Grande with San Felipe Spring at Del Rio. Then come major ones at Brackettville, San Antonio, New Braunfels, San Marcos, Manchaca, Austin, Round Rock, Georgetown, Salado, Belton, and Waco. Some of them (Manchaca, Salado) are of moderate size and privately owned. San Felipe Spring at Del Rio produces 65 million gallons of water daily, enough for the city, a nearby military installation, and a large irrigation project. Barton Springs, at Austin, fills a swimming pool that has roughly the area of a football field. In summer the huge pool is drained twice a week for cleaning, and the springs refill it in nine hours.

The biggest of all the Balcones springs, Comal Spring at New Braunfels, produces 200 million gallons of water daily. It pours out through several openings and makes the Comal River, which winds four miles through town and beyond, to join the Guadalupe. The lovely spring at San Marcos has been heavily commercialized and polluted.

Most of the great springs are now enclosed in concrete, or submerged under dammed-up water, or at best drastically landscaped. Some day, maybe, a more enlightened society will dig out the concrete, let the ferns and frogs and shade trees return, and treasure the Balcones springs as the natural wonders they are.

Meanwhile, the small one at Salado is still pleasantly unimproved. Anyone in town can direct you to it. A heavy, slow, clear stream of water rises soundlessly from the bottom of a little pool. Its surface writhes as if the water were simmering, though actually it is cool, almost cold. Green mounds of watercress grow in the shallows. The long streamers of aquatic plants undulate in the current day and night, year after year. In just a few yards the water from the spring flows into Salado Creek.

Rainwater dissolves limestone. The process is slow, but the rock of the Edwards Plateau has been there since the Age of Reptiles. Porous to begin with, it holds water somewhat as a sponge does, and the water has dissolved out innumerable caverns and sinkholes and tunnels which carry underground streams. The plateau, and especially the Hill Country, makes up the most notable cave region in Texas.

More than two thousand caves are known to exist, and more are found every year. If a frontier remains in Texas, it is this complex and sometimes dangerous underground world.

The easiest and safest caves are rock shelters—overhanging bluffs and shallow grottos, lit by the light of day. Archaeologists and casual arrowhead collectors dig in their middens, for they were favorite dwelling places for prehistoric men and some recent Indians. The commercial caves, with their paved paths and underground snack bars, are heavily advertised along our highways. Most of them are "scenic"—decorated with stalactites and other rock formations.

Then there are the undeveloped caves, dark and hard to explore, lacking the pretty formations that would attract tourists. They interest certain scientists, and the people who explore caves for excitement and adventure. Beyond the known caverns lie the unknown ones, probably a vast, deep realm whose extent will never be known.

Some of the wild caves are dry, some contain streams and pools, and some have parts and passages completely filled with water. All contain living things, and certain obscure Texas caves are famous among biologists for the rare and curious little animals that live in them.[10]

Ezell's Cave, at San Marcos, has many pools of water. A blind white salamander which lives in these pools is found nowhere else in the world. This animal, about three inches long, is probably more highly adapted to cave life than any other creature. Its legs are too thin to support it except in water. It has eye spots but they see nothing. It has no eyelids and no thyroid gland and it never develops lungs. It remains in the larval stage throughout life and breathes with gills, like a pollywog which fails to become a frog.

Ezell's Cave also contains a primitive crustacean less than a tenth of an inch long called *Monodella texana Maguire*. It is kin to the shrimps and crabs. In the Western Hemisphere it has been found only in Ezell's Cave. But around the Mediterranean, in Italy, Tunisia, and Yugoslavia, certain caves contain other small animals so much like it that they are unquestionably close relatives of the ones in Texas.

The question arises, how did they get from Texas to Italy and Yugoslavia? Or perhaps from Yugoslavia to Texas? The animals are blind, minute in size, and unable to live outside the wet blackness of caves. They are barely able to move a few yards in a lifetime, much less across the Atlantic. Yet their structure proclaims that the Mediterranean and the Texas species are descended from a common ancestor as surely as Percherons and Clydesdales both came from an ancestral horse.

One possible answer to the question involves the theory of continental drift. When there was only one great land mass on the earth, Pangaea, the little crustaceans were all one family, living in some complicated cave system. About 200 million years ago the land mass broke apart and the pieces formed up into the present continents, slowly drifting to their present positions. *Monodella texana Maguire* and its Mediterranean kin (or rather their ancestors) drifted with their respective continents, surviving as time built and destroyed many systems of caves, carried by underground water from one cavern to the next and keeping their race alive until man evolved to muse over them. This may be what happened or it may not. It is merely a fairly reasonable solution to a pleasant puzzle.

Cave animals tend to be small, unattractive to housewives, loved only by the scientists who study them. Worms, snails, scorpions, spiders, roaches, centipedes, salamanders, frogs, fishes—these are typical cave dwellers. Most of the world's cave fishes are catfish. Even in surface streams, catfish have characteristics useful in darkness. They have poor eyesight, sensitive whiskers, and a strong sense of smell, and are most active at night. It is easy for them to adapt to permanent darkness.

Tooth Cave, near Austin, ranks among the top few caves in the world in the number of terrestrial troglobite species it contains. (A troglobite is any animal so completely adapted to cave life that it cannot survive anywhere else. It is an aquatic troglobite if it lives in water, terrestrial if it lives in the dry parts of a cave.)

But Tooth Cave, with its hearty population of spiders, scorpions, and centipedes, is now owned by a scientific organization and closed to the public. So is Ezell's Cave, after being nearly ruined by visitors who emptied kerosene and carbide into the underground pools and killed many of the rare animals. The white salamander was almost exterminated by people who broke into Ezell's Cave even after metal bars were put over its entrance, captured the living animals, and shipped them off to be sold as curios at carnivals.

Harvestmen, better known as daddy-longlegs, live in the twilight zone near the mouths of caves, and so do such poisonous spiders as the black widow and the brown recluse. They are not troglobites, but belong to the class of animals which can live either in caves or in the upper world. Owls like to roost in caves, where they cough up "owl pellets"—the undigestible fur, feathers, and bones of small animals they have eaten.

Large animals from the surface do not particularly like to go into caves, at least not very far. They don't get around well in total darkness, and feel uncomfortable away from the sounds and textures of their normal habitat. Most of the bones of surface animals which turn up in caves are there because the animal fell in (through a vertical opening) or because its remains were washed in by a flood, or brought into the cave by a predator—man or animal—which made a meal of it there.

The stable environment of a large cave is good for preserving fossils. Friesenham Cave, in Bexar County, has yielded a huge assortment of fossil mammoth bones, all from young animals, and the bones of saber-toothed cats of all ages. Analyzing the find, scientists concluded that in Pleistocene time, about a million years ago, the cave was a den for saber-tooth cats, and that the adults had killed the young mammoths on the surface and brought them in to feed their young.

Four Texas caves are known for their huge populations of Mexican free-tailed bats, also called guano bats. They are Ney Cave, the Frio Bat Cave, and Bracken's Cave, in the Balcones Escarpment, and the Devil's Sinkhole on the Edwards Plateau. Each is said to contain a greater bat population than Carlsbad Cavern, though nobody really knows; bats are hard to count.

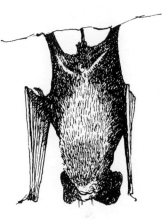

The bats arrive at the caves in spring, coming from the south—Mexico or South America. The females give birth to the young in the Texas caves. The little naked creatures, unable to fly, cling to the cave walls in what are called nursery colonies. There are so many of them that their mothers, returning from feeding flights, don't try to find their own babies but allow any random pair of infant bats to nurse. By the time they are a month old, the young bats can fly and catch insects.

Turn a funnel upside down, and you have the basic shape of the Devil's Sinkhole. It is a big hole going straight down through rock for 140 feet, then widening out into an enormous cone-shaped room. The big room is largely filled with a huge pile of rock, the "breakdown mountain" of debris whose collapse made the cave in the first place.

Leaning over the rim and peering down the hole—it is sixty feet in diameter—you think you see the bottom. But it is merely the summit of the rock pile, and if you could suddenly be lowered to it you would still have to scramble down its steep slope for 160 feet to reach the floor of the cave.

Around the rim of the cone-shaped room are other, smaller rooms containing pools of water. Divers have gone down eighty feet in one of them without reaching bottom.

The Devil's Sinkhole isn't pretty and it doesn't smell good. Getting into it isn't easy, and neither is getting out. The sides of the hole are tricky, with ledges and over-hangs. If you want to go down, you have to rig a rope or cable and be let down by friends, dangling and revolving in the air. Two cave explorers have fallen to their deaths in the Devil's Sinkhole.

Because the entrance descends like a well, direct sunlight reaches only a few feet down from the rim. Shrubs and vines grow in crevices near the top, but in the twilight farther down, there is little but rock. A big yellow-brown lump, projecting from an overhang, is seen through binoculars to be a mass of honeycomb. It must contain several gallons of honey.

A lifetime ago cowboys, unable to get down to the honeycombs, used to shoot into them from the rim and watch the honey drip into the hole. Before their time, bees probably nested in the cave in total security for hundreds of years.

One estimate of the number of bats in the Devil's Sinkhole is eight million. I watched their flight once with a cousin who lives nearby. We came early, before twilight, when cave swallows swirled overhead, or flew in and out of the hole on corkscrew paths, eating insects. From down in the hole came the sound of dripping water and a steady, puzzling hiss, like that of escaping gas.

At a certain point in the twilight the swallows dived in for the night, and immediately afterward, with a rubbery flutter, the first bats came out.

There are merely lots of bats at first. Then the rising column thickens and there are bats in unbelievable numbers. They fly just inches apart, not even brushing each other's wings, and the fluttering mass fills the big round hole completely, like smoke in a stovepipe. Their upward movement seems to draw air up from the underworld. The air near the rim turns thick and foul.

The stream of bats holds its round shape after leaving the cave. An undulating rope of bats trails off to the south, a little higher than the treetops, for perhaps half a mile. Beyond that it frays out into the darkening air. In the top of an oak, a big hawk has been waiting for its supper. It flies into the stream of bats and plucks one out, causing a momentary eddy of alarm. Owls do the same, though on this evening we didn't see one. A slow orange sunset fills more than a quarter of the horizon, and the half-moon high overhead is diffused by thin clouds.

There is no such thing as a collision of bats. Clearly their radar is as good in its way as eyesight, and works in a swarm of bats just as eighty thousand pairs of human eyes will work in a stadium. Years ago four men were exploring the Devil's Sinkhole and the last man out was caught in the bat flight, hanging suspended from a cable while the swarm enclosed him. They didn't touch him. The worst of it, he said later, was the smell, and the psychological shock.

Now it is dark, but a flashlight beamed into the hole shows the same density of ascending bats. Occasionally one of them lands on the rim of the hole and flutters about erratically before taking off again. Is it ailing, and resting after the steep climb, or is it chasing an insect? Bat movements are too fast for the eye to follow.

After an hour it begins to seem that if all the bats that have come out of the sinkhole were shoveled back into it, their bodies would surely fill it to the brim. But then the flow of bats suddenly lessens to a fifth of what it has been.

We didn't wait for the last bat to come out, that time. We left, driving in a pickup truck at three or four miles an hour down stairsteps of rock to the gate that let us out of the pasture.

Bats don't catch flying insects in their mouths as swallows do. Their mouths are busy sending out high-pitched sounds, their ears picking up the echoes that return, and their heads serving as aiming devices for this radar. When a bat "hears" an insect in the air nearby, it flies alongside and grasps it with a wing. The long, frail wing bones are modified finger bones anyway, and a bat can actually use them as fingers to seize its prey. The wing membrane doesn't get in the way; it helps. Then the bat puts the insect in its mouth just as we feed ourselves a cheese dip by hand. You can sometimes see a brief irregularity in a bat's flight, aside from its constant dodging. This is the moment when the bat is flying with one wing and feeding itself an insect with the other.

It can also bend its tail membrane forward to make a scoop and catch an insect in that. Then it can bend its head downward while flying and pick out the insect held in the scoop of its tail.

Thirty-two species of bats live in Texas. Most of them eat insects. A few species are adapted to other foods like fruit, nectar, fish, or blood. The fruit-eating bats have excellent teeth for chewing, while the nectar-drinkers have almost no teeth at all. Fish-eating bats use their radar to locate ripples made by tiny fishes which feed in schools just under the surface. The bats swoop over the water, drag their claws through the ripples, and often enough hook a fish. Vampire bats have channels in their tongues which work like a small intestine. By squeezing movements these channels carry blood from the victim's vein to the bat's mouth.

Long before DDT, people tried to use bats to clean the mosquitoes out of a city's air and control malaria. In 1915 San Antonio built a bat tower for this purpose.[11] It looked somewhat like a wooden church belfry with no church beneath—just some long concrete stilts to hold it up and a sign which said Municipal Bat Roost.

New developments in medicine and sanitation made bat towers old-hat while they were still new, and San Antonio abandoned the project. Some say it wouldn't have worked anyway because bats and mosquitoes fly at different levels in the air and one rarely encounters and eats the other.

In World War II, Dr. L. S. Adams planned and carried out an imaginative experiment with Texas bats.[12] He theorized that thousands of bats, fitted with delayed-action incendiary devices, could be released from airplanes over Japan to roost in the wood-and-paper buildings and start thousands of small separate fires which would combine into conflagrations and destroy entire cities. The War Department thought he was right and financed the project.

Dr. Adams and his helpers built a screened structure over the mouth of Ney Cave, in Medina County, and captured thousands of Mexican free-tailed bats. Each bat was then fitted with a one-ounce incendiary bomb, which it could easily carry. (Experiments showed that a bat can fly with a load amounting to three times its own weight.)

The experimenters built a dummy town in a remote place, and used airplanes and parachutes to drop containers closely packed with bats. When the containers neared the ground a timing device opened their doors and the bats flew out.

It was dawn. Sure enough, the bats went to roost in the dummy buildings, the incendiaries worked, and both the bats and the "town" were destroyed by fire. Two million dollars were spent on the experiment, but no bats were ever released over Japan. The atomic bomb had meanwhile been perfected, and it was used instead.

3 | THE LLANO UPLIFT

The Llano country is the smallest and strangest region in Texas, if any part of nature can rightly be called strange. You can drive across it, from east to west, in about an hour and a half. The north-to-south trip is even shorter. But hardly anyone crosses the Llano country in a hurry because there's so much to look at.

Geologically the region is different from all the rest of Texas, and looks it. (There's a point on the edge of Burnet where the dirt beside the road actually changes color from limestone-white to granite-pink as you move west off the Grand Prairie and onto the Llano Uplift.) Its granite crags suggest a miniature Scottish Highlands. Great lumps and bumps of schist and gneiss—rocks the size of bathtubs, cars, houses—stick out of the soil, making much of the land impossible to plow. The Llano River flows between banks of pink rock, its pink sandbars and small rock islands bearing almost no vegetation—a lone dwarf oak, perhaps, or a prickly pear. In the spring the wildflowers here are unusually bright and thick, their growth stimulated by the many minerals in the soil.

People who have spent seventy years in the Llano Uplift say they have never been able to see what's uplifted about it. You won't be able to either. What you see is a very large valley, ringed by rough hills.

"Uplift" is a geologist's term. It refers to something that happened far back in geologic time. A tremendous mass of magma—molten rock—was forced up from deep inside the earth. If the magma had been lava, the result would have been volcanoes. Instead, it came close to the surface but never actually erupted. It made a bump on the earth just as a blister makes a bump on your palm. Then, over a long period of time, the magma cooled and hardened into granite.

The bump is seventy miles across and about a thousand feet high, and *that* is the Llano Uplift—an area so large that, as with the State of Texas, you would never suspect it existed if you were not told it was there.

More millions of years passed. The surface rocks—the skin on top of the blister—eroded away, exposing both the granite and the rocks into whose cracks and crevices it had flowed when it was liquid. These, too, began to crumble and wash away, and rivers cut through the region to make the valley we see now.

The valley floor is covered with what may be the oldest rocks in Texas, and the soils that derive from them. We have to say "may be" because rocks from the same geologic era (the Pre-Cambrian) exist at Van Horn and El Paso. Pre-Cambrian time—roughly the first four billion years of the earth's history—was a period when comparatively few life forms existed on the earth, and those few—worms, sponges, algae—were simple and soft and did not make good fossils. Thus few fossil remains are embedded in Pre-Cambrian rocks to aid in dating them. The rocks themselves have been so greatly changed by earth movements and the high heat of magma that whatever messages they may once have contained for geologists to decode have been blurred and lost. Whether El Paso or Van Horn or Llano has the oldest specimens, all three, in any case, are old beyond our power to comprehend. They may be as old as the Pre-Cambrian rocks at the bottom of the Grand Canyon.

Huge intrusions of magma like the one that made the Llano Uplift are called batholiths, stones from the depths. They are scattered here and there about the world, and usually are rich in minerals. A batholith in Arizona is mined for copper, and one in Mexico for years yielded 85 percent of the world production of silver.

The Llano country was not so lucky. The richest deposits of minerals are normally concentrated in the upper layers of a batholith, nearest the surface. These layers, with whatever mineral wealth they contained, were eroded away from the Llano Uplift long before men came to live there.

What remains is a great variety of minerals in the rocks and soil, but always in small quantities. Gold, silver, and many even rarer substances turn up all over the Llano country, but never enough in one place to make mining them pay. An old name for the area is the Central Mineral Region, but the old hope that mining would one day make it rich is about dead.

Rockhounds find unusual specimens. In Mason County, topazes can be dug out of the ground, which is why the topaz is the Texas state gem. Trace elements in the Llano soil are credited with many local oddities, including the remarkable longevity of some of the people who live there.

Small deposits of iron ore are found all over the Llano area, and there's a hill called Iron Mountain near Valley Spring. In the 1880s a mining boom began, but soon ended for lack of iron. Llano still has a street called Bessemer, named optimistically in the hope of steel mills and prosperity.

What the earth does yield is less spectacular: granite of high quality, and also graphite and talc. The quarries that produce these things are

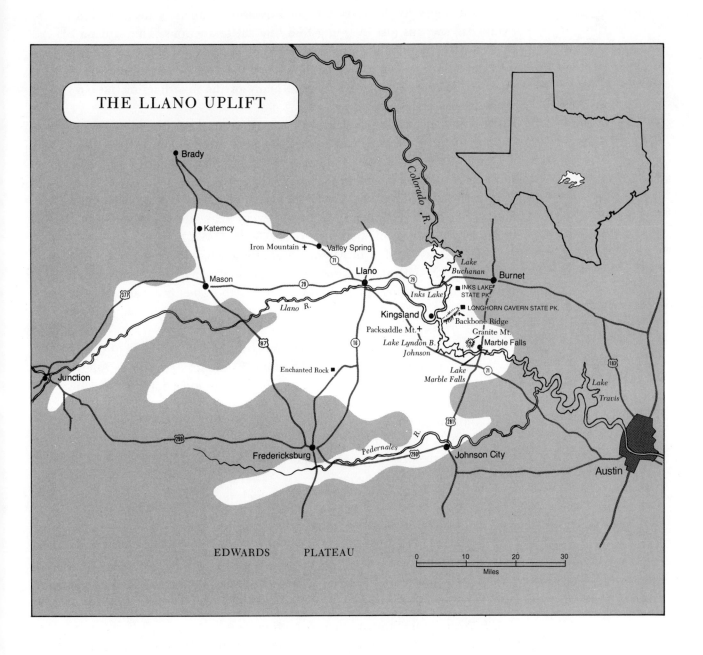

THE LLANO UPLIFT

Brady

Katemcy

Iron Mountain + · Valley Spring

Mason

Llano

Colorado R.

Lake Buchanan

Burnet

Inks Lake

INKS LAKE STATE PK.

LONGHORN CAVERN STATE PK.

Llano R.

Kingsland

Packsaddle Mt. +

Backbone Ridge
Granite Mt.

Lake Lyndon B. Johnson

Marble Falls

Enchanted Rock ■

Lake Marble Falls

Junction

Fredericksburg

Pedernales R.

Johnson City

Lake Travis

Austin

EDWARDS   PLATEAU

0   10   20   30

Miles

important, but they don't set the tone of the region. Cattle raising does that.

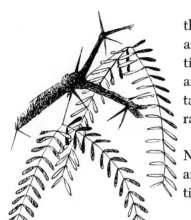

Llano ranchers claim that their cows grow bigger and better than those raised just to the west on the Edwards Plateau. They say that anyone can see this just by going to a few cattle auctions. The explanation, many of them believe, is the variety of minerals in the Llano soils and grasses. Yet ranching in the Llano Uplift is steadily declining. Estate and inheritance taxes have forced many of the inheritors of the old ranches to sell to developers.

When the land was first settled, its grasses grew three to five feet tall. Now it is heavily infested with mesquite and a shrub called whitebrush, and the grasses are of different species—shorter, sparser, and less nutritious than those that grew there when ranching began.

The suburbanization that is now taking place will be hard on the wild animals, which are still plentiful. Almost every year more deer are killed in Llano County than in any other Texas county. "We Buy Pecans, Furs, Deer Hides," says a sign in Mason, suggesting what the region is like: rural and quiet, with much wooded country and many ringtails, skunks, raccoons, and opossums. In both Mason and Llano, steel traps are sold in grocery stores.

Mason was settled in the 1850s and '60s by families overflowing from the prospering German communities around Fredericksburg, forty miles to the south. German craftsmen built stone houses and churches, which still stand and make Mason one of the more beautiful small towns in Texas. Until 1947 no municipal water system existed. Every house had a windmill and a cistern in its yard, and the sight of all the mills spinning together gave the place a nineteenth-century look. A few of the windmills are still there, still working.

The town was named for Fort Mason, which protected the first settlers from Comanches and Apaches. It was one of a series of outposts strung across Texas from the Red River to the Rio Grande, along what was then the frontier. (More than one line of forts was built across Texas in the nineteenth century, as the frontier moved west.) Fort Mason was bigger and better than most of the others, with stone buildings that involved arches and ornamental work. Robert E. Lee, then a lieutenant colonel in the U.S. Army, was stationed there for a time.

The place was abandoned in 1869, when Indian raids were no longer a problem. Its stones were gradually and haphazardly used to build houses and stores. No trace of Fort Mason remains except a few foundation stones buried under dirt and weeds.

Outside the town lies ranching country. Near the western edge of Mason County the Llano River comes off the Edwards Plateau and enters the Llano Uplift, to which it has given its name. In the assortment of things named Llano—the town, the county it's in, the physiographic region that both are in, and the river that flows through all of them—the Spanish meaning of *llano* has been lost sight of, and ceases to fit. Llano means *plain,* as in Llano Estacado, Staked Plain. At least the North and South Llano Rivers start out on a plain of sorts, the Edwards Plateau. They come together at Junction, and thirty miles or so farther on the single river enters the Llano Uplift.

It is a friendly stream with fishing holes and swimming holes—one of those small, pretty rivers, like the Guadalupe and the San Sabá, beloved by the people who live nearby. Its major floods are rare but terrible. In 1935 the river uprooted all the ancient native pecan trees along its narrow floodplain and wrecked the high bridge at Llano. Today people put very little in its path more substantial than a barbed-wire fence.

The town of Llano, built on a huge mass of nonporous granite, has almost no water beneath it. Dams make two small lakes—really, mild widenings and deepenings of the river—and Llano gets its water from them. From time to time, some of Llano's water has had to be shipped in by railroad tank cars.

The older dam is a friendly patchwork structure that people like to fish and swim from. It makes an old-fashioned river scene just upstream from the bridge that connects one part of Llano with the other.

Much of the river, as it flows east through its big valley, is bordered by ranches and left pretty much in its natural state. It runs for many miles uncrossed by bridges and untouched by towns. Some years ago the Llano emptied into the Colorado River at Kingsland, but today the Colorado, through the Llano Uplift and beyond, has been made into a string of lakes. The Llano now becomes, at its lower end, a green lagoon laden with water-skiers and fishermen, one of the many arms of Lake Lyndon B. Johnson.

The Highland Lakes, as they are called, are spaced along the Colorado River like beads on a string. The upper reaches of one lake extend to the dam of the next. There are no stretches of river left between. Four of the six lakes lie entirely within the Llano Uplift: Lake Buchanan, Inks Lake, Lake Lyndon B. Johnson, and Lake Marble Falls.

All of them are artificial. Their dams generate electricity, their fish are raised in hatcheries, and they have had a powerful effect on nature in the Llano country. For one thing, they cover some thirty thousand acres of what used to be wooded bottomland and floodplains along the Colorado, rich in wildlife and plant life. For another, they have changed the austere, thinly populated ranch country along their shores into resort country, and this has increased erosion and pollution. Side canyons, old gristmills, and archeological sites now lie beneath the water. So does Bluffton, one of the first towns to be founded in the area. The marble waterfalls—natural, not man-made—over which the Colorado once dropped twenty-one feet are now covered (and memorialized) by Lake Marble Falls. The shores of all the lakes are lined with resorts, camps, summer homes, marinas. Inks Lake, the smallest, is four miles long, with a surface of only 800 acres. Beside it, in Inks Lake State Park, a few acres have been left to wild animals and birds, somewhat as reservations were set apart for Indians in the last century.

The lakes provide water sports and bring in money, and only a few people in this dry country would want the free-flowing Colorado back again in place of them. They supply water and electricity for a series of towns and for Austin, and they serve to control floods. Disastrous major floods used to occur on the Colorado every twenty to thirty years.

Ordinary floods are easy to handle, but there have been some big ones that were not. In April and May of 1957, for example, a series of heavy rains fell on the Colorado watershed. It rained on the lakes themselves, on the rivers which feed them, on Austin. Lake Travis, the only lake with room specially provided for floodwaters, rose thirteen feet in one twenty-four-hour period—and Lake Travis is sixty-five miles long. Nearly two million acre-feet of water entered the system of lakes—that is, enough to cover two million acres of land to a depth of one foot.

But the water could not be released, except in small amounts, because heavy rains had also fallen downstream from the lakes, and throughout its length the Colorado River was dangerously full. A little too much water released by opening the dams would have flooded a dozen river towns between Austin and the Gulf of Mexico.

It was a tricky situation and it lasted thirty-five days. The basic procedure was to store flood water in the two largest lakes, Buchanan and Travis, to let enough of it out after one downpour to make room for the next—and to do this without flooding the towns and farms downstream.

Measuring stations were set up all the way to the Gulf, and the Colorado was kept filled with racing muddy water for weeks, until the entire runoff of the tremendous storms had drained into the Gulf of Mexico. At one point Lake Travis was thirty-eight feet deeper than when the rains started.

But there was no flood. Without the dams there would have been one, perhaps the worst in the river's history. The Lower Colorado River Authority claims, no doubt correctly, that its territory is "one of the most completely managed river areas in the nation."

A vigorous minority opposes the dams, saying they are the wrong approach to flood-control, somewhat like treating skin cancer with cosmetics. The real solution, they say, is to work with nature instead of against her—to stop the erosion brought on by bad farming and ranching practices, which leads to excessive runoff; and to stop building in the flood plains of rivers, which by definition are going to be flooded every twenty to fifty years.

They say that nature once handled the floods much more effectively than dams do now—by maintaining plentiful vegetation on the land to hold the soil in place and trap water where it fell. The water sank into the ground, maintained the water table, and gave life to the land, instead of draining away in destructive floods. The great pecan trees along the Llano River, for example, were centuries old and had never known a flood like the one that washed them away in 1935. Such a flood was possible only after the land had been abused.

The levels of the artificial lakes fluctuate considerably, sometimes leaving boats stranded and fishing piers standing in dry ground. This is partly due to the fact that rice farmers nearly three hundred miles down the river have a legal right to Colorado river water. They started irrigating their rice fields with it about 1905, long before the dams were built. When they need water it must be supplied, whatever the inconvenience to fishermen and water-skiers northwest of Austin.

When the lakes get low, some people announce darkly that their water is draining off into vast, mysterious, unexplored lower reaches of Longhorn Cavern nearby. It is not, but there are always people who prefer ingenious theories to provable facts. In this case the water can all be accounted for by hydrologists and engineers.

Longhorn Cavern lies hundreds of feet above the levels of the nearby lakes, inside a small mountain. Lake water would have to flow uphill to fill even its lower passages. It is the biggest scenic cave in Texas, and is less crudely exploited and commercialized than some of the others. The Texas Parks and Wildlife Department gets credit for this, for it administers the cave as part of Longhorn Cavern State Park.

The cavern is not hollowed out of granite; granite does not dissolve readily to make caves. It occurs instead in Paleozoic limestone. This rock is deeply buried in other parts of Texas, but here a huge block of it known as Backbone Ridge has been pushed upward by earth movements that were part of the Llano Uplift.[1]

Geologically, Longhorn Cavern is young, formed over the last few million years. Water did most of the work, seeping through cracks in the rock and dissolving the limestone. Eventually the passages got big enough for floods to roar through them after heavy rains, carrying sand and gravel, which enlarged the cave by abrasion. Next the slow process of decoration began—the creation of stalagmites, stalactites, columns, draperies, and flowstone by dripping and seeping water. In some parts of the cavern these formations are elaborate. In others they are missing entirely, and the walls are smooth, bare, and elegant.

Some people think the plain parts of the cave more interesting than the decorations. I am one of them. The creamy colors of the scoured walls, and their complex flowing lines, suggest a piece of abstract sculpture that people can wander around inside of. The stalactites and flowstone, on the other hand, often have a muddy, lumpy look. What is the mysterious appeal, to so many people, of a rock which looks like a deformed man or a damaged owl?

Men and animals have been wandering and falling into Longhorn Cavern for a long time. (Several of the main openings are vertical holes in the ground.) An elephant bone was found in the cave, from Pleistocene time when elephants lived in Texas. Grizzly bear and buffalo bones have also turned up, and the skeletons of two human beings.

Confederate gunpowder was made in the cave during the Civil War, the raw material being bat guano, which is rich in potassium nitrate and was then superabundant in Longhorn Cavern. The powder, once made, was stored in a small room of the cave where the air is fairly dry. The rest of the place feels faintly chilly and damp. The temperature holds steady at 64 degrees regardless of the weather or the season outside. In the 1930s, when air conditioning was rare, a room of the cave was floored and a nightclub opened there, with an orchestra for dancing.

The public tour covers about two miles. Beyond that lie more than seven miles of passages which have been explored but not cleared of debris or fitted with lights and trails. Beyond this region the passages turn downward and are filled with water. They have not been explored. The water, of course, is what makes some people certain that the cave connects with the lakes below.

On the surface above the cavern is a rambling, casual nature trail, which is perhaps the best kind. It winds through a scrubby forest growing mostly out of rock—mesquite, cedar, and oaks, and a sprinkling of yuccas and cacti. On its farthest stretches, if you go quietly, a deer may stare at you for a moment before it runs away.

Deer are so plentiful in the Llano area that it's hard not to see them. They are also small—smaller than deer on the nearby Edwards Plateau, which in turn are smaller than those on the Rio Grande Plain.

Local theory says that minerals from the soil make deer capable of high reproduction rates, and then insufficient food (from overcrowding) makes them small. Some biologists agree, tentatively, while pointing out that no one has any idea what the magic minerals are. The deer population makes a fast comeback after die-offs caused by droughts or hard winters. Llano County was the first in the state to allow the hunting of does and young bucks without antlers. Yet heavy hunting pressure for decades has not depleted the herds.

At the same time the Llano country shows a very different phenomenon—deer that don't reproduce at all. At intervals large numbers of animals called velvet-horn bucks appear. These males have dwarfed, misshapen antlers which remain coated with "velvet"—actually modified skin and hair—long after the normal bucks have shed this covering. In fact they never lose their velvet at all, and their horns, instead of dropping off cleanly at the end of the breeding season, tend to rot down to oddly-shaped stumps.

The testicles of velvet-horn deer are only about one-sixth normal size. Their general appearance is more doelike than bucklike, and they are never observed in sexual activity. In some years one buck in ten of those killed in the Llano area is a velvet-horn. Hunters like to shoot them because their meat is more tender and tastes better than that of the other deer.

Velvet-horn bucks manage to be well-fed in spite of being social outcasts from September through February, which is the mating season. Normal bucks, does, and even some of the bigger fawns will fight them. They come timidly to the feeding grounds and are tolerated, if at all, only on the outer edges. Yet as soon as the breeding season ends, all deer seem to forget about sexual differences entirely, and the velvet-horns are fully accepted by the rest of the herd.

Llano hunters and ranchers have been pondering the velvet-horn question for decades. They blame nuclear bombs, insecticides, and a hypothetical deer disease resembling mumps. They theorize that old bucks effect something like castration of the young fawns by nipping their testicles, or that the fawns do it themselves jumping barbed-wire fences.

In the 1960s, wildlife biologists made a detailed study of velvet-horns. They found that more than 90 percent of all those killed in a four-year period were killed on soils derived from the Llano granite, and that all the rest had such soils within their territory.[2]

The biologists tried to turn normal male fawns into velvet-horns by limiting their diets, injecting female hormones, etc.—and failed. They found no signs of disease in the velvet-horn animals. But they did find that most of those they studied had been born within a four-year period, and very few in the years since then. The "causative agent," it seemed, had been active in the environment for four seasons, and inactive thereafter.

What could it be? The biologists admitted they didn't know, but theorized that some obscure plant grows in the Llano region on soils derived from granite, in cycles controlled by drought or some other factor. And this plant, harmless to does, will stunt the sexual development of bucks that eat enough of it. The theory is just a theory, but the investigators were left with it after eliminating all the other possibilities they could conceive.

To date, the mysterious plant has not been found, and may not exist. But it is true that plant life in the Llano country is highly cyclic. Many plants are not seen for years, then suddenly reappear in large numbers.

With no new velvet-horns developing, the biologists closed their investigation. They could not expect to find a causative agent if it had withdrawn from the scene and no one knew when it would return. In any case, their chief interest had been in the reproductive power of the deer herds—did the presence of so many sterile bucks lower the birth rate? It did not. Apparently nothing slows the birth rate of Llano deer. The inquiry was ended, the cause of velvet-horn bucks remains a mystery, and the area goes on producing velvet-horns at intervals.

Llano granite catches the eye and the public fancy, but there are other rocks too. They were there before the granite, and its coming changed their nature. These are the *metamorphic* rocks. Packsaddle schist is one of them, named for Packsaddle Mountain, a lump of rock clearly designed by nature to be a landmark. It stands isolated near the shore of Lake LBJ, its shape unmistakable. Even today, any stranger blundering into the country would name it Packsaddle Mountain.

The Packsaddle schist is called "winter country" by the local cattlemen. Grass thrives in its gray soil through the mild winters and dies in the hot summers. The other old rock is Valley Spring gneiss, named for the town of Valley Spring. These three—the schist, the gneiss, and the granite—are the Pre-Cambrian rocks of the region.

But granite dominates. It makes the most picturesque hills and streambeds, and is the best source of mineral curiosities. Near Katemcy are a few square miles of land which appear at first glance to be solid rock, plain granite with no soil at all. Smooth pink domes and mesas, ten to thirty feet high, lie under the wind as naked as eggs. Nothing grows on them but an occasional prickly pear or a stunted oak in a crevice. It seems pure desert. But there is soil between the mounds of rock. Streams flow through this country, springs rise in it, it has its modest share of birds and wild animals, and cattle eat the grass.

The biggest quarry is at Granite Mountain, a smooth pink dome near the town of Marble Falls. Compared with a real mountain it is merely a knob. Every cubic inch of it is granite, a generous if somewhat cumbersome gift of nature to man. The fine-grained, high-quality stone needs only to be sliced off the mountain like pink meat from a ham, and consumed.

The quarry machinery lies at Granite Mountain's base, patiently chewing away. With occasional interruptions for depressions and such, it has been chewing for nearly a century. But it has removed only a small fraction of the visible mountain, and no one really knows how much granite lies out of sight underground. People in Marble Falls like to say that their supply is inexhaustible. At the present rate of consumption, perhaps it is.

This granite was used to build the Texas State Capitol. Originally white limestone was to be used, from a quarry near Austin. But the first limestone delivered to the building site was too soft and in other ways inferior, and there probably wasn't enough of it anyway. (The Texas Capitol is by far the biggest of any state's. The National Capitol is bigger, but the dome in Austin stands a little higher than the dome in Washington.)

Public favor, perhaps helped by early-day public relations, swung from limestone to the granite at Marble Falls. The quarry was new then—the year was 1885—and known as the Big Rock Granite Deposit. Its owners signed over to the state, free of charge, all the granite needed to build the Capitol. And so the job was done, in pink stone. Some call it red but it is pink—a muted, dignified, grayish pink which looks dusty and withdrawn in daylight but now, in our era, glows under tinted floodlights at night.

Huge new state office buildings have been erected just outside the Capitol grounds. Their basic construction is modern steel. But their outside surfaces are slabs of pink granite from Marble Falls.

Not all of Granite Mountain's rock is of top quality. Some is flawed with streaks of quartz or other minerals. These make it unsuitable as building stone and unthinkable as tombstones but leave it entirely functional as *rock*, in very large chunks. Such stone is sent by rail to the Gulf Coast for use in breakwaters and jetties. The rocks are in fact called jetty stones, and they weigh six to eight tons each. The Gulf shore has almost no rock—just sand and shell. The big rough boulders which lie at the base of the Galveston seawall, mile after mile, look foreign to that coastal country, and they are. Most of them are jetty stones from Granite Mountain. Their function is to break up big storm waves just before the waves hit the seawall.

Granite domes are scattered throughout the Llano country—remarkably smooth rounded forms, bald except for a few tufts of grass, and bushes. By far the best known is Enchanted Rock, in southern Llano County, far from any town. It rises 450 feet above the surrounding ranchland. The curve over much of its surface is so regular that a person a hundred yards away is out of sight, like a ship below the horizon.

Liking Enchanted Rock is probably a matter of temperament. Some visitors find it bare and boring, worth a ten-minute stay on its top and no more. To others it is a melancholy, clear echo of the Texas of Indian times. They like its simplicity, the spaciousness of the world around it, and the persistence with which life clings to it—a few plants and animals keeping stubbornly alive on what seems to be nothing but hard granite.

Enchanted Rock looks a lot like Granite Mountain. Both are domes. But Enchanted Rock's granite is too coarse for commercial use and has been left alone. It also seems safe from damage by casual visitors. They leave a little litter, which decays; the rock remains. The only serious threat to it was a scheme to carve it up like Mount Rushmore into the faces of famous Texans. So far this has not been done.

Indians, not real-estate men, gave the rock its name. They believed it *was* enchanted, that spirits lived on its top. From nearby camps they saw strange glimmers of "spirit fire" at night, and heard mysterious noises coming from the rock. Some Indians would climb up it—in daylight—to leave offerings. Others feared the spirits and would not touch even the base of the rock. When white men first came, they found well-worn trails leading to the rock from all around the horizon. It was a major place of worship.

The strange night noises can still be heard. They are made by the granite's cooling and contracting after a hot day. The "spirit lights" are no longer seen and are harder to explain. Some people theorize that they were wet patches of rock, or bits of mica, which reflected moonlight.

The rock, with its moody majesty, seems to attract religious observances. In the 1880s and '90s, local people held a church service there each year, climbing up or riding horses to the top. The text of the sermon usually came from Matthew: "Upon this rock I will build my church." No trace remains of any of these past events. Enchanted Rock seems to have survived, unchanged, from prehuman times, impervious to anything man has done.

But it is not impervious to time. Slowly it erodes and crumbles. In some places the rock breaks up into enormous boulders. In others it exfoliates— that is, large, thin sheets of granite come loose from its curved surface. They may be three inches thick and fifteen or twenty feet square. They remain in place, taking a long time to disintegrate.

Disintegration is what gives plants a foothold. The cracks on the surface are filled with grasses and wildflowers, little rambling strips of vegetation two inches wide. A few crevices near the top of the dome contain healthy live oaks and blackjacks, and small hickory trees that bear full crops of nuts. Although from a distance the rock looks bare and forbidding, on a hot day there is coolness in its deep crevices, and breezy shade in its miniature groves of trees.

Near the top of the dome, where the surface is almost horizontal, shallow depressions catch rainwater. There are more than a hundred of these, of various sizes. Some contain only gravel. In others, plant life has slowly, over long periods, built a small amount of soil out of granite dust and decayed plant materials. The first plants to take hold are lichens, which grow directly on the rock. Their decay eventually creates a bit of humus in which mosses can grow. The mosses in turn decay, create a slightly richer environment, and are replaced by ferns.

As soil accumulates, the vegetation changes—to grasses, wildflowers, prickly pear, yucca. The tiny mats of vegetation grow from the center of their depressions outward, because the hollow is deepest in the middle and soil collects there first. Sometimes the entire succession of plants can be seen in one pothole, from the pioneer lichens on the circle's rim to luxuriant grasses in the deepest soil in the center.[3]

If visitors realized how many centuries it takes for nature to establish these tiny wild gardens on a knob of pure granite, they might treat them with more respect. But to most people the swaying grass stems are merely stuff they would cut from their own yards with a power mower. Sometimes, when the grass is dry, a tourist sets one of the little patches on fire just to see it burn.

Though the rock looks like desert even to people standing on it—only a minute fraction of the surface supports plants—more than a hundred species of plants have been found growing here. Some are minimally represented. On my last visit I spied one mullein plant and one Virginia creeper.

The vegetation attracts a thin population of insects and lizards, and these in turn draw a few birds. Life on the rock is sparse but secure.

In the warm months a steady wind comes from the Gulf, two hundred miles away. It is deflected upward by Enchanted Rock and makes a "wave" in which two dozen or so vultures circle and soar. Clearly it's the best updraft for miles, an aerial playground. It is the only place I know where you can see, and be sure that you are seeing, vultures having a good time.

Enchanted Rock is just a small bump on the great granite mass that underlies the Llano Uplift. But it has a special quality—of brooding, of loneliness, a hint of what the world was before man made it over. Toward sundown the few sightseers return to the camping ground and picnic area below. Darkness simplifies the landscape until nothing is left but the sky, the wind, and the rock. Only far to the west, in the Trans-Pecos mountains, are there other such simple places left in Texas.

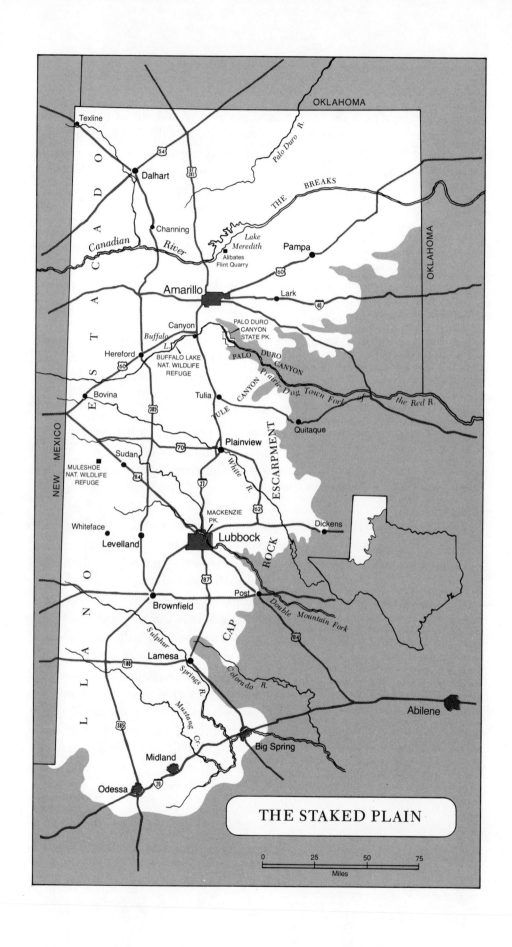

THE STAKED PLAIN

OKLAHOMA

Texline

54

Dalhart

87
281

L L A N O

Channing

Canadian   River

E S T A C A D O

Hereford

60

Bovina

385

Sudan

MULESHOE
NAT. WILDLIFE
REFUGE

84

Whiteface

Levelland

NEW MEXICO

Amarillo

Canyon

Buffalo
L.

BUFFALO LAKE
NAT. WILDLIFE
REFUGE

Tulia

70

Plainview

27

White R.

MACKENZIE
PK.

Lubbock

87

Brownfield

Lamesa

180

385

Sulphur

Springs R.

Mustang Cr.

Midland

70

Odessa

Lake
Meredith

Alibates
Flint Quarry

60

Lark

THE   BREAKS

Palo Duro R.

Pampa

40

PALO DURO
CANYON
STATE PK.

PALO   DURO   CANYON

CANYON

TULE

Prairie Dog Town Fork   of   the Red R.

Quitaque

E S C A R P M E N T

62

R O C K

Dickens

Post

84

Double Mountain Fork

Colorado R.

C A P

Big Spring

Abilene

OKLAHOMA

OKLAHOMA

0   25   50   75
Miles

4 | THE STAKED PLAIN

Before the white man came, the Staked Plain was a land without trees, hills, rocks, firewood, or water, except in a few odd places; and it had no human inhabitants. It was just a huge expanse of wind-fluttered grass, almost perfectly flat, reaching to the horizon and hundreds of miles beyond.

The Spaniards named it the Staked Plain, Llano Estacado, and no one now is absolutely certain what they meant by it, chiefly because the word *estacado* has several meanings: staked, fenced, stockaded. Maybe they meant, as tradition says, that the plain was so featureless that men had to drive stakes in it in order to find their way back across. Maybe they meant they had to stake their horses in camp because there were no trees to tie them to. Maybe they meant that the western edge of the plain, in New Mexico (which is an abrupt escarpment) was like the wall of a stockade. Or maybe they meant something we haven't guessed.

People have added trees, thousands of them, and houses and highways and towns. They have drilled for water and turned the Staked Plain into a big irrigated farm. But it is still in one sense a grassland, for most of the crops they grow—oats, corn, grain sorghum—are grasses too. It still lacks hills and rocks and rivers, and the wind still blows.

The steady prairie wind, in fact, has led people to set up miniature windmills on their lawns. The little towers are six or seven feet high, with fans spinning endlessly in the breeze. They are much like big windmills, but lack certain details and pump no water. Some yards have several windmills, one for each child.

The celebrated flatness of the Staked Plain amazes all visitors and depresses some. In the 1920s when cars were young and roads were few, people drove across the smooth grassland wherever they wanted, as they do in motorboats on water. On trips beyond the horizon a kind of dead reckoning was involved.

As a young man I crossed the plain on the old Fort Worth and Denver Railroad. When the train left Dalhart I wandered to the last car and stood on the rear platform. The tracks raced backward from me, perfectly straight, and vanished over the horizon, or perhaps into their vanishing point. It seemed uncanny, unearthly. I resolved to stay on the platform until the tracks curved. Minute after minute passed and they flowed on from under the train, straight as a ruler. A kind of suspense built up. It seemed impossible that this could go on any longer; surely the world and railroads weren't made like that. But it did go on, and forty minutes went by before the train lurched around a faint bend and stopped in Texline.

Recently I learned that a railroad which crosses Australia, the Indian-Pacific, runs straight for 297 miles across the Nullarbor Plain. But it goes distinctly uphill and down, which the one between Dalhart and Texline doesn't.

Both Holland and the Lower Rio Grande Valley are flatter than the Staked Plain, though both are tiny in comparison. How, one wonders, did this enormous platform of land get built, three to four thousand feet above the sea?

The upper layers of the plain washed down from the Rocky Mountains. And not just into Texas. The Staked Plain is merely the southern tip of the High Plains, a long flat bench of land that runs east of the Rockies, from the Texas Panhandle all the way to Canada.

Rivers of rain and melted snow came down from the Rockies, moving fast because they went sharply downhill, carrying material eroded from the mountains. When they got to flatter country, they slowed. The sand and clay, gravel and rocks, settled out of them. And in that low, hot region, the rivers didn't continue to the sea. They just dried up—some water sank into the ground and the rest evaporated.

The rivers kept this up for millions of years, bringing material and leaving it there, and so, layer on layer, constructed the smooth surface of the High Plains. Geologists can take clay or sand from the Llano Estacado into the Rockies and there match it up with the rocks it came from.[1]

Beneath its surface the Staked Plain is soft and crumbly—layers of bright-colored sandstones and clays and shales that erosion could easily carry away. But the Cap Rock lies on top of all this crumbly stuff, like concrete icing on top of a cake, and prevents erosion, or anyway slows it down.

The Cap Rock isn't concrete, of course, but it's a pretty good natural substitute. It is a mixture of marl, chalk, and gravel, plus a lot of caliche. Caliche is a white substance, kin to limestone, that forms in certain soils (and only in dry climates) when water evaporates and leaves behind calcium carbonate which cements the earth into hardpan.

If caliche were the final, topmost layer, nothing much would grow on the Staked Plain. But it isn't; above it lie several feet of rich, red-brown sandy soil or, in some places, sand alone. The soil and sand were not brought by rivers from the Rockies. Instead they were *blown* onto the plain by southwest winds, probably from the valley of the Pecos River. Out of this soil grew the great sea of grass that once covered the Llano Estacado. In it today grow endless square miles of wheat and corn, vegetables and cotton.

The plain tilts slightly away from the Rockies, like a big marble table. If you had an enormous ball, say three hundred feet high, you could set it down west of Clovis, New Mexico, and it would roll steadily southeastward across the Staked Plain for perhaps 150 miles and drop off the Cap Rock near Dickens, Texas. It would, that is, if it were light enough not to sink into the ground, and heavy enough not to be blown off course by the wind.

The slope of the land is about nine feet to the mile. This is just right to make water flow nicely through irrigation channels. Thirty or forty miles west of the Texas border, in New Mexico, the highest points along the western edge of the Staked Plain lie a full mile above sea level.

The rivers which built this big tableland ceased to exist millions of years ago. The Llano Estacado is no longer being built up. Instead, it is wearing away. But very gradually, since the cement-like cover of the Cap Rock makes erosion slow.

Slowly, the eastern and western edges are crumbling, washing down into the Pecos river on the west and the Brazos and Red Rivers on the east. The Prairie Dog Town Fork of the Red River has made the beautiful Palo Duro Canyon, reaching back many miles into the plain. And the Canadian River, crossing the Panhandle north of Amarillo, has cut a broad, shallow trough all the way across it. Part valley, part canyon, the trough is only a few hundred feet deep but ten to twenty miles wide from rim to rim. It is known as the Breaks of the Canadian.

Coronado and his men crossed the Staked Plain in 1541, on their way (they thought) to the Seven Cities of Gold.[2] They found buffalo, and Indians in Tule and Palo Duro Canyons who lived off the buffalo, making use of its hide, meat, sinews, bones, and blood. The Indians craved and drank the stomach juices of the buffalo, squeezing them out of grass cuds. The juices no doubt supplied Vitamin C and other nutrition that the meat lacked. And of course the Indians cooked their food, when they cooked it at all, on fires of buffalo chips.

"Not a stone, not a bit of rising ground, not a tree, not a shrub, nor anything to go by," Coronado reported, and didn't remain on the Staked Plain long. His army's crockery and tents were broken by hailstones.

Two centuries passed. Then in 1786, Spanish-speaking men from New

Mexico began venturing across the Staked Plain to trade with Comanches and other Plains Indians. *Comancheros,* these traders were called. Guns, beads, whiskey, bread, and cloth were their trade goods, and they exchanged these for horses and cattle, most of which the Indians had stolen from settlements in Texas or Mexico, and some of which they stole back from the *Comancheros* and sold to them a second time. The *Comancheros* did business on the Llano Estacado for a century—until, in the 1870s, the Indians they had traded with were marched off to reservations.

In 1849 Captain Randolph B. Marcy, U.S.A., exploring the headwaters of the Red River, climbed onto the Staked Plain and found it "one vast, dreary, and monotonous waste of barren solitude." But he liked the mirages. They turned pronghorns into buffalo or horses, or created beautiful lakes with shade trees on their banks. Maybe for some people they still do, but not for me. I never get more than a watery shimmer on the horizon, where the land and sky seem to blend.

Josiah Gregg, the author of the brisk and entertaining *Commerce of the Prairies,* crossed the Staked Plain in 1840. As a businessman hauling American trade goods to Santa Fé, and then on down to Chihuahua, he traveled the Santa Fé Trail eight times and pioneered the southern route across the Llano Estacado.

Prairie fires were one of his concerns. They could explode the trader's gunpowder and wreck his prairie schooners. "A keg or two of twenty-five pounds each is usually to be found in every wagon."[3] Gregg didn't worry much about being burned in a prairie fire. He could always get to a spot where the grass was short, he said, and be safe. Apparently the most serious threat of fire, at least from the human point of view, was in later times, to the ranchers' grass. Colonel Charles Goodnight himself said that he had never known a man to be killed by a fire on the prairie.

Seen from far away on the plain to the east, the Cap Rock escarpment is like a big smooth bluff on the western horizon. Headlands jut out into the lower plain, and canyons cut back into the Llano Estacado. The country below the rim is rough and scrubby, with mesquites and junipers and yuccas. Here and there people have dammed the little canyons and made small fishing lakes and resorts, with cattails, redwing blackbirds, and imported bullfrogs. Aoudad sheep, natives of Africa, have been released below the Cap Rock and have found the steep, rocky country to their taste. The big males, weighing 300 pounds and bearing horns nearly a yard long, are craved as trophies.

When people say they "live up on the Cap Rock," they mean they live on the Staked Plain. Climbing the Cap Rock has always been a kind of ceremonial event. It isn't very high—just a few hundred feet (or, on the New Mexico side, a thousand). But it is an abrupt, highly visible shift from one kind of country to another, and there is no doubt that life on the Staked Plain is somehow different from life on the lands below.

Perhaps the difference is no more than this: you are always conscious of being there. Among hills and valleys, people take their surroundings for granted. But that flat world, overwhelmed by the sky, cannot be shaken off. You can no more forget you are on the Llano Estacado than you can forget you are at sea.

The names of some towns suggest the look of the plain and what grows there: Levelland, Plainview, Pampa, Bovina, Kaffir, Sudan, Whiteface, Hereford, Lark. Spanish and Indian place names are rare, for the land was largely without settlers until the Anglo-Saxons moved in in the 1880s.

Tradition says that mountain dwellers all over the planet are clannish, close-mouthed, and suspicious of outsiders. This may or may not be true. But it is certainly true that no place on earth resembles mountains less than the Llano Estacado, and here the people are markedly open and sweet-tempered. They enjoy telling strangers about their land and their way of life, and they talk well. Their easy courtesy is so noticeable everywhere that you end up wondering if indeed there is a cause-and-effect relationship between this spacious world and the character of its people.

There are still only a few trees per square mile on the Llano Estacado. A century ago there were none. Trees grew, then as now, in the various big canyons—Palo Duro and the Breaks of the Canadian—but on the flatlands not at all.

Northeast of Amarillo on Route 60, an historical marker is set beside the remains of the first tree planted on the Staked Plain. It is a dead bois d'arc stump. A man named Thomas Cree put it there around 1888 and it lived until an overdose of an agricultural chemical killed it in 1969.

Understandably, people hunger for trees on the prairie. Many farm houses have rows of trees to the north and south, one to break the icy winds of winter, the other for the hot south winds of August. Some people fill their yards with ornamental trees—willows, maples, sycamores, catalpas—and pamper them to help them survive.

But the common workhorse tree of the Staked Plain is the Chinese elm, planted not for its beauty but simply because it can survive the weather and the wind.

In both country towns and big cities like Amarillo, Chinese elms give most of the shade. They have been planted in rows along highways, and in hot weather travelers gratefully park and rest in their shade. Their long, drooping brittle branches swing in the wind, and their leaves rustle pleasantly. They make a pleasanter rest stop than the official ones of concrete and steel.

Chinese elms are heavily attacked by insect pests. They drop a steady litter of dead twigs and branches, and they rarely become stately. But on the Llano Estacado they can carry on doggedly through the beating winds and the violent weather, and that's a virtue most other trees don't have.

Violent weather is one of the Staked Plain's specialties. "The weather phenomena of the Panhandle may be described under five types of occurrence," says Fred Rathjen, writing in the *Southwestern Historical Quarterly.* "The thunder storm, hail, the norther, the blizzard, and the dust storm."[4]

The lowest temperature ever recorded in Texas, 23 degrees below zero, occurred at Tulia, south of Amarillo, in 1899. A friend of mine in the western Panhandle once picked up thirty mourning doves killed by hailstones. Farmers dread the hot, wilting south winds of July and August, and everyone dreads the lashing north winds of winter, when the Panhandle is far colder than the rest of Texas.

Once, looking down from an airplane at the Llano Estacado under snow, I kept trying to recall where I had seen something like it before, from another plane. At last I remembered—the frozen Arctic Ocean west of Greenland, flat, white, and featureless.

But fine weather comes too. Spring on the plain is infinitely gentle, with fiestas of wildflowers in the breaks and canyons and along the roads. The hot summer days are followed by cool high-altitude nights. And the strange, nostalgic power of autumn is as strong here as anywhere, even without bright colors or burning leaves. Autumn, more than any other season, seems to be a change of mood in the air and sky. The Llano Estacado has plenty of both.

Most of the western third of the Panhandle was once occupied by a single ranch, the XIT, almost certainly the largest ranch ever to be put under fence. It covered three million acres in parts of ten counties, and stretched about two hundred miles from north to south.[5]

The ranch came into existence because the State of Texas wanted a new capitol building at Austin. Lacking cash, the state traded an enormous chunk of uninhabited Panhandle land to the Capitol Syndicate, an organization of Chicago businessmen. The syndicate built the Capitol— the one still in use—and set about raising cattle on its three million acres of short-grass prairie, far out on the Llano Estacado.

The big ranch was unique in various ways. Eventually it was enclosed and divided by six thousand miles of fence. The barbed wire was held to the posts by enough staples to fill a freight car. For convenience the ranch was split into seven divisions, each with its own headquarters, foreman, and cowboys. A private and somewhat unreliable telephone system was strung on fence posts.

The name XIT had nothing to do with the word Exit, or with much of anything else. It was merely a brand that could easily be made with five strokes of a single bar of hot iron, and one that rustlers found hard to alter.

A single prairie fire burned nearly a million acres of XIT grass in 1885. Cowboys sometimes killed two hundred lobo wolves a year. Blizzards, hailstorms, and droughts did great damage. Rustlers, coming out of New Mexico, stole hundreds of head of cattle.

But the ranch was successful. It made money for its owners, who had never intended to operate it indefinitely. Ranching was merely a way to make the three million acres pay off until settlers moved into the Panhandle and the land could be sold to farmers and smaller ranchers. The last of the XIT cattle were sold in 1912.

Traces of the XIT—windmills, buildings, bits of fence—remain scattered over the ten counties, and the main headquarters building stands in downtown Channing. People who spent their childhoods on various divisions of the big ranch still hold reunions, but the men and women who actually worked on the XIT are nearly all dead.[6]

Anglo-Saxon history on the Staked Plain goes back a mere hundred years. Until recently a few people still lived who had experienced it all. And virtually all of it is contained in the Panhandle-Plains Historical Museum at Canyon, Texas, one of the best regional museums in the country.

As an institution, it seems bravely to have accepted and put on display whatever people gave it. But though it has a lumber-room aspect, as a museum of the Staked Plain it is superb. Its collections of books and other papers about the Panhandle are the best there are, and its exhibits are imaginative and handsome.

My favorite is the upper parts of a huge windmill, of a kind no longer seen in the countryside. Even its fan blades are multiple slats of wood. Dominating a central hallway, the splendid old windmill sets the nostalgic mood of the whole museum.

There is a chuck wagon, a real one, set for cooking a meal on the open range. The iron skillet and Dutch ovens and a big coffee pot are deployed on the ground. Huge cans which held a gallon of baking powder, two gallons of coffee, sit on the chuck-wagon shelves, their old paper labels still bright and readable, showing brand names now forgotten.

There are collections of barbed wire, of fine saddles, of beautifully restored horse-drawn wagons and buggies. A huge map shows all the major cattle trails ever used, from Texas to Montana. And there are exhibits on the geology, climate, and Indian tribes of the Panhandle.

But there is no dugout, that curious dwelling which the early settlers sank into the ground for lack of building materials. A sort of re-created dugout is in Palo Duro Canyon State Park, a few miles east of the museum. And the ruins of many real ones can be discovered all over the Llano Estacado.

Dugouts were remarkably snug dwellings, warm in winter and cool in summer, like adobe houses. In the breaks, people dug them into hillsides and canyon walls, and roofed them over with poles, then cowhides, and finally a thick layer of dirt. They had a door but no windows.

On the plain, men dug a big rectangular hole in the ground and put a roof over it, with perhaps a small amount of sod or wooden wall between roof and ground. My informant, Ida Arbuckle, says their wall was wood. The Staked Plain was not much settled until after railroads had come near, and lumber was shipped in. "Four feet of it was underground and three feet above ground," she told me. "The chickens in the yard would look down at you through the window. And nothing ever froze. A little fire in the cookstove would keep us warm in a blizzard."

The Canadian River, cutting its trench across the Llano Estacado, has exposed layers of petrified wood, gypsum, and colorful flint. The flint is some of the best in North America for making arrowheads and tools, though the demand for it has dropped to zero in the last century or two.

Twelve thousand years ago, men were taking flint from a place now known as the Alibates Flint Quarry, a carefully protected area on a bluff above Lake Meredith. Spear points and arrowheads of Alibates flint were used by early men to kill animals now extinct in the area—camels, mammoths—and have been found with the animals' bones.

Slowly, the fame of Alibates flint spread across the primitive world that was to become the United States. The people who worked the Alibates quarry five hundred years or so ago built pueblos along the Canadian River, like those of New Mexico and Arizona. Theirs is the only pueblo culture known in Texas. They traded their fine flint for seashells from the Pacific coast, pipestone from Minnesota, and pottery from the Southwestern pueblos.

All these trade items have turned up in archaeological sites near the quarries, and in turn spear points and arrowheads of Alibates flint—identifiable by its rich colors, its fine crystalline structure, and sometimes its translucency—have been found as far as a thousand miles from the source.

Allie Bates, a rancher who settled near the quarries around 1880, gave

A diamondback rattlesnake west of Circleville.
(The Edwards Plateau)

OVERLEAF: The granite domes of Enchanted Rock
north of Fredericksburg. (The Llano Uplift)

A white stone beach and boulders in the Frio River
south of Leakey. (The Edwards Plateau)

Grass and granite outliers east of Llano. (The Llano Uplift)

Ferns and lichened rocks northwest of Marble Falls. (The Llano Uplift)

Lichen colonies on granite northwest of Marble Falls. (The Llano Uplift)

At the edge of the Great Plains, Palo Duro Canyon
east of Canyon. (The Staked Plain)

Mirabilis blooming southeast of Amarillo.
(The Staked Plain)

Badlands,
Palo Duro Canyon
east of Canyon.
(The Staked Plain)

Layered bacon rock of gypsum and sand southeast of Goodnight. (The Staked Plain)

Palo Duro cedar north of Wayside. (The Staked Plain)

Sage, goldenrod, and grasses southeast of Amarillo. (The Staked Plain)

LEFT: Caprock and cottonwoods south of Goodnight. (The Staked Plain)

Eroded caprock and grasses east of Canyon. (The Staked Plain)

his name to a little creek that runs below the quarries and thus to the flint. Alibates Creek now empties into Lake Meredith, a thirty-mile stretch of cool blue water made by damming the Canadian River. It laps against cliffs of the same bright colors that one finds to the south in Palo Duro Canyon. The rocky hills on the lake shore grow numerous showy wildflowers and a few species of scrubby trees.

Western collared lizards, eighteen inches long, beautifully marked and colored, and harmless, sit on boulders in the hot sun for hours on end and allow you to come close and take their pictures. When alarmed, they rise and run over the ground on their hind legs only, dragging their long tails.

On both sides of Lake Meredith and the Canadian River's trench, the flat plain reaches north and south for hundreds of miles. Its flatness is faintly broken by thousands of depressions called playa lakes, or dry lakes, or sinks. A newcomer may fail to notice them for a while because they are so slight and seldom contain water.

But he notices them eventually: big dimples, as shallow as saucers, from a few hundred yards to a mile in diameter. After a rain, they collect a little water in the center, but it soon evaporates. Sometimes a farm road makes a precise half-circle around a dry lake, and then runs straight again for many miles. Sometimes it crosses a small one on an embankment.

Early travelers theorized that playa lakes began as buffalo wallows, and that wind erosion made them bigger and bigger. But geologists now believe that gypsum and other materials beneath the surface have been slowly dissolved and carried away by the movement of water underground, and that the surface of the plain has sunk down to fill the cavities.

Playa lakes are hard to farm because part of the crop may end up rotting under shallow water. But the cattle business has found a use for some of them. Here and there, businessmen have built a feedlot in a very large playa lake. I visited one that contained 46,000 head of cattle, all in small pens on the sloping sides of a dry lake.

The animals' manure and urine drained down the slope to the low spot in the middle, or was washed there by rain. The result was a vast central puddle of sludge-like excrement which from time to time was pumped out, diluted with water, and used as fertilizer.

Standing on the shore of this puddle I was awed by the sight of so many cattle. The animals are brought in when they weigh about 600 pounds, and are fed a carefully blended diet until they weigh a thousand. Then they are trucked off for slaughter. The pens are lighted at night, to encourage eating.

The men who work in the cattle pens are called cowboys, though their life seems to bear no resemblance whatever to the cowboy life of the past. Feed lots (more often called feed yards in the Panhandle) are a big new industry. Corn to feed the cattle is now a major crop, and meat-packing plants have risen on the Staked Plain and in nearby New Mexico.

Palo Duro Canyon has attracted Indians, ranchers, geologists, tourists. You come down off the featureless plain and find a running stream, colored cliffs, side canyons, strange rock formations, and the breezy shade of huge old cottonwood trees. You can even swim, or at least get wet, in the Prairie Dog Town Fork of the Red River, which is the name of the stream at the bottom. It and its little tributaries made the canyon, though after a hard rain they are not little, but tumbling torrents.

The formations in Palo Duro Canyon would be remarkable even if they were a uniform gray. Instead they are deep red, satiny white, lavender, yellow, salmon-pink, orange, and pale green—the most intense earth colors I have seen, brighter than those of the Grand Canyon or the Painted Desert. The colors lie one above another in precise horizontal bands, so that from a dollar guidebook you can figure out the geological age of each one.[7]

Many geological epochs are missing from the walls altogether. Their rocks may once have been there in layers thousands of feet thick, but erosion stripped them away. Between the bright-red Permian beds of the lower canyon wall and the varicolored Triassic strata of its middle region, about 50 million years of earth history are missing.

The Technicolored scenery is what brings most people to the state park which occupies the best part of Palo Duro Canyon. But visitors also come to hunt geodes and fluorescent opal and mastodon bones, and in the hope of finding yet one more Indian archaeological site.

Junipers grow on the canyon's walls, and mesquites in the bottom. A few wild turkeys wander through the park, not much alarmed by visitors. And because there are trees, there are birds you never find in the grassy plains above the canyon's rim.

The theatrical production called *Texas,* staged on summer nights in the park, uses as its backdrop a magnificent stretch of the canyon wall and the Panhandle sky, with its sunset colors and its stars. The show is famous for its accurate reproduction, in light and amplified sound, of a High Plains thunderstorm.

The Sad Monkey Railroad, named for a rock formation which looms above it, is a miniature affair with a mile or so of track. It offers a geological and biological train ride through a canyon, with a running lecture by the engineer. For the more active visitors, hiking trails lead to the tall rock column called The Lighthouse, and to the intensely colored cliff called The Spanish Skirts. Park officials can point out more obscure trails, and it is also possible to explore and climb for miles where there are no trails at all.

In the park, Palo Duro Canyon is roughly two miles wide and eight hundred feet deep. A few miles downstream, where Highway 284 crosses the canyon, it is seven miles wide, an expanse of brilliantly colored badlands. From there it grows wider and wider until it is no longer a canyon at all.

The first ranch established in the Staked Plains country was not on the flat prairie but in Palo Duro Canyon. Charles Goodnight, who lived one of the most adventurous and satisfying lives of any nineteenth-century Texan, set it up in 1876, driving out thousands of buffalo to make room for his cattle.[8]

The canyon made an almost ideal ranch. Its steep walls took the place of miles of fence and protected livestock from the winter winds. There was plentiful water from the central stream, shade from cottonwood trees, and good grass. Game birds, including turkey, were plentiful when the ranch people wanted a change from beef and buffalo, and the canyon grew wild plums and grapes.

Molly Dyer Goodnight, the rancher's wife, was for a time the only woman in the Texas Panhandle. A cowboy brought her three live chickens which became her pets and companions. "No one can ever know how much pleasure and company they were to me," she said, years later. "They knew me and tried to talk to me in their language."

Charles Goodnight spent fifty-three years ranching in the Panhandle and died in 1929 at the age of ninety-three. He invented the chuck wagon, kept a private herd of buffalo, made and lost fortunes, served as a military scout, and bred an animal called the cattalo, a cross between Polled Angus cows and buffalo bulls.

In a lawless country he carried no gun. He made personal pacts with Indians and outlaws, agreeing to leave them alone if they stayed off his land and spared his cattle. He said that he never knew an Indian to go back on his word. He lived outdoors, and knew the Plains and the Rocky Mountains when men had only faintly begun to tamper with their wildness. It is no longer even possible to live the kind of life he had.

He was a careful student of animals, plants, and weather. "A man should be able to tell from watching birds and animals whether they are going to or coming from water," he said. "If wild mustangs are strung out and walking steadily along, they are going to water. If they are scattered, frequently stopping to take a bite of grass, they are coming from water."

In the early days of his life on the plains, water was not pumped from the ground. It was where you found it, and very little was found.

In the 1840s and '50s it was generally supposed that human beings would never live permanently on the Llano Estacado. There was nothing to build with, neither wood nor stone; but worse, there were no springs, no rivers. There was only grass. The water that collected in playa lakes was soon gone.

But water, it turned out, lay *under* the plain—a magnificent reservoir of it just a hundred feet down, waiting to be pumped out by windmills. Then came pumps run by gasoline and diesel engines, and the era of irrigation began.

"The supply of underground water in this area is unfailing," said a pamphlet circulated by the Santa Fé Railroad in 1933. But the supply is failing now. After forty years of irrigating millions of acres, the water table has dropped, the wells produce less, and the cost of pumping has grown. The irrigation goes on. "People are going to irrigate," a pump salesman's wife told me recently, "even if they haven't got no water for the house."

I have asked various people on the Staked Plain what will happen when the water gives out, and have received various answers.

"Just dry up and blow away, I reckon."

"I don't know. I just don't know."

"Go back to dry-land farming, and ranching."

"Most folks will move away. They'll have to."

"Oh, they'll come up with something."

And "they" are trying to come up with something. A grandiose scheme, costing billions, to pump water from the Mississippi River to the Staked Plain was heavily defeated by Texas voters. There is talk of designing windmills far bigger than any ever seen, to lift water from underground more cheaply than fuel-driven pumps do. There are attempts to drill out the centers of playa lakes and make deep cisterns with little surface area, to hold rain that now evaporates. There are hopes that hundreds of feet down beneath the present aquifer (water-bearing sand and gravel called the Ogallala Formation) another great reservoir will be discovered.

Meanwhile, farmers drill more and deeper wells, to get what water is left. Native grassland is still being broken by the plow, and irrigated. The common aim, obviously, is to get while the getting is good.

The people of the Staked Plain have loved their abundant, good-tasting water and have been proud of it. "They're putting a lake in Tule Canyon," a man at Silverton told me, "and before long we'll be getting our water from there. But it will be runoff. It won't be as good."

A friend in Dalhart urged me to empty my canteens of Amarillo water and fill up at her kitchen sink with water from deep underground. "Amarillo water comes from Lake Meredith," she said. "It has everything in it—gas and oil and I don't know what." Signs along Lake Meredith say "This Is Your Drinking Water. Help Keep It Clean." Some campers and boaters help; some don't.

Perhaps because of its curious name, Deaf Smith County has had most of the publicity about the natural fluoride content of its water. Hereford, the county seat, is called the Town Without a Toothache. But in fact much of the underground water of the Staked Plain contains two or three times more fluoride than is needed to prevent cavities in teeth. This excess causes the teeth of young children to be mottled with brown. No Panhandle city *removes* fluoride from its water, however, for that is a costly process. Some parents try to deal with the problem by diluting their children's drinking water with distilled water from a jug.

Quite a bit of dry-land farming has always been done on the plain, because there are areas which lack the big underground reservoir and have only "windmill water"—enough for the family and the livestock. Such farming produces thirty bushels of wheat per acre in good years. Irrigated farming will yield forty-five to sixty-five bushels whether it rains or not. The dry-land farmers, with their low yield, can't afford fertilizers or insecticides. Some of them have made a good thing of this hardship by carefully excluding all chemicals from their land and selling their grain as natural food at premium prices.

The Staked Plain's two national wildlife refuges are both sanctuaries for birds, mostly migrating waterfowl. In every other way they are drastically different. The Buffalo Lake refuge, near Canyon, has a long blue lake that attracts campers and fishermen in summer. But on November 1, most of the lake is closed to boats, and ducks and geese by the thousand drop down out of the Central Flyway to rest, or spend the winter.

The harshly alkaline lakes of the Muleshoe refuge, south of the town of Muleshoe, contain no fish and only a few frogs. They often go dry in summer, becoming lifeless alkali flats. But the autumn rains refill them, at least partly, and in winter the Muleshoe refuge attracts the country's largest concentration of sandhill cranes—sometimes 100,000 at once.

No one knows exactly what caused the depression in the plain that contains the Muleshoe's three little lakes. They get all their water from runoff, and lose it by evaporation. There are no drainage outlets.

The summer mood of the place is of silence and dryness. Tourists come, but quickly go. The prairie dogs ignore the drought—they don't drink water anyway—and the songbirds, also plentiful, know where to go for a drink. Rattlesnakes, jackrabbits, cottontails, and burrowing owls are easy to find. The owls, which like to live in abandoned prairie-dog holes, are small, long-legged, cross-looking birds which sit around on posts or

stalks in the daytime, or on the mounds that the prairie dogs make. Any small owl that you see on the Llano Estacado in daylight is probably a burrowing owl.

Golden eagles are not common, but they are there. Prairie dogs are eagle food, and the eagles in turn are shot illegally by hunters—not on the refuge but in the country nearby. The manager of the Muleshoe refuge has a big wire cage in which he cares for wounded eagles. When I was there it was occupied by a golden eagle, handsome and healthy, but with most of his right wing shot away. The wound had healed, leaving the bird unable to fly. Below it were the skins and bones of rabbits and prairie dogs which the manager had shot for its food.

In winter the sandhill cranes—big gray birds with six-foot wingspreads—attract bird watchers from many states. Thousands of ducks and geese stop to rest or spend the winter. The lakes offer almost nothing to feed these masses of big birds, and so they range out for miles in all directions—to eat grain left in the harvested fields, forbs and grasses, insects.

"But the prairie dogs own this place," the manager told me. Prairie dogs are not exactly thriving anywhere in Texas, having been massively poisoned by ranchers and government agents for many decades. Some of the best remaining prairie-dog towns are on the Staked Plain. The most famous one is in Mackenzie Park in Lubbock. It is almost like a zoo.

A more natural situation exists at the Muleshoe refuge. The visitors' campground is also a prairie-dog town. There is no real fraternizing—no petting or hand feeding. The prairie dogs keep a cautious distance, just right for seeing them in detail with field glasses.

Prairie dogs are as appealing as puppies or chipmunks. They have cheerful dispositions and clean eating habits, being vegetarians, and are themselves good to eat. They are not dogs at all, of course, but rodents—relatives of the squirrel. They engineer their holes and tunnels to prevent flooding, and their digging is good for the soil. Rabbits, snakes, lizards, and burrowing owls live in prairie-dog towns, usually in abandoned burrows, and the prairie dogs don't mind.

They stay underground at night. They like to lie, totally relaxed, in the sun. Whenever they bark, their tails twitch. Prairie dogs often kiss on meeting, and sometimes two of them stand upright on a mound, chattering, each with an arm around the other's shoulders.

Man, when he settled the plains, set about killing the prairie dog's natural enemies—hawks, coyotes, eagles, owls, badgers, etc.—and soon the prairie-dog population was enormous. Vernon Bailey, in 1905, reported a single prairie-dog town 250 miles long and 100 miles wide in western Texas, with an estimated population of 400 million prairie dogs.[9]

Because prairie dogs eat grass, ranchers concluded that their grazing lands were threatened. And cowboys' horses, stepping in prairie-dog holes, sometimes broke their legs. So millions of prairie dogs were poisoned and shot, and the process of extermination is still going on. It is now clear, though, that while the prairie dogs lived on the Great Plains for many thousands of years without hurting the grasslands at all, a mere century of ranching has damaged them severely.

Prairie-dog society is highly organized and cooperative. There are lookouts to warn of danger—a big bird overhead, a coyote, a man. When the call comes, all hands dive into their burrows. After such an alarm, an hour or more may pass before the tops of prairie-dog heads begin to show, each one lifted just far enough above the mound for its owner to see out. If all is well, the town comes to life again. Young prairie dogs scamper around their home mounds playing games, and are treated with indulgence by all their elders. The grownups feed and groom each other, and lie happily in the sun.

Killing prairie dogs had the side effect of nearly exterminating the black-footed ferret, one of our most beautiful wild animals and now one of the rarest. Long, lithe, quick-moving, masked like a bandit, it lived in prairie-dog burrows and ate them for every meal. The arrangement worked well for a long time. The black-footed ferret, though never numerous, had a secure ecological niche. It disappeared from the Llano Estacado in the 1920s. A few ferrets may yet survive in remote prairie-dog towns in the Dakotas. But the poisoning of prairie dogs continues in the Dakotas, too, and the black-footed ferret may soon be gone for good.

When buffalo lived on the Staked Plain, they were preyed on by the gray wolf, or lobo. Once the buffalo were exterminated, the wolves naturally turned to ranchers' cattle. Cowboys used to chase them for miles across the grassland, and down the rim of the Cap Rock where they hid in dark dens and caves. One way of killing a wolf (and often a litter of pups as well) was to crawl into its cave with a lighted candle, which the wolf stared at from the depths, silently. The cowboy then shot between the two points of candlelight which glittered in the wolf's unblinking eyes.

But killing wolves by candlelight was time-consuming, and the species survived. The great demand for beef in World War I led to a more systematic form of destruction—by trappers working for the U.S. Government—and the wolves were soon extinct in Texas and elsewhere. There are still a few in the wilder mountains of northern Mexico.

Coyotes, though, are surviving handily. They do well on the big plain, where space itself is so plentiful that it makes a kind of hiding place. A scientist once examined the stomach contents of eight thousand coyotes and found that 76 percent of the total consisted of rabbits, carrion, and various species of mice. Such food is plentiful on the Llano Estacado.

A man I know near Quitaque has a curious hobby, which involves chasing coyotes over the plain in a pickup truck. From it, while moving at thirty miles an hour or so, he releases greyhounds by springing open the doors of "drop boxes" along the sides of the truck. The greyhounds then take over the chase. One or two of them must be trained to "take hold"—that is, to bring down the coyote. Otherwise the dogs would simply pursue it until it dropped from exhaustion. There is little pleasure in shooting an animal that lies gasping for air, so tired it can no longer run.

The large mammal of the prairie now is the pronghorn, usually miscalled the antelope. It must have treeless country, where it can see for great distances and run from danger. It shuns woods, and can't survive in them. And, having lived for millennia in lands without barriers, it does not know how to cope with even a simple barrier like a fence.

Pronghorns will not jump fences, even low ones that they easily could, nor will they break through one that is ready to fall. This means that every rancher's pronghorn herd is his own. People pay well for hunting leases, though pronghorn meat has an unpleasant flavor. Hunters usually kill them for trophies. Or, in many cases, just to be killing something.

Several species of animals are found mostly along the rough edges of the Cap Rock or in the canyons, because grassland alone is not enough for them. They must have trees. This is true of porcupines, those curious vegetarians whose important necessities include weeds, tree bark, and salt. Porcupines can live on the treeless plain in summer, when green leafy plants are growing. Intensely cold weather does not bother them; they grow fur under their quills. But in winter they must have trees whose bark they can eat when fresh forbs are lacking.

Even a few trees around a farmhouse will do, and thus porcupines sometimes manage to live all year on the prairie. They are far more common, though, in the breaks. The first one I ever saw on the Staked Plain was in Tule Canyon, where it lay dead on the highway. A traveler from Mississippi had stopped to look at it. He had no idea what it was.

Most people regard porcupines as only slightly less desirable than rattlesnakes. According to David Costello, who has written a good book about them,[10] they make placid and cheerful pets. Baby porcupines have great charm and are easy to raise. Porcupines can be picked up and even stroked, if you work from head to tail. If you stroke the other way, pliers may be required to remove the quills from your hand.

There are no longer black bears in the canyons below the Cap Rock, but they were once fairly plentiful, feasting on wild honey, grapes, and plums when they could get them, and getting along on fish, roots, and acorns when they couldn't.

Black bears are shy animals, not happy in the neighborhood of men.

They like to raid garbage dumps, but also sometimes kill calves and lambs. This made ranchers their enemies and now Texas has bears only in the remoter Trans-Pecos mountains.

The Llano Estacado's big dome of sky makes it a good place for watching clouds, stars, and thunderstorms. The watcher has a sense of drifting through the universe on a little round platform, much as if he were an astronaut.

In summer, camped in a farmer's pasture, I have watched violent nighttime thunderstorms move across the landscape, sometimes five or six at once, all of them so far away that I could hear nothing. Sometimes one came on and swamped me in thunder and rain.

The plain lies directly under the Central Flyway. On October afternoons, if you're lucky, you can see flight after flight of southbound geese far overhead, sometimes a dozen wavering wedges in the sky at once, each line as light and strong as a spider's strand.

The spectacle never palls. The sight and the faint, wild sound of migrating geese remain one of man's great experiences, a link to an older, cleaner world that we have almost destroyed.

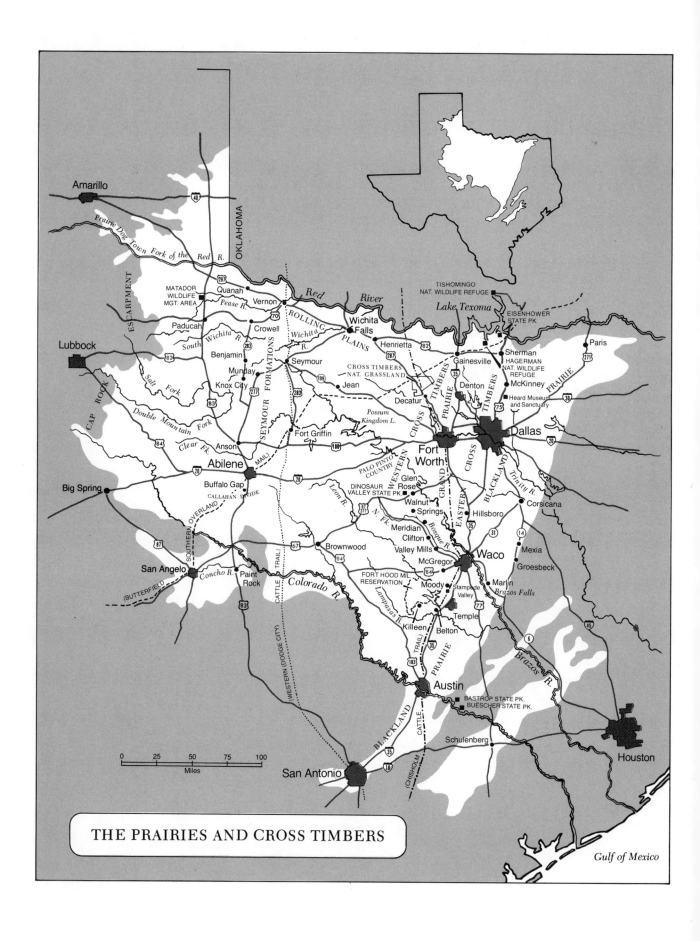

THE PRAIRIES AND CROSS TIMBERS

5 | THE PRAIRIES AND CROSS TIMBERS

All the prairies, plains, and woods of north Texas are strips running north to south. If you drive Interstate 20 from Abilene east to Dallas, you thread through them all in 182 miles: the Rolling Plains, the Western Cross Timbers, the Grand Prairie, the Eastern Cross Timbers, and the Blackland Prairie. Each region has a distinct geological underpinning, but intensive land use and tree cutting have muted the differences and blurred the edges.

The overall region occupies almost a quarter of the state and has two exact boundaries, the Red River and the Cap Rock Escarpment. On the south the Colorado River provides only an approximate borderline, while on the east there is a fairly smooth line where the Blackland Prairie soils stop and the post-oak trees, rooted in sand, begin.

Almost the entire area is farmed or ranched except for the small river bottoms, and sometimes they are too. Many of the state's biggest towns and cities—Dallas, Fort Worth, Wichita Falls, Austin—are here, and nothing anywhere that resembles wild country. But there are wild animals and flowers and birds, and some of the most varied and beautiful lands in Texas.

Two famous old routes run, or ran, across this country. The Butterfield Overland Mail went east and west for a few years just before the Civil War, and the Chisholm Trail went north and south for a few years just after.

Of all the cattle trails, the Chisholm is the best known and probably always was, merely because its name sounded best in songs and stories. It began with various feeder trails converging on San Antonio, then went past Austin, Waco, and Fort Worth. It crossed into the Indian Territory at a place called Red River Station (north of today's Henrietta, Texas) and went on to Abilene, Kansas, where the longhorns were loaded on Kansas Pacific cattle cars for the eastern slaughterhouses.[1]

D. E. McArthur described the Chisholm Trail thus:

From 200 to 400 yards wide, beaten into the bare earth, it reached over hill and through valley for over 600 miles, a chocolate band among the

green prairies. . . . As the marching hoofs wore it down, and the wind
blew and the waters washed the earth away, it became lower than the surrounding country and was flanked by little banks of sand, drifted by the
wind.[2]

And no doubt it was like that at certain times and places. But the
whole point of a cattle drive was to move slowly, letting the herd graze
and gain weight on the way to market. A chocolate band of bare earth
would have made poor grazing; and banks of drifted sand are unlikely in
country known for the richness and blackness of its soils.

The Chisholm Trail, like other cattle trails, was actually a corridor a
few miles wide. One herd might go along its eastern edge, the next much
farther west to get untrampled grass. And there were various crossings at
big rivers like the Colorado, Brazos, and Red.

Jesse Chisholm, for whom the trail was named, was an Indian trader,
known for his honesty, who established a trade route from Kansas southward into Oklahoma. This short stretch was the original Chisholm Trail.
Jesse Chisholm died before the big cattle drives began. When they did,
they passed over the stretch he had pioneered with his trade wagons, and
in a few years his name had spread over the whole length of the trail,
from Abilene down to San Antonio.

The first cattle went up the as-yet-nameless Chisholm Trail in the fall
of 1867. Its promoters (men who bought and shipped the cattle in Abilene) described it—correctly—as having "more prairie, less timber, more
small streams and fewer large ones, altogether better grass and fewer
flies, than any other route yet driven over."

The cost of moving huge herds of cattle from ranches in Texas to
northern Kansas was less than a dollar a head. The animals moved under
their own power, ate free grass, and drank free water. Almost the only
expenses were food and pay for the trail boss and cowhands.

Fort Worth lacked a railroad. Otherwise the trail would have ended
there. But it did become an outfitting center where the drovers bought
saddles, pistols, groceries, whatever was needed for the long haul that
still lay ahead. Fort Worth also became a cattle market where men who
did not want to drive on to Abilene sold their cattle to men who did, for
the sake of still higher profits. And it is a cattle market still.

All of the Prairie-and-Cross-Timbers country is favored by the scissor-
tailed flycatcher, the only bird I know of which has caused Roger Tory
Peterson to abandon scientific detachment. He calls it (in *Field Guide to
the Birds of Texas*) "A beautiful bird." It is. But its fine colors—silver,
salmon pink, black—are hard to see except through binoculars.

Scissor-tails are handsome, they give pleasure, they do no harm, and collectively they eat many tons of insects every year. Given this excellent record, you would expect them to be nearing extinction in a world which seems geared for the casual destruction of whatever is harmless or handsome in nature. But no: there are as many scissor-tails now as forty years ago. Along with mourning doves, they are the telephone-wire birds of the central plains and prairies.

Their long tails are folded shut most of the time. They scissor out handsomely when the bird climbs an invisible peak in the air to capture an insect, or when several scissor-tails are playing around the top of a telephone pole. Then they look like flying orchids. A glimpse of the bird's axillary feathers—deep in its "armpit" where the salmon color is most intense—is a kind of bonus for those with enough patience.

Scissor-tails depart for southern Mexico and Central America in October. They come back in March. This may seem a short stay for so long a trip. But the good-sized birds, for whom a flight to Panama is no strain, have to go somewhere. There aren't enough winter insects in Texas to feed the big scissor-tail population, and they eat almost nothing else.

The Rolling Plains don't always roll. North of Abilene for many miles they are as flat as any land in Texas. In places, long mesas, with names like Flat Top and Skin Out, rise above the general levelness. Other places are distinctly hilly, and there are still others where the plains do really roll.

But what name could be exactly right for this varied country that runs from Cap Rock to Cross Timbers? It has been given many. They suggest that people can't decide either where it is or what it is: Central Basin, Central Lowland, Northwestern Lowland, North Central Plains, Osage Plains, and (in an effort to get everything in) Central Rolling Red Plains.

My favorite name for it is Central Denuded Region. This is a geologists' invention, totally unpopular with chambers of commerce in the area. They prefer upbeat names like the Big Country. "Denuded" comes from the fact that the red Permian earth—the famous Red Beds—is loose and crumbly and has been eroding fast for thousands of years.

You see it in the brightly-colored country north of Benjamin, where the small South Wichita River has made a wide badland of gullies and crumbling buttes, not only Permian red but also white with gypsum and blue with veins of shale. You see wind erosion in the big red dust devils that whirl across the summer fields, like ghosts from the 1930s' Dust Bowl (which included these plains). And above all you see erosion in the rivers. They carry so much silt after any rain that they are as red as the land itself. Orange-red hills and fields are fine, but orange-red water is not. It looks as thick as hand lotion and entirely unpalatable.

The major eroding rivers are the Colorado, the Brazos, and the Red. Before dams were built on the Brazos, people in the white limestone country of central Texas noted "red rises" on the river and knew that rain had fallen far out on the plains. Now the red mud sinks into the lake above Possum Kingdom Dam. In the upper parts of the lake, where the Brazos's current slows, silt lies seven feet deep on the bottom.

The eastern quarter of the plains has been denuded most of all. The Permian rocks, if they were ever there, long ago crumbled and drained down the rivers and left even older strata at the surface—Mississippian and Pennsylvanian, which are not so red. Otherwise the two pieces of country are much alike. They raise cotton, cattle, and cattle feed. They are monotonously infested with mesquite. And their small towns are among the drabbest in Texas.

Yet it is prosperous country. Until the soil washes away, it produces good crops. And there is enough variety in the landscape so that a change of place, a cast of light, may make you feel briefly that you are not in Texas at all, but in Saskatchewan or Durango.

And why not? Saskatchewan is on the Great Plains, and so is this big red piece of Texas. Back in the days when the settlers feared the open prairies, Captain Randolph Marcy, U.S.A., wrote this:

> This barren district, however, exhibits one characteristic which compensates for many of its asperities. Perhaps no part of the habitable globe is more favorable to health and the continuation of human existence than this. Free from marshes, stagnant water, and all other sources of malaria, and open to every wind that blows, this immense grassy expanse is purged from impurities of every kind, and the air imparts a force and vigor to the body and to the mind which repays the occupant in great measure for his deprivation.[3]

Those are the Great Plains, all right. Captain Marcy's nineteenth-century prose still fits the country. It was at Fort Griffin, in the clean October air of the Rolling Plains, that I finally coaxed a pair of miniature binoculars to show all four of Jupiter's biggest moons.

A few miles south of Abilene a line of striking white hills and mesas rises above the red beds and mesquite. They are the Callahan Divide, a high, broken ridge and separator of waters. Rain that falls on the north side of the Callahan Divide flows toward the Brazos. On the south side it goes to the Colorado.

The two rivers have carried away the hundreds or maybe thousands of feet of limestone which once covered these plains. They exposed the

Permian rocks, and are now draining them away. All that remains of the limestone is the Callahan ridge between the river basins. Eventually it too will go. It is no longer a solid line, but broken. The biggest gap in it is the mile-wide Buffalo Gap, through which buffalo herds funneled and plodded for thousands of years on their seasonal shiftings. The Goodnight-Loving cattle trail went through this gap too, and the Butterfield Mail Line, and many wagon trains bound for California. For the Callahan Divide, with its vertical white cliffs, is a long and serious barrier.

The village of Buffalo Gap (population 320) stands where Comanche Indians once wintered under big live-oak trees. The trees are still there. The children of Buffalo Gap may ride their bicycles to school but not their horses—a sign says, No Horses on School Ground.

A few miles south of the village, Abilene State Park contains hundreds of big pecan trees along Elm Creek. This is another Comanche camp ground. The Comanches, nomadic plainsmen, disliked real forests and avoided them except for raids. But a grove of shade trees beside a pretty stream made a nice change from the sun-beaten plains and pleased them very well.

You can cross the Callahan Divide on U.S. 277 (Abilene to San Angelo). When you do, you'll think you're on the Edwards Plateau: junipers, yuccas, sheep. And you are, for the limestone which once covered all or part of the Rolling Plains was essentially just a northward extension of the Edwards Plateau.

But so little is left of it now that after fifteen miles or so the highway drops down again from white country to red, from cedar to mesquite, and it remains red and mesquite-ridden to San Angelo and beyond.

The plains are well seasoned with two common minerals: salt and gypsum. Much of the area is drained by various forks of the Brazos—Clear Fork, Double Mountain Fork, etc., and they don't all get together until just above Possum Kingdom Lake. If you ever find yourself crossing the Salt Fork, get out and taste it. It is saltier than the Gulf of Mexico, and has coatings of salt on its sandy bottom. Yet the pollywogs and minnows in it don't mind at all.

Gypsum, unfortunately, dissolves. The result is the "gyp water" of the plains, a notorious purgative and stomach-cramper. A cotton farmer near Paducah told me he irrigates his fields with gyp water pumped from 250 feet below the surface. It is plentiful, he said, and good for cotton. But his hoe hands, who are migrant laborers, sometimes get thirsty and ignore his warnings. The big flow of cold, clear water from the irrigation pipe tempts them on hot afternoons, and soon they are down with diarrhea.

This same farmer's drinking water comes from a little well fifty feet deep beside his house. It is *not* plentiful. And this situation is common all through the Rolling Plains.

I have never lived out there, and so have never tested two statements often made about gyp water: that it makes excellent coffee, and that Navy beans cooked in it never get done but only grow harder and harder. It does no good to ask about these matters; you get conflicting answers. Some day I'm going to bring a few gallons of gyp water home with me and test it on beans and coffee.

All of this country was once called by the Spaniards the *Comancheria,* the land of the Comanche Indians. Their culture was simple, totally intertwined with two animals, the horse and the buffalo. They rode one and hunted the other.

If buffalo herds had actually covered miles of the plains like a solid brown blanket, if they had existed in the scores of millions the pioneers thought they saw, they would have drunk the rivers dry and eaten the earth bare. Scientists today, basing their calculations on what the grasslands will support—or rather on what they would have supported when they were far lusher than they are now—estimate that the North American population of buffalo in their heyday was about thirty million.[4]

Railroad builders fed their construction crews on buffalo meat as the transcontinental railways were built across the plains. The estimated cost of it was less than a penny a pound. Buffalo Bill earned that name as a commercial hunter for railroad gangs in Kansas, where he killed 4,280 buffalo in eighteen months. It was only much later that he organized his Wild West Show.

Hunting buffalo for their hides began when someone devised a tanning process that would turn tough buffalo hide into workable leather. (One of the big buyers of this leather was the British Army.) The first big hide shipments from the plains were made in 1871. By 1881 it was all over. All but a few of the thirty million buffalo (if that was their number) had been slaughtered. The U.S. Army wanted the buffalo killed, since it would simplify the job of subduing the Plains Indians. The Army, in fact, supplied many hide hunters with ammunition. And ranchers wanted the buffalo killed, so there would be more grass for their cows. Toward the end some journalists urged people to go west and shoot a buffalo before they were all gone. Some men hoped to manage the distinction of killing the last buffalo of all.[5]

The center of hide hunting in Texas was Fort Griffin, on the Clear Fork of the Brazos, on the Rolling Plains. There hunters could get outfitted with guns, horses, and supplies, and there they could sell the hides when they got back. Fort Griffin was also on the Dodge City cattle trail, and for a few years, drovers and hide hunters and prosperity made it the roughest frontier town in Texas.

The fort itself was on high land above the river. The civilian town (saloons, hide buyers, outfitters, dance halls, hotels) was down on the Flat, part of the Clear Fork's floodplain. The Flat is now the sedate public camp ground of Fort Griffin State Park, with children's swings and running water at the campsites.

Some of the fort's old buildings have been restored, which generally means rebuilt from the ground up so that they look and smell brand new and have no historic aura whatever. But the thickets of oak and mesquite around the real ruins are good places for birdwatching, and the annual crop of prickly-pear apples is varied and abundant.

The Flat's boom faded when the buffalo were all killed off, and the fort itself was closed in 1881. Fort Griffin is now far from any town. It is headquarters for the official state herd of Texas longhorns. The animals' horns are truly magnificent, and they themselves look rangy and rawboned, capable like their ancestors of surviving in wilderness or walking to Kansas and gaining weight on the way. Actually they get range pellets, salt blocks, and veterinary care, and they answer the horn of a pickup truck calling them to their feed.

As for the official state herd of buffalo, there is none. The larger buffalo herds which exist today are well to the north of Texas, some of them in Canada. But small private herds are scattered over the state. There is one near Jean, Texas, beside Highway 199. It contains calves, cows, and very large bulls, visible at close range. The greedily grazing buffalo are indifferent to visitors and are upstaged anyway by a large and lively llama which, through their owner's fancy, lives with them. It comes bounding down the hillside to the highway fence, clean, light, and graceful. The buffalo, by comparison, look so stupid and dirty that it's possible to feel momentarily, and unfairly, that extinction was about what they deserved.

The basic ecological change on the Rolling Plains has been from buffalo and grass to beef cattle and mesquite, but also to cotton and other crops. Old farmhouses are scattered over the land, abandoned as dwellings when family farms were absorbed into agribusiness empires. Often the old kitchens and bedrooms are stacked to their ceilings with baled hay. The black skeletons of mesquite trees, poisoned in various ways, fill thousands of pastures, and other pastures, cleared of mesquite a few years ago, now show it coming back.

In somebody's yard, pruned and shaped, a mesquite is handsome. At the Amon G. Carter Museum of Western Art, in Fort Worth, a big mesquite holds the place of honor, virtually enthroned, in front of the building. And Fort Worth has sensibly planted mesquite trees in some of its huge civic parking lots, where they relieve the monotony of acres of pavement and yet survive the heat waves that rise from it. A mesquite's thin, shimmering leaves look cool on the hottest day. But infesting ranchland, mesquite trees steal ruinous amounts of water and nutrients that might otherwise go to grass.

Millions have been spent in efforts to eradicate it, but mesquite keeps bouncing back—tough, tenacious, and equipped in many ways to survive and multiply. Big trees may send tap roots down sixty feet, reach water, and grow heartily while everything else is dying of drought. The tree blooms at intervals through the summer and produces several crops of seeds—in pods, for the mesquite is a legume. The seeds may lie in the ground up to fifty years before they germinate. The earth of many parts of Texas is literally saturated with them. If all vegetation were scraped away, millions of little trees would pop up each year for decades into the future.

Before mesquite became a pest, people were fond of it. They made folk remedies out of almost every part and they brewed "coffee" from roasted mesquite beans when they lacked the real thing.

But the great early-day use of mesquite was as firewood—for branding irons, wash pots, barbecues, fireplaces. The wood makes a hot flame and long-lasting coals. Its smoke is sparse and aromatic. It gives a good flavor to meat, and to coffee boiled in an open pot.

Birds and animals eat mesquite beans. Human beings—some of them —favor the pods. They contain so much sugar that they taste sweet, and so much protein that they're good for you. Back-country Mexicans grind the pods into a meal which they make into bread, or ferment into an alcoholic drink.

In the days of the cattle drives, cows excreted mesquite beans all the way to Kansas, and Kansas is still the northern limit of their range.

The mesquite is so skilled at survival that it gets credit for a kind of consciousness, or shrewdness. Mesquites never put out their leaves, people say, until the last frost is safely past. Somehow they "know" which one is the last. But anyone who observes them long enough will find out some late spring that they don't know. They merely leaf out late, and some years not late enough. It may be true, however, that mesquites bear heavier crops of beans in a hot, dry summer than in a rainy one. Botanists are now checking out that belief.

To the question, "What do you hunt here?" the answer on the plains is often "Varmints." "I'll bet you there's a bobcat within two hundred yards of us right now," said a man in Stamford. He was behind a counter, selling tractor parts in a downtown store. Somehow bobcats, which are supposed to prefer rocky canyons and thickets, have taken hold on the heavily-farmed plains. They live as usual on mice, rats, rabbits, and birds. Coyotes are also numerous. The gamebirds are doves and quail.

North of Paducah on the Pease River, the Matador Wildlife Management Area occupies 28,000 acres which were once part of the east pasture of the old Matador Ranch. Turkeys and quail—scaled quail as well as bobwhite—flourish despite the many coyotes which eat their eggs. There are even a few deer.

And the Matador area gives the Mississippi kite a hope of survival. Mississippi kites are slim-winged graceful hawks, designed not for power flight like most hawks but for gliding. They are handsomely done up in black and white and gray, and when you see one for the first time you sense that you've seen something unusual. In flight they manage to look a little like small gliders. (Their wingspread is about three feet.) Mississippi kites are becoming rare in Texas. The Rolling Plains and the adjoining Staked Plain are the only places in the state where they breed.

West of Knox City, the Plant Materials Center stands out like a bizarre truck garden of improbable plants. It is obviously a government operation; otherwise it would not bear such a flat-footed name. The Soil Conservation Service runs it, and grows and tests plants that farmers and ranchers might find valuable. More or less incidentally it constitutes a museum of grasses and forbs, all alive, aggressively healthy, and growing in patches and rows. The work of the place goes on while visitors wander through on their own, consulting a map-guidebook to identify the plants. The Center is assembling a collection of rare and endangered plants, many from Texas but also some from other states; the Soil Conservation Service is a federal agency and does not limit its interest to Texas.

Pleasant anomalies, sudden changes of mood or texture, turn up on the Rolling Plains. The Permian Red Beds are topped here and there with islands of sandy soil up to fifty miles long which somewhat resemble the top layer of the Staked Plain. This soil is called the Seymour Formation. It generally lies on high land between two watersheds and it may have been blown there by winds from the west. Quanah, Crowell, Benjamin, and Munday are among the towns on Seymour deposits. The town of Seymour itself is just off the edge of one.

At Paint Rock, on a long, graceful bluff above the Concho River (and on privately owned land) is the fading gallery of Indian pictographs which gave the town its name in 1879. The youngest of these paintings, not counting the work of Anglo-Saxon vandals, were made after the white man came to the plains, for they show cowboys with lariats and spurs.

Far over on the eastern edge of the plains rise the Palo Pintos, an unexpected and picturesque little range of mountains. They are largely Pennsylvanian limestone. The Brazos River cuts through them in a deep, crooked canyon. A dam has formed Possum Kingdom Lake, one of the older and better-looking of the state's "impoundments." The lake is crooked too, not by any means filling the Brazos canyon; and along some of its shoreline are fine gray limestone bluffs. Petroleum geologists like to study them because these same strata are buried several thousand feet underground at the western edge of the Rolling Plains, and there have yielded large amounts of oil.

The Palo Pinto Mountains are covered with cedar brakes as thick as any on the Edwards Plateau. "Post Yard" say signs along the roads, and that lifetime outdoorsman, the cedar chopper, has survived here and bred cedar-chopping descendants as he has in parts of the Edwards Plateau. But a little to the east of the Palo Pintos the cedar thins and disappears, and country with a different look begins: the Cross Timbers.

The woods called Cross Timbers, East and West, are small, frayed, and partly forgotten, the most nearly wiped out of all the physiographic regions of Texas. I suspect that in this century many people have grown up in the Cross Timbers without knowing they were doing so, for millions of acres of the original post-oak and blackjack woods have been cut down and made into farmland.

From 1850 to 1880 or so the Cross Timbers were important. Then, everybody in Texas knew where they were and what they were. They were the very last strips of forest before the Great Plains began, long bands of oak running north-south across the grasslands. They extended up through Oklahoma and on into southern Kansas.[6]

Since the rivers of all this country ran essentially from west to east, flowing through the Cross Timbers, they formed a kind of grid in a region then without roads or settlements. And so the two halves of a scouting expedition could agree to meet in a month's time "where the Trinity flows out of the Upper Cross Timbers," or "two miles below the Lower Cross Timbers on the North Canadian." (The Western Cross Timbers were often called Upper and the Eastern Cross Timbers Lower, since one lay upstream, in fact up many streams, and thus uphill from the other.)

In those days the Cross Timbers had character. They were not just scraps and patches of woods sheltering birds and small mammals, as they are today. They were full of black bear and wild hogs and turkeys. They had grape vines and wild-plum thickets. Captain Marcy, writing in 1852, said:

At six different points I have found the Cross Timbers with the same peculiarities—the trees standing at such intervals that wagons can pass between them. The soil is thin, sandy, poorly watered. This forms a boundary line between the country suited to agriculture and the great prairies, which for the most part are arid and destitute of timber. It seems to have been designed as a natural barrier between the civilized man and the savage. . . .[7]

And a natural barrier it was, until the late 1870s. The white man tarried in the familiar woods, not knowing how to live on the treeless plains. In any case, the Comanches were on those plains, to keep him back. And, conversely, the Comanches distrusted the woods. They regarded the beginning of the Western Cross Timbers as the limit of their world.

Prairie fires would burn across the Rolling Plains and stop at the Cross Timbers, finding too little grass to feed on. Sometimes buffalo would hide in the timbers to escape hunters on the prairies.

What caused these strips of forest to exist in an immensity of prairie? The answer has to do with geology and the remote past. Most Cretaceous formations are limestone. (*Creta* is Latin for chalk.) But some Cretaceous strata are mixtures of sand, gravel, and clay. Two of these, the Woodbine Sands and the Travis Peak formation, thanks to erosion and upheavals of the earth's crust, have lain exposed for some millions of years in the areas that for a century or more have been called the Cross Timbers.

Sand and gravel make a loose soil, easily penetrated by tree roots, better for tree growth than for grass. But it is not a rich soil, so the Cross Timbers did not grow the deep forests that East Texas has, but savannahs of post oak and blackjack. And these were skimpier than the post oaks and blackjacks of the Post Oak Belt because they lay farther west and got less rain.

Sandy soils are great absorbers of water. The Woodbine and Travis Peak formations slope eastward underground and lie beneath Fort Worth and Dallas. When the two cities were small, wells drilled down to the sands yielded all the water they needed. Now Fort Worth and Dallas must dam rivers for their water. But many small towns on the Grand and Blackland Prairies still get soft artesian water out of the Cross Timbers strata.

Technically the Hagerman National Wildlife Refuge lies in the Eastern Cross Timbers, along that stretch of Red River which some decades ago became Lake Texoma. But being largely riverbottom and lakeshore and marsh, it doesn't look like Cross Timbers country.

It's a pleasant place, lacking in swank, perhaps run as much for the benefit of plants and animals as for people. The roads are not particularly good. Stretches of them are sometimes under water. The basic pamphlet advises visitors to "be alert for rattlesnakes and cottonmouth moccasins."

Three thousand acres of the refuge are marsh and water, and make an important stop on the Central Flyway for migrating water birds. Some of them spend the winter. The big show is Canada geese. With the possible addition of other species of geese, they may total 25,000 at a time. Not in one mass, of course; the refuge covers 11,000 acres of which several hundred are planted in grain for the birds to feed on. Geese can be found both on the water and in the uplands.

Because it has a variety of habitats, Hagerman is a good place for seeing birds. The golden eagle turns up there (rarely) and so do the brant and the pileated woodpecker. More than 250 bird species have been spotted on the refuge, but it would be a life's work for one person to see them all. Mink and beaver live along the little streams, which in places are completely arched over by trees and tangled vines. When a north wind raises whitecaps and pounding breakers on Lake Texoma, the refuge seems to be on the shore of a fresh-water sea.

It is, however, merely the shore of the Big Mineral Creek arm of the enormous reservoir, which has 580 miles of shoreline. Half an hour's drive east of Hagerman is Eisenhower State Recreation Park, with its screened shelters, hot showers, acute litter problems, and full-length view of Denison Dam, which is what keeps Lake Texoma from draining away and is nearly three miles long. And thirty miles north of there, in Oklahoma, the Tishomingo National Wildlife Refuge covers even more territory than Hagerman does. It too is on an arm of Lake Texoma.

Wise County, north of Decatur, has a patchwork of old farms which the federal government bought up and made into the Cross Timbers National Grasslands, more than twenty thousand acres of them. Not forest, you'll notice, but grasslands—an indicator of the extent to which the Cross Timbers have been wiped out. But bits of woods remain among the fields, and it is in them, if anywhere, that you can get some idea of what the old Cross Timbers looked like. The trees still stand, as in Captain Marcy's day, far enough apart so that wagons could pass between them. Your imagination must add black bears and wild turkeys, but you will still see red-tailed hawks, skunks, foxes, quail, and of course squirrels, which appreciate the acorns.

You will also see armadillos. They are strangely-put-together animals. Their armor is really a specialized form of skin. It is not hard to break; coyotes, dogs, and javelinas can do it. It does not, therefore, do the armadillo much good to roll up into an invulnerable ball because he isn't invulnerable. What the shell really seems useful for is letting the armadillo burrow unscratched into thick tangles of briars and thorns where its enemies don't want to go.[8]

In one respect armadillos are unique among North American mammals: a mother armadillo in normal birth produces four babies per litter, all of the same sex. They are in fact identical quadruplets which start out as a single egg, then divide into two and then into four.

This reproductive procedure seems to work extremely well at supplying the world with armadillos. They have spread into the United States from South America and have extended their range enormously, though people kill them in great numbers—for food, to make their shells into curios, or just to be killing something. In 1880 armadillos were found in Texas only in the state's southern tip. They had appeared in Louisiana by 1925, and now live all along the Gulf coast to Florida. They don't go far north, though, because, lacking fur, they don't survive well in cold weather.

Armadillo is Spanish, meaning little armored one. The animal lives mostly on insects, grubs, and worms, which it finds by nosing around in fallen leaves and digging into the ground. If you are careful to move when an armadillo's head is down and stop when it looks up, you can sometimes come up behind one and touch it. It will then run away fast, for armadillos have good muscles and heavy bones. And their claws, long and sharp, are useful for digging and fighting.

Their solid construction makes armadillos heavy for their size, denser than water. They cross small streams just by walking across on the bottom, completely submerged if the water is deep enough. But armadillos must breathe, and when the river is wide and they have to swim they swallow air until their bellies bulge with it and they float. Once ashore, they work the air on out through their intestinal tracts.

The nine-banded armadillo is the name of the Texas species and it is our only one. Various larger relatives live in South America. The Texas variety is such an efficient digger that abandoned armadillo homes, which are numerous, supply living quarters to various other animals. Skunks, rats, rabbits, possums, and owls have all been found living in old armadillo holes.

The farther away the horizons are, the better I like a piece of country. By that standard the Trans-Pecos is my favorite part of Texas. There, one can see mountains rising a hundred miles away.

By the same standard, the Grand Prairie is my second favorite region. I was born on it, and after many years of absence I live there now. It is the big prairie with the big views, and hardly anyone ever says so, but its white limestone hills, Irish-green pastures, and cedar brakes so dark they are black-green make it one of the most beautiful regions of Texas.

Like the Blackland Prairie, the Grand Prairie is limestone laid down in Cretaceous time. But it is harder than the Blackland limestone, it gets less rain, and has formed a thinner, rockier soil. In places you can see the blackest possible dirt dotted with the whitest possible stones. Yet it is the white stones that decompose into the black soil. In pastures south of Fort

Worth you may still be able to find ammonites, fossilized shellfish like big stone snails a foot or more across. People have been collecting them for a long time.

Getting about thirty-five inches of rain a year, the Grand Prairie is a transition zone between the wet east and the dry western parts of Texas.[9] Fort Worth, on the prairie's eastern edge, has as its slogan "Where the West Begins." This is no mere Chamber-of-Commerce boast. It is ecologically correct.

In its narrow northern strip (Decatur, Gainesville) the Grand Prairie is dairy country, rolling, grassy, and almost bald of trees. Farther south it widens out and those matchless, mournful, white-walled mesas begin. One good view of them is from the well-tended hilltop park a few miles west of Glen Rose on Highway 67.

Some of the Grand Prairie is ranched, some farmed. There are ranching areas where live oaks dominate, usually as small trees in mottes. These are the same trees that, on the wet Gulf shore, become century-old moss-hung giants. On the higher, dryer Grand Prairie they never do.

This country has the prettiest small rivers in Texas except for those on the Edwards Plateau. The three little Bosque rivers, North, Middle, and South, make miles of small bluffs and rock shelters and swimming holes before they run into drab Lake Waco. The Leon River has rich floodplains with native pecan trees. Stretches of the Lampasas River west of Belton, with huge square-cut slabs of gray limestone, make a design as formal as the gardens of Versailles.

One of the handsomest stretches of Grand Prairie country lies along Highway 6 between Valley Mills and Clifton, where the North Bosque has made a flat, fertile valley. Actually it is not a valley but a floodplain. The true Grand Prairie is found in the fortresslike hills that rise on either side.

Near Walnut Springs, the Flat Top Ranch has been a showplace for decades, and for the right reasons rather than the wrong ones. It is not one of those ranches made splendid by oil money massively spent. It is, rather, twenty-seven square miles of fields and pastures exhausted by misuse which a single man, Charles Pettit, brought back to rich grass, clear streams, and a variety of wild game along with his Hereford cattle.

Mr. Pettit (he died in 1964) was that rarity, a businessman who understood that conserving the natural world is more profitable than plundering it. He wanted to make money, and he did so by stopping erosion, planting grass, and stocking his land not only with cattle in moderate numbers but also with wild turkey, beaver, quail, pronghorn, and deer. People still pay a premium to hunt on Flat Top lands.

Charles Pettit was neither an all-out conservationist nor much of an ecologist. He paid bounties for rattlesnakes, coyotes, bobcats, and foxes killed on his ranch, and would have liked all these animals exterminated. His aim was not to restore his piece of the Grand Prairie to what it had been before the white man came. His aim was to make a profit from crops, cattle, game, fishing ponds, everything.

Thirty years before there was general awareness that the land was being damaged, he was restoring his and making it pay. People came from everywhere to see what he had done. One of the many showpieces was East Bosque Creek. It entered the Flat Top Ranch as a waterless gully, ruined by the misuse of lands upstream, and left it five miles farther down as a small, full stream, alive with fish and birds and beavers and enclosed by banks deep in grass.

Near Glen Rose the bed of the Paluxy River contains tracks made by dinosaurs more than 100 million years ago. They are excellent specimens. One set of them was dug up in the 1920s and taken to the American Museum of Natural History in New York. Another set is at the Texas Memorial Museum in Austin. The best remaining ones, still in place, are now within the new Dinosaur Valley State Park, a few miles from Glen Rose.

There was no Paluxy River when the dinosaurs lived at Glen Rose. The climate was wet and warm, the land was marshy, and the huge animals left their tracks in limey mud flats which since have turned to stone. That stone is now the riverbed, and most of the tracks, much of the time, are under a foot or two of water.

Some of the footprints are isolated—that is, not one of a series—and some a bit indistinct. But there's one place where you lean against a cedar-log fence, look down a fifteen-foot bank into the river, and see a series of clear, large, alarming three-toed tracks. It's as if a dragon had just waded the stream and disappeared into the thickets of the other side.

The maker of these tracks was Acrocanthosaurus, a small ancestor of the huge Tyrannosaurus Rex. It stood and walked on its hind legs and was only fifteen feet high, but trailed a long reptilian tail. Its tracks are the most numerous in the park. The largest footprints were left by a forty-ton vegetarian, seventy feet from nose to tail tip, called Pleurocelus.

All of the dinosaur tracks, both in and out of the park, are contained in the same stratum of rock. A few yards from the river this stratum is buried under alluvium. Experimentally, Parks and Wildlife scientists probed an old river-bottom field which is now within the park. They wanted to see if the limestone layer was down there. It was. They dug a hole. And not only did they reach the rock, twenty-eight feet down, but they came upon more tracks within it. It's possible that the washed-in dirt of the old field covers twenty acres of dinosaur tracks and trails. But the cost of removing twenty-eight feet of earth from twenty acres would be large, so we may never know.

The little park itself is still pleasantly undeveloped. One fork of its hiking trail leads to a high point which overlooks the Grand Prairie at its best. In a distant pasture some members of the state's longhorn herd are couched or grazing on emerald-green grass. Seen through binoculars, with their huge horns curving in silhouette against the afternoon sun, they seem legendary beasts of infinite grace and gentleness, capable of vanishing if you came too near. Unfortunately you *can* come near; and then they turn out to have runny noses and stupid stares, like any other cattle in any other pasture.

A few miles south of Dinosaur Valley is Meridian State Park, notable for its thick stands of cedar. These attract the golden-cheeked warbler, and the warblers in turn attract people who hope to see one or at least hear its simple song.

The military men of Fort Hood, ever alert to the possibilities of public relations, have reserved a patch of cedar on their vast shell-shocked acreage for the golden-cheek, but none has yet been seen there. They do turn up sometimes in Mother Neff State Park, which is nearby, and has been enlarged to include some old cedars. This park, on the Leon River near McGregor, has ancient riverbottom oak and elm trees of championship size. And native pecan trees. People camp in the park in the fall, or drive out from nearby towns, to gather pecans.

Fort Hood, which is near Belton, covers 341 square miles, and the Army is trying to expand it. It was established during World War II, and within a year or two its streams were running clear and native grasses were coming back, as the land began to recover from overgrazing and bad farming. You can find there a portion of the Grand Prairie that looks somewhat as it did before farmers plowed and ranchers ranched it.

Fort Hood is a tank and gunnery training post, mostly open to the public. Anyone who isn't unnerved or ear-damaged by the sound of eight-inch guns may drive its paved roads, looking at a Grand Prairie without fields, fences, barns, or houses. A central region called the Impact Area, twelve miles across in its greatest dimension, is where the shells land, fired from points around its rim. It is, in effect, a small wilderness, inhabited only by wild animals.

Surprisingly the Impact Area is not full of holes like a French battlefield of 1917. It looks normal. It is large and the shells fall far apart, and I suspect that they are not, in any case, loaded with all the explosive they would carry in real war. Deer and doves and wild turkey are plentiful in the Impact Area. In season the big guns are silenced and the public may come in and hunt.

Fort Hood is not an ecological paradise. Dirt roads and tank trails scar the landscape. The headquarters, called the cantonment area, is a city of forty thousand soldiers and civilians. Killeen, right beside it, was a pretty country town until fast, haphazard growth made it one of the ugliest small cities in the state. But Fort Hood has at least given some hundreds of square miles of land a needed rest. Bombardment has proved less damaging than cultivation.

Among the animals that don't seem to mind the guns are horned frogs. Despite the name, they are not frogs but lizards. They live all over Texas except in the moist eastern woods. The Grand Prairie is where I played with them as a small boy. They were easy to find then, and are now, around anthills, for ants are their favorite food. Any hill of big red ants supplies far more than they can eat.

Yes, horned frogs can shoot a tiny stream of blood ("fine as a horsehair" according to Dr. Raymond Ditmars, who saw it happen) from the corners of their eyes, or perhaps from their eyelids. They can't be made to do this on demand, and they don't do it often, so this performance has not been well observed. Dr. Ditmar's horned frog, a large one, squirted its blood four feet onto a nearby wall, and kept squirting for a second and a half.

And yes, horned frogs are harmless. They don't bite, sting, cause warts, or scratch you with their claws. They are easily tamed, but make rather listless pets and die without plenty of sand and sunshine and live food. It is more fun to watch a horned frog free and active in a vacant lot than one boringly imprisoned in a wire pen. Killing or selling horned frogs is now against the law. Even the ten-year-old who trades one to a friend for bubble gum is a lawbreaker.

Horned frogs live all over the western U.S. and in Mexico. There are seventeen species altogether, with only three in Texas. Of the three, the most widespread is called the Texas Horned Lizard. It is also the largest (four to five inches long) and has the longest horns projecting backward from the back of its head. Skeletons in museums show that the various horns (six or eight on the back of the head, a dozen or more small ones along the lower jaw) are part of the animal's skull bone, as the claws are part of a claw hammer. They are not a separate substance, as cows' horns are.

Several monster movies have starred horned frogs as monsters, using camera tricks which make them look as big as dinosaurs. And Texas is full of tales about horned frogs cemented into the cornerstones of courthouses in horse-and-buggy days and found alive when the buildings were torn down thirty-nine or fifty-three years later. There are still people who know this is so because their grandfathers saw the cornerstone opened and the horned frog blink.

I have looked for solid evidence that such stories can be true—I would like them to be true—and have found none. In view of the elaborate preparations that many animals must make before hibernating or estivating for just one season—forming special burrows, storing fat or water, coating themselves with slime, etc.—it seems unlikely that a horned frog, clapped without warning into a cornerstone, would be equipped to survive in the airless dark for thirty years. But a lot of people still believe it can.

"What we should have put our money into twenty years ago," a Waco businessman said to me recently, "are diamonds and blackland farms."

He's right. The Blackland Prairie, appropriately shaped like a Horn of Plenty, runs about four hundred miles from the Red River down to San Antonio. It has by far the best soil in Texas—rich, black, waxy, and many feet deep.[10] Though this earth contains no gold or silver, it is pay dirt all by itself.

The land lies in smooth, rolling hills, like enormous green waves, their crests a mile or more apart, the curves interlocking. The long bowed lines that airplanes draw in the sky match exactly the lines of the hills. The valleys, where they exist, are as shallow as saucers, miles across, rich, and immensely calm. Stampede Valley, near Moody, is one of the best, and best seen early or late in the day.

There are few trees. Originally there were none, except along stream bottoms. If ever there was truly a sea of grass, it was the Blackland Prairie in its prime. Day after day the sun sets clear, often in that nameless, luscious, orange-peach color that a few wild plums have on every tree. Sometimes the sun, even as it touches the horizon, is still too bright to be looked at with the naked eye.

For some reason winter twilights on this prairie are royal blue. Maybe it's all that black plowed land. The famous Blue Hour of dusk in Paris, France, is washed-out compared with that of Paris, Texas (which lies on the edge of the prairie).

This grassland is the place where trees look their best. Not merely because trees are rare on the prairie, though that's part of it. Chiefly because there is room enough to see them. In the eastern woods you can't see a tree for the forest. On the prairie a tree often stands alone, outlined from the ground up against the sky. In January, when a tree's last leaves have been blown away, its structure is totally revealed, and one begins to think that Euclid is not the only one, after all, to have looked on beauty bare.

The commonest Blackland tree is the homely hackberry, usually found along fencerows in a ragged line. Even it looks good in the prairie setting. Hackberry limbs are clumsy, their bark is warted and rough, they are heavily victimized by mistletoe. But birds nest in them and eat their berries, and many a cotton chopper has been grateful for their shade when he came to the end of a row.

I once lived for three years in Austin, not a place for claustrophobes. When its hot little hills and hollows, its oppressively dense vegetation began to wear on me, I used to drive a few miles east to the prairie, to feel the long, smooth wind and see 180 degrees of sky.

Toward sundown nighthawks fly in their strange, jerky manner above the fields, shifting the rate of their wingbeats as they zigzag after insects. The males come out of their power dives with a roar of fluttering feathers. They seem to do this for fun. Most people know nighthawks from nighttime cities and ball parks where they beat about over bright floodlights, eating insects. But open country and open air are their original habitat. They are as much a part of the Blackland Prairie as meadowlarks and mourning doves.

The Blackland weeds are still cockleburr, broomweed, and Johnson grass, as they have been since farming began. A few landowners still let the priceless soil erode, and you can see in the gully walls how amazingly deep it is.

The virgin blacklands were entirely tall-grass prairie. (Tall grasses are four feet high and up.) Here is what it looked like, seen from a ridge on its eastern edge in 1854:

> Below lay a sea of pale green, flowers of every variety, shade, and form interspersed over the surface; a dark green belt of verdure here and there marking the ravines and watercourses, scattered in such perfect arrangement over the whole, as to seem as though some eminent artist had perfected the work.
>
> —W. B. Parker, Notes Taken on the March Expedition, 1854.

The first settlers put animals to grazing on the prairie. Then they started cutting the wild grasses to make hay, and finally they got plows that would break the heavy sod and started farming. Farmland is what the Blackland is today. You don't see flowers of every variety, shade, and form. You see endless acres of cropland and pasture.

One tenth of one percent of the Blackland Prairie remains as it originally was, unplowed and unpaved.[11] Nearly all this virgin grassland is old hay meadows, cherished and carefully mowed once a year by farmers now feeble or dead. If you want to see some of the great variety of grasses and insects and small animals that lived on the original prairie, you have to find one of these meadows. Even they are disappearing, as housing developments spread and new owners plant them in the ever-present, ever-profitable grain sorghum.

The Brazos River cuts across the blacklands, flowing through Waco and past Marlin. Its floodplain interrupts the hills, as broad and flat as the Rio Grande Valley. In places it extends almost to the horizon on each side of the river. Here there are trees, big pecan groves or sketchy little woodlands. But more often there are pastures of fat cattle, for the richness of the Brazos plain matches the richness of the hills on either side. Indeed some of their richness has been allowed to wash down onto it.

The Brazos (Los Brazos de Dios, the Arms of God) is not a handsome river anywhere along its course. Below Marlin it makes a waterfall, the only one in the river's long trip from the Staked Plain to the sea.

The Falls of the Brazos are not vertical. They are not falls at all, they are merely rapids. But no one calls them rapids, and they were considered remarkable enough to give Falls County its name. The river slides downhill over a natural limestone ramp. It's a big river, and its visible descent—perhaps twenty feet in a hundred yards—is impressive. It lets you know how much water is actually moving at all points along that placid-looking stream.

When the water and weather are right, the thrashing Falls of the Brazos are a joy to cool off in. And they give some idea of what serious barriers the big rivers of Texas were in the days of dirt roads and no bridges. The Falls, with their smooth rock bottom, were a principal fording place for east-west traffic when people traveled in wagons and on horseback.

Seventy million years ago the Blackland Prairie was ocean bottom. The water above it was the home of big ocean-going lizards called mososaurs. They swam in the warm, shallow sea and some of them, when they died and sank, became fossils. Many people have found odd bits of mososaur bones in creekbeds and other washed-out places on the prairie. In 1934, two geology students discovered an almost complete skeleton, thirty feet long, in the bed of Onion Creek, a few miles from downtown Austin.[12]

Reconstructed, the Onion Creek Mososaur now dominates the main hall of the Texas Memorial Museum in Austin. Somehow mososaurs, seen as skeletons in museums, seem even more bizarre and improbable than dinosaurs do. They are truly satisfying monsters. The power-filled curve of the Onion Creek Mososaur's body and tail is beautiful. The big jaws and sharp, hooked, backward-pointing teeth are fairly awful. If man had existed and gone swimming in Cretaceous times, this animal could have eaten him in three bites.

Another rebuilt mososaur, more recently discovered on the Blackland Prairie, is now on exhibit at the Corpus Christi Museum. It was found near Corsicana.

Near McKinney, a woman named Bessie Heard bought 256 acres of land a few years ago and turned it into a wildlife sanctuary. Then she built a small museum of natural science at the edge of the property, assigned enough money to the enterprise to keep it running well, and appointed a board of directors. The result shows what a single wealthy and determined person can do for the hard-pressed wildlife and exploited land of Texas.

The refuge is being kept as nearly as possible in its natural state, or returned to it, with its original vegetation and wild animals. High grassland and low stream bottom both occur in the sanctuary, startlingly different from the nearby farmland. More than 230 species of birds, mammals, reptiles, and amphibians live in the woods and ponds and meadows.

Admission to the Heard Museum and Sanctuary is free. To discourage vandalism, a guide accompanies hikers over the trails. The museum has an exhibit of wild animals along with the usual mounted habitat groups, and special rooms containing Miss Heard's personal collections. The whole operation is modest compared to a single national wildlife refuge. But it represents one woman's gratitude to the land from which her family's fortune came. And it may lead other wealthy Texans to consider giving back to the land some small part of what they have taken from it.

At Groesbeck, where the Blackland prairie fringes away into the Post Oak Belt, Fort Parker has been restored and made a state historic site. It was not a military fort but a private stockade enclosing several pioneer cabins—a crude walled village with fields outside—from which Cynthia Ann Parker, age nine, was kidnapped by Comanche and Kiowa Indians in 1836.

She was recaptured twenty-four years later, a red-haired, blue-eyed, freckled Indian squaw, the wife of Chief Peta Nocona and the mother of two sons and an infant daughter. When recaptured (at the Battle of Pease River, on the Rolling Plains) Cynthia Ann could speak no English. She recognized her name when her uncle pronounced it, and indicated that it was hers.

Her family taught her to spin and weave and "perform the domestic duties," and thwarted all her attempts to escape and return to the plains. She survived less than four years as a prisoner of her own kind, and died in Anderson County in 1864. Her small daughter, Prairie Flower, who had gone with her into captivity, died a short time before Cynthia Ann.

The Blackland Prairie is, or anyway was, a matchless kindgom of grass. And grass, not oil or gold, is man's chief source of wealth.[13] Bread, most meat, whiskey, beer, leather, sugar, syrup, and the work that horses do—all are transformed grass.

Grass leaves are made of two parts. The sheath surrounds the stem like a tube split along one side, and the blade curves or leans away from the stem. No matter what grass grows in your yard, you can pick a piece of it and find it made this way. And because grass grows both from the base of the sheath and the base of the blade, it recovers faster than other plants from being grazed or mowed. If the main stem is cut off, a new stem will grow from a place in the sheath.

Grazing animals—cows, buffalo, pronghorns—obviously benefit from eating grass. It's not so obvious that grass benefits from *being eaten* by the animals, but it does. Their hooves chop and aerate the soil. Their manure is fertilizer. They carry grass seeds to new places in their excrement or clinging to their hides. Their grazing is a kind of pruning which encourages grass to grow.

The relationship between grazers and grazed has been neatly worked out by nature over millions of years and is good for both. It perhaps worked best in Texas in the time of the buffalo. The grass grew in a luxuriance we can hardly imagine. It held the world together, the buffalo ate it, and things stayed neatly in balance.

Then came ranching. In *Cattle Ranges of the Southwest*, H. L. Bentley tells of a meeting of cattlemen in the 1890s where a botanist pointed out that the ranchers present knew a lot about horses and cattle but almost nothing about the native grasses on which their business depended. He then tried to discuss the habits and needs of the better wild-grass species, but the ranchers weren't interested. Someone interrupted the botanist and offered a resolution:

> Resolved, that none of us know, or care to know, anything about grasses, native or otherwise, outside of the fact that for the present there are lots of them, the best on record, and we are after getting the most out of them while they last.[14]

The resolution was adopted, Mr. Bentley says, without a dissenting voice and with a shout. Only a few ranchers were at that meeting, but their view was that of nearly all the cattlemen of the West. So the great

natural grassland that in the 1880s constituted 80 percent of Texas became the depleted grasslands of today. Or mesquite thickets, or chemically treated farmland.

As for the remaining 20 percent, half of it was desert lying west of the
Pecos. The rest, a deep forest, lay along the rainy eastern edge of Texas
and was called the Piney Woods.

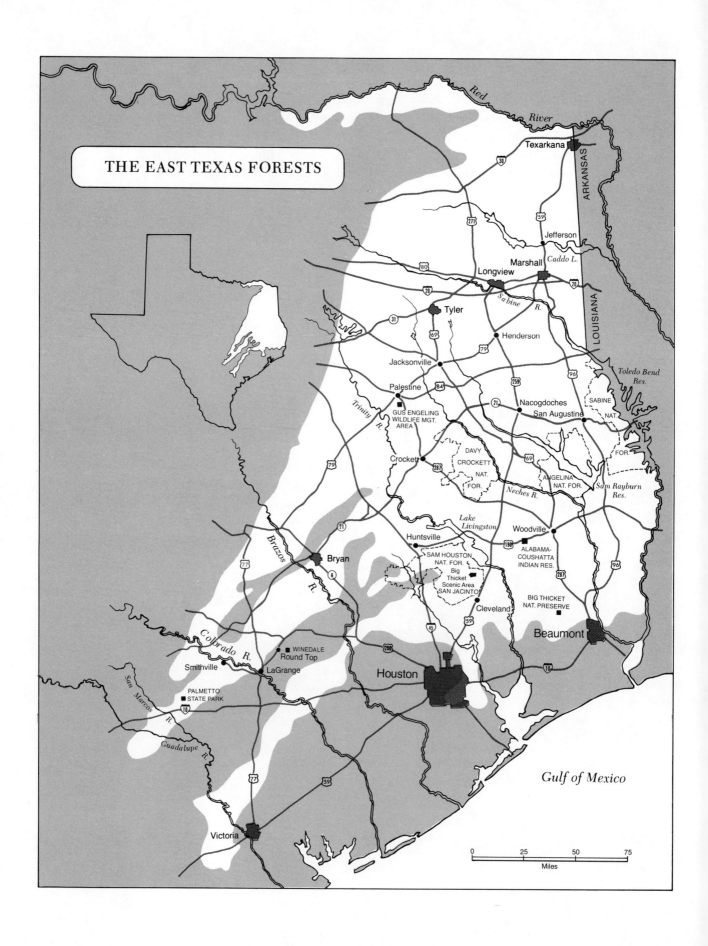

THE EAST TEXAS FORESTS

Red River

Texarkana

ARKANSAS

Jefferson

Marshall

Caddo L.

Longview

Sabine R.

Tyler

Henderson

LOUISIANA

Jacksonville

Toledo Bend Res.

Palestine

SABINE NAT.

Nacogdoches

San Augustine

GUS ENGELING WILDLIFE MGT. AREA

Trinity R.

21

FOR.

DAVY CROCKETT NAT. FOR.

Crockett

ANGELINA NAT. FOR.

Sam Rayburn Res.

Neches R.

Lake Livingston

Woodville

Huntsville

Brazos R.

ALABAMA-COUSHATTA INDIAN RES.

Bryan

SAM HOUSTON NAT. FOR.

Big Thicket Scenic Area

SAN JACINTO

BIG THICKET NAT. PRESERVE

Cleveland

Beaumont

Colorado R.

WINEDALE
Round Top

Smithville

LaGrange

Houston

Gulf of Mexico

San Marcos R.

PALMETTO STATE PARK

Guadalupe R.

Victoria

0   25   50   75
Miles

Two hundred years ago, they say, an energetic but purely imaginary squirrel lived in Virginia, near the Atlantic shore. He decided to travel west, and went all the way to the Mississippi River by moving through the treetops, without ever touching the ground. Such, in those days, was the continuity of the great Southern Appalachian Woodland.

With a lift over the Mississippi, that wandering squirrel could have continued across Louisiana and a fourth of Texas before he stopped in some final post oak and gazed westward across the treeless, squirrelless grasses of the Blackland Prairie.

For the westernmost reaches of the southern woods cover all East Texas from the Red River down almost to the Gulf. Most of the Texas forest is called the Piney Woods. South of them is the Big Thicket, and both areas are bordered on the west by the lovely open savannah called the Post Oak Belt.

"The best childhood you could possibly have was where I had mine, in the Piney Woods of East Texas," a woman told me once. She must have been a child about 1940.

"That soft, sandy land is good for going barefooted, and the woods are full of wild animals and things to eat. We had black children for play-mates—they're the most fun—and trees so big you could spend the day in them. At night the owls were loud and close to the house. We kids were *glad* we had to sleep two and three in a bed."

Some children still live that way in East Texas. The Piney Woods from the beginning fostered a way of life that involved growing garden vege-tables in a little clearing, hunting squirrels and deer and turkey for meat, gathering wild foods in the woods, and getting along on very little money.

Young people who buy small farms in East Texas, aiming to escape the strains of modern life, find elderly neighbors who have never known those strains, who have lived all their lives in the woods.

There are other life-styles too. Oil, cattle, lumber, and cotton have kept a few families rich for generations. The Southern plantation system reached westward into the broad riverbottoms of East Texas. Cotton and slavery and white-columned mansions had their day there, and some of the mansions remain.

Cotton is grown in the far western parts of Texas now, and the Piney Woods are becoming cattle country. "The cows have come east, the cotton has gone west, the niggers have gone north, and the Yankees have come south," is a standard joke, or perhaps complaint, in small East Texas towns.

The towns often seem to have been built in forests, there are so many trees. They are older than the general run of Texas towns, partly because East Texas was what settlers struck first when coming out from the United States, and they stopped there. And partly, too, because the settlers were woodland people by birth and feared the western prairie, with its Comanche Indians and its scarcity of trees and water.

San Augustine thus has a number of houses dating from the Republic and the early days of statehood, and a little wooden church that is plainly New England. The town of Woodville, in the Big Thicket, is in its entirety a bird sanctuary.

Almost every college campus in the East Texas woods seems steeped in dignity and tradition (even when it isn't) because of stately trees and flowering dogwood and plum. Stephen F. Austin University in Nacogdoches is especially handsome with its tall, quiet pines, and the town has various old buildings that figured in Texas history. At Huntsville, a pretty compound contains several houses in which Sam Houston dwelt or practiced law, one of them a gem of nineteenth-century comfort and good design.

Some people find mystery and a sense of wonder in the hidden depths of forests, some in remote Trans-Pecos mountains, some in water, some in the black windings of underground caves. East Texas casts so powerful a spell that prairie dwellers can't live there. They suffocate. But those whose temperaments fit it love the easy shelter of the woodlands and the thousand small adventures they contain.

Of all the state, only this eastern region can show the full splendor of trees. They grow in hundreds of species, to great size and age. "Hardwood" in East Texas means any tree that isn't a pine. In certain East Texas soils the pines and hardwoods grow together. In others the forest is almost pure pine.

Besides hardwoods that the rest of Texas doesn't have—beeches, maples, hollies, magnolias, sweetgums—the East Texas forests have those little understory trees with spicy or tasty products: persimmons and paw-

paws to eat, sassafras for tea, witch hazel to make a fragrant lotion, bayberries for scented candles.

And the chinquapin, the best-tasting of all nuts—I have never had enough of them. Chinquapin trees are small and not very common, the tiny round nutmeats are enclosed in prickly burrs, and squirrels, the gourmets of the rodent world, beat you to most of them anyway. A pound of chinquapin nutmeats ought to sell for about a hundred dollars, if a pound could be assembled. Try to find one and taste it if you can.

We read yearly of smoke jumpers in California, and the forests of Arizona are like tinder before the summer rains start. But in East Texas, forest fires are not much of a problem.

The heavy annual rainfall not only helps trees grow; it makes a humid climate in which they are often too wet to burn. Many an East Texas morning is steeped in deep fog until the sun cuts it away around nine or ten o'clock. Perhaps pine trees are never more beautiful than when they fade down a long perspective, each tree a paler gray than the one before, to a vanishing point made not by distance but by fog. Fog on the woodland lakes sometimes makes the shore you stand on seem the edge of the world, with nothing beyond but gray space.

In 1800 the land now called East Texas was almost totally virgin forest. A few small meadows existed where the soil wasn't right for trees, and the Indians—chiefly the various Caddo tribes—had cleared some patches of bottomland where they farmed. The rest was trees, and they must have been a splendid sight.

From the 1820s on, Anglo-Saxon settlers hacked at the forest, trying to make room to grow cotton and corn and kitchen gardens. Their tools were small and simple—axes and mattocks. The forest fought back. It would reclaim in a few seasons land that was not regularly plowed, just as the brush does today on the Rio Grande Plain. Even at the end of World War II, East Texas had relatively little farmland.

Then came bulldozers, and the discovery that cattle raising was more profitable than farming. Much larger tracts of land were cleared, and converted to grass. Now truly vast stretches of forest land are being turned into prairie.

This is not to say that trees and cattle can't be mixed. They can. Cattle graze in the four national forests of East Texas, and on private woodlands as well. The first fresh grass of spring, called "woods grass" appears on the protected forest floor while the open pastures are still brown.

The soils of East Texas are better adapted to trees than to grass. The level of nearly all plant nutrients is low, so the cattle-raisers have to fertilize their pastures heavily. But if this is done, two acres will support a cow in East Texas, whereas on the thin-soiled, rarely-rained-on Edwards Plateau it takes twenty-five or thirty acres. The result is that East Texas, having got into the cattle business, now produces more cattle than the traditional ranch country does.

Two little sawmills were built in 1819, one near San Augustine, one at Nacogdoches. They were the first in Texas; they sawed one log at a time. From this beginning the lumber industry grew, until by the 1940s all of the East Texas forests had been cut except for a few odd scraps and some large areas in the Big Thicket.

"Cut and move on" was the motto, and cutting and moving on left a clumsily butchered forest behind. Yet East Texas is so superbly made for trees that new forests grew up in the cut-over lands, sometimes almost indistinguishable from the old. But only sometimes, and only almost. The second-growth forests did not contain the centuries-old trees that the virgin forests had, or develop an ecology of such immense richness.

Eventually people realized the cutting and moving on was hardly any smarter than chopping down a tree to get the apples. They began raising trees as cash crops—planting, thinning, and harvesting them just as one does corn, but over a longer timespan. There are now about four million acres of tree farms in East Texas.

And there the situation stands today: the land is covered in second-growth forest, much of it not really forest but tree farms, with cleared areas growing rapidly as cattle raising expands.

Texas's four national forests are so big they seem empty. But a lot goes on in their 659,000 acres. They have a few large lakes and many small ones, with recreation areas on the shores and fishermen hard at work. Cattle graze among the trees—their owners pay for the privilege —and deep in the woods you'll come upon man-made ponds which water both cows and wildlife. Two state parks lie inside the national forest boundaries.

You may find patches of ten to a hundred acres where all the trees have been removed by a lumbering operation called clear-cutting, and other patches where ground thus bared has covered itself with brambles, and still others where the trees have grown back. In odd corners little patches of special habitat are left alone so that certain endangered species, like the red-cockaded woodpecker, may continue their struggle to survive.

Forest Service crews fight the southern pine beetle, usually by removing the trees from an infested area. Hunters hunt whatever is in season, except in a few spots reserved for game management. Lookout towers stand empty in all but the rare dry periods. Logging operations are in progress here and there. Hikers, birders, botanists, and photographers walk the back trails, carrying their equipment like badges of identity. Yet all this activity is lost in the sheer expanse of the woods.

They are not quite as large as they look on ordinary maps. Road maps, for example, show the four forests (Angelina, Sabine, Davy Crockett, and Sam Houston–San Jacinto) as big solid areas. Detail maps reveal that each area is actually a crazy-quilt patchwork of national forest land and land that is privately owned—much of it by lumber companies, hunting clubs, and developers, but also by cattle raisers, small farmers, and people who have just an acre or two of land on some edge of the Federal preserve.

There is no intent to deceive here. It's just that small-scale maps can't show everything. If they could, they would show that only about half the acreage that appears to be national forest actually is.

Many people think of these forests as places where a splendid chunk of the natural world is preserved and protected for its own sake—as places where wild plants and animals find every possible advantage. They are not. Our national forests are multiple-use areas, but the use that counts more than all the others put together—more than recreation, wildlife, watersheds, and hunting—is the production of lumber. Everything is subordinate to that.

In Texas, for example, 95 percent of the national forest lands are lumbered. There is no virgin timber whatever in the four forests, but then it had all been cut before they were established, in the 1930s. Private lumber companies now buy and cut the trees, then Forest Service crews replant the cut-over areas with seedlings.

The favored procedure is called even-aged management. This means, to begin with, clear cutting: when an area is lumbered, all the trees, usable or not, are removed, leaving bare ground. Then pine seedlings are planted, and the resulting new growth consists of trees of the same age and size which will all be ready for cutting at once, when they reach the age of seventy.

Pines produce more lumber than hardwoods like magnolia, beech, hickory, and oak. Pines can be planted close together, they have few bothersome small branches, their shape makes them easy to handle when cut. Selective breeding has produced "super-pines" or "genetic trees" which grow faster than ordinary pines and yield more lumber.

Super-pines are to ordinary pines what hybrid corn is to ordinary corn. They are new. There are not yet enough super-pine seedlings to supply the demand. Eighty-five percent of the replanting done in the Texas national forests is in pine seedlings—if possible, super-pine seedlings.

Even-aged management, then, produces sections of forest where all the trees are pines of the same age and size. This has advantages, most of them connected with the convenience of lumbering operations and higher production. But quail and doves benefit too, for a while, and so do deer and rabbits.

The first thing to grow back on clear-cut land is a briar patch of weeds, bushes, grasses, and flowers, and it is full of seeds and berries and tender shoots that the game thrive on. But growing among the briars are the pine seedlings planted by Forest Service crews. After a few years, they rise and cast thick shade, so that the brush dies for lack of sunlight. After that there isn't much of anything but pines, with the gloomy forest floor a brushless, deerless, quailless, and (except for bacteria, worms, etc.) life-less layer of brown pine needles.

This is what biologists call a monoculture, as opposed to the natural forest which has many species of trees, shrubs, vines, etc. Many animals can make no use whatever of pine trees, either for food or shelter. So a stand of pure pine contains only a small fraction of the living things that a mixed pine-hardwood forest will support. Ecologically, a pine planta-tion is out of balance.

And it is vulnerable to insects and disease. Infection goes from pine to pine like cold germs from child to child in the third grade. If something kills the pine trees, there's nothing left. Thus disease has to be fought with pesticides. And a monoculture of pines exhausts the soil just as a monoculture of cotton does. Fertilizers are needed.

Corn is a grass, but a cornfield is scarcely a natural grassland. And super-pines are trees, but a stand of them can't be called a natural forest. Our four national forests are tree farms, not different in any significant way from the four million acres of commercial tree farms owned by lumber and paper companies in East Texas.

Still, the land is better off than when it became national forest land, in the 1930s. And a piece of it—five thousand acres—has been set aside and lumbering stopped. It may eventually be declared a back-country area, a place where wildlife will be undisturbed by clear-cutting and pesticides, and maybe even by hunters.

The tract is on the Neches River and is called the Big Slough Area, which suggests that cutting it may have been a boggy, low-profit job anyway. But whatever the reason for setting it aside, there it is. Many birds, mammals, and reptiles will find it not too boggy at all, but just right.

Among Texas Indians, the glamorous Comanches are best remembered nowadays (by laymen, at least) for their boldness and horsemanship, or perhaps for their cruelty and horsemanship. But the Caddoes, living in Louisiana and in the East Texas woodlands, had by far the most advanced culture.

One Caddo confederation occupied the country around Nacogdoches, which claims to be the oldest town in the state, based on the fact that it was a Caddoan village long before the Spanish put a mission there in 1716. Other Caddoes lived along the Red River in the Texarkana area. All were farmers, which was the key to their population density and their culture.

Their little fields in the riverbottoms grew two crops of corn a year, plus squash, beans, and tobacco—the usual Indian crops. Their only farm implement was a crude hoe, but the harvests were usually good. Each fall the Caddoes celebrated Thanksgiving.

The forest supplied a fine variety of wild berries, nuts, and fruits (it still does) and the Caddoes caught fish on trotlines like those Texans use today. They hunted deer and black bear in the woods, and ventured out on the prairies for buffalo.

Their hunting bows were so good that Southwestern Indians would trade turquoise and blankets to get them. The Caddo bows were made of strong, springy Osage orange, a tree the French called *bois d'arc*, the wood for bows. It grew in the Caddoes' forests but not on the plains.

In hard times the Caddoes ate their dogs. But hard times were rare, and normally they lived so well that only they, of all Texas Indians, could afford specialists—chiefs, priests, and craftsmen who did not hunt or farm but were fed by the community in return for their special skills.

Sociologists and social anthropologists consider this important. When some members of a primitive society can be spared from the eternal effort to get food, and can devote their time to arts and ideas, civilization is on the way.

The Caddo tribes built round houses as much as fifty feet in diameter, wove good baskets, and made Texas's handsomest pottery. They were expert tanners of deerskin. They painted their bodies, dyed their hair, and (in the opinion of the Spaniards) ruined their native good looks with elaborate tattoos on their faces and elsewhere. And they piled up huge mounds of earth like small flat-topped hills, and built temples on top. In this they resembled the tribes in the forests east of them, to whom they were culturally kin.

Several of these mounds, thoroughly excavated, are within the city of Nacogdoches. One that can still be climbed lies in the floodplain of the Neches River near the Highway 21 crossing. It is one of three such surviving mounds in the area, where a Caddoan town of beehive-shaped houses once covered a hundred acres and was surrounded by cultivated fields.

Caddoes divorced and remarried with great ease, over and over. In this they even outdid us. Yet women were not mere servants and childbearers, but powerful individuals in their own right. Sometimes a woman was chief or priest. Caddo women could be cruel to war prisoners, torturing them ingeniously and gruesomely. Warriors scalped their victims and sometimes ate bits of them—ceremonially, to absorb the enemy's power. This is called ritual cannibalism and is regarded (by some, at least) as less barbaric than eating a man merely because you are hungry.

But the Caddoan culture, rich and complex though it was, was fading even before the first white men arrived in the seventeenth century. No new ceremonial mounds had been built for hundreds of years, the population was declining, crafts and traditions were being forgotten.

Then the collapse was hastened by epidemics of white man's diseases. The Caddoes, still fairly hardy in the eighteenth century, resisted the Spaniards and refused to become Christians. They did this so firmly that in 1731 the Spanish abandoned the Caddoan missions and drew back to San Antonio. But by the time Texas became a republic the Caddoes were too weak to resist the white settlers pouring in from the east.

"The onrushing American frontier," writes W. W. Newcomb in *The Indians of Texas,* "hardly took notice of the Caddoes, the dregs of what had been two centuries earlier rich, splendid, barbaric theocracies."[1]

What remains of the Caddoan cultures is mostly what has been dug out of the earth, or what still lies undiscovered in it. But they also left us the word *Tayshas,* which meant allies or friends. The Spanish made it *Tejas,* and it passed into English as Texas.

People who think Texas is all lonesome prairie are surprised to learn that it has one of the most complex and magnificent forests in the world. It's called the Big Thicket, and it happens to be in East Texas because of a series of coincidences involving geography, climate, and the soil.[2]

First, it stands where the eastern woodlands begin to change into the western plains. In effect, it's where east meets west. On the north-south axis, it's where the subtropics fade into the truly temperate zone. So bits of land characteristic of all four of these regions occur in the Big Thicket, together with their appropriate trees, shrubs, vines, mosses, weeds, flowers, and grasses.

That's not all. The Big Thicket grows on sandy soils laid down in Tertiary time as dunes and beaches and sea bottom. This sand is easily penetrated by tree roots, and it soaks up water and holds it like a sponge. There's plenty of water to soak up, for the Big Thicket lies just a few miles inland from the Gulf of Mexico and gets fifty-five to sixty inches of rain a year. The growing season is about 245 days.

The result of this combination of factors is trees which achieve great age and size, and a swarm of other living things, both rare and common. Fifteen of the nation's champion trees grow in the Thicket, and fifty-six others which are merely Texas champions.

The sandy soil releases water in a steady, even flow, well-filtered, so that the Thicket is filled with bayous and running streams of extraordinarily pure, sweet water.

In its prime, which was before the white man came and briefly thereafter, the Thicket was the home of black bears, panthers, and wolves. Indians hunted in the forest but didn't live there. The Spaniards avoided it altogether. The Old Spanish Trail (now Highway 21, connecting San Antonio, Bryan, and Nacogdoches) went well to the north of it, and when the first Anglo-Saxon colonists began to move into Texas from the east, they flowed around the Big Thicket, not because it was an impenetrable tangle, for it wasn't, but because wagons sank to their hubs in its sloughs and sandy-bottomed streams.

There may also have been elements of awe, or fear. The early settlers came from woodlands to the east, and felt ill at ease on the western prairies. But they had never known a woodland like this one—mysterious, seemingly endless, full of unnerving silences and sounds.

For nearly a century the Thicket was chiefly a hiding place. Runaway slaves, Confederate draft-dodgers, outlaws, misanthropes dwelt there. It offered easy living. Game, water, and firewood were plentiful. The climate was mild. The only bad time was the summer which brought more than anyone wanted of humidity and mosquitoes.

The misanthropes and badmen gave way gradually to small farmers, hunters, and sawmill workers, both black and white. People moved timidly into the Thicket, beginning at the edges. At first the main means of transport were little river boats that plied the larger streams, taking general-store commodities in and produce out.

A special way of life grew up in the Thicket, linked to the rifle, the hoe, hunting dogs, and perhaps a mule. Most of the meat on the table was wild game, and the total cash income of a family might be less than a hundred dollars a year, from a patch of cotton or sweet potatoes.

But that was enough. The forest provided most of what was needed. And it bred its own folklore, recipes, customs, and legends, now available in many books about the Big Thicket. A few old-timers live in approximately the old way in the woods, though they are likely to have electric lights and television. Most of the wooden dog-trot houses are ruins, but you can still find a few, with chimneys made of mud bricks bound with Spanish moss instead of straw.

The Big Thicket has eight separate plant communities, from the sandy upland forests down to cypress bogs. There are even little bits of prairie. Southern magnolias grow to great size. So do sugar maples, Ohio buckeyes, beeches, and pines. Southwestern plants like mesquite and tumbleweed live in sunny sands. Forty species of wild orchids grow in the

Thicket, and nine of carnivorous plants. Many plants whose native ranges are hundreds of miles away in New Mexico or Tennessee turn up in the Big Thicket, alive and flourishing in some microclimate.

It's the best place in Texas to see forest layering. Any little piece of woodland will have three layers—the tallest trees, the understory trees, and some weeds or bushes on the ground. The Big Thicket has *six*, and no one has yet described their interdependence better than William Bray did in his *Distribution and Adaptation of the Vegetation of Texas*, which was published in 1906:

> A tree grown in the forest is entirely different in essential respects from one grown in the open. It is taller, slenderer, less ample of crown, freer from limbs, less sturdy and independent than its open-air brother.
>
> In this forest there are the masterful, dominant species like the white and the red oaks, hickories, ash, walnut, gums, magnolia, and the loblolly pine, which demand the best illumination and so over-top the others. They make the top story. Others like beech, hornbeam, ironwood, lin, and holly content themselves with less of the direct sunlight and submit to, perhaps even depend upon, the dominance of their superior neighbors. They constitute the second story counting from the top.
>
> Others yet, of normally still smaller stature and perhaps positively dependent upon the shade and protection of their superiors, constitute a third layer or story. Such would be the flowering dogwood, hawthorn, mulberry, witch hazel, etc.
>
> Lower in stature than these and correspondingly more shaded and dependent, are shrubs like the swamp honeysuckle, Virginia willow, corkwood, sweetleaf, blueberry, bay-gall holly, and others. Still beneath these stories of woody vegetation is a stratum of herbaceous plants such as wood-fern and partridgeberry, with, finally, the carpet stratum of sphagnum, green mosses, and liverworts.
>
> Now all these plants are, in a sense, messmates at a common table. They share the soil space and the air space together, and the sunlight, each according to its needs. They are commensalistic. They are not equally important or important in the same way, but they are all helpful rather than harmful in the community. The partridge-berry and the wood fern, the blueberry and the swamp honeysuckle would not be there at all if the environment of soil, moisture and shade due to the presence of the canopy were wanting, while they, in turn, form a mulching of green that gives coolness and moisture to the earth about the roots of the great trees, preventing the sunlight from striking in to dry out this loose soil.[3]

Naturally there are insects and animals to fit the various habitats. Roughly three hundred species of birds can be seen in the Thicket. A third of them live there; the rest stop on their migrations. There are so many streams and ponds that water birds inhabit the place in great numbers. Deer, alligators, mink, otter, opossums, and squirrels all find the food and housing they need.

There may even be wildflowers and insects unknown to man, waiting to be discovered and named. The same is true of mushrooms, lichens, and mosses. Scientists have been exploring and classifying in the Thicket for a century and still aren't sure they have found everything.

If the ivory-billed woodpecker still lives in the Big Thicket, only two or three people know it: those who have actually seen one. No one else can be sure, because too many people lie about having seen one, for the brief notoriety that it gets them. Some have even offered fake evidence. In one case it was a photograph of a stuffed ivory-bill mounted in a tree.

The last authentic sighting of an ivory-bill was in 1904. If a few birds do survive, they are probably the most highly endangered of all endangered species. There may be only four or five of them.

Ivory-bills are (or were) big birds, larger than a crow, and memorable for their beauty. Deep black, snow white, and bright red were their colors, with bills of ivory white. The males had a flaming red crest, the females a black one. If anyone should spot one today, the big white wing patches would distinguish it from the pileated woodpecker, at distances at which the bird's ivory-colored bill might not show up at all.

Ivory-bills were the biggest of all woodpeckers. They are believed to have preferred their woods undisturbed by man, and to have required very large, very old pines for nesting. Lacking them, the birds stopped breeding and died out. Hunters may have helped them die out. They made big targets, and their plumage was attractive.

Some theorize that a bird as big as the ivory-bill would have to range over miles of territory to get food, as other big birds do. They aren't seen doing this, the argument goes; therefore they don't exist. And probably they don't.

What many people see in the Big Thicket and excitedly report as ivory-bills are pileated woodpeckers, which come in the same colors (but differently arranged) and are almost as large. Their cheerful, clucking call is one of the loudest bird sounds you will ever hear.

Pileated woodpeckers are not quite rare, but not common either. This, and their size, and their flaming red crests, make seeing one an experience to remember. I had a pair of them for neighbors once, through a summer in the Missouri Ozarks. I heard them almost every day, but saw them only four or five times.

The little red-cockaded woodpecker does live in the Thicket, and is endangered. Tree-farming does not tolerate the elderly pine trees, afflicted with red-heart disease but still alive, that red-cockaded woodpeckers require. (Other woodpeckers nest in dead trees.) Various efforts are being made to preserve a few bits of this kind of habitat, but critics say the bits are too small to do much good.

The red-cockaded woodpecker, we often hear, has almost specialized itself out of existence. But the opposite view is also possible: a forest in ecological balance would contain plenty of suitable trees for this little bird. One can equally well say that man has homogenized the forests so that many plants and animals can no longer exist in them.

Originally the Big Thicket covered three and a half million acres. The first lumbering started in the 1850s. Little railroads were built after the Civil War, to haul trees to sawmills. From then to the present, the lumber industry has grown steadily and the Big Thicket has shrunk.

As late as 1936 it was possible for biologists to write: "The Big Thicket still exists and still holds for those who wish to see nature untouched by man, mile after mile where neither the axe nor the plow has taken either the forest or the sod."[4]

But much has happened since 1936. The last good-sized stand of virgin loblolly pine has survived only because of a tangle of lawsuits over the land that have dragged on for seventy years.

Another part of the Thicket has been preserved by the Alabama and Coushatta Indians. These two tribes were moved to Texas around 1800. Long cheated and pushed about, they were at last given a firm claim to some four thousand acres in the Big Thicket, then regarded as worthless. Parts of these forests have remained uncut to this day. Even when they were starving, in the 1930s, the Alabama-Coushattas did not sell their trees. Now they operate a small Indian Disneyland for tourists, with dances, foods, crafts, and a pleasant bus tour through their forest.

The Alabama-Coushatta tour is one way for strangers to get at least a beginning idea of the Big Thicket. Another way is to walk the neat trails of the Big Thicket Scenic Area near Cleveland, Texas. It is an eleven-hundred-acre bit of the Sam Houston National Forest which was cut over long ago, but where big, crooked hardwoods unsuitable for lumber were left intact. These huge old trees, combined with second-growth timber, give a rough approximation of the Thicket.

Such tours are handy for families with small children, or for those lacking outdoor skills. The real Big Thicket is still a place where strangers can get lost. It has rotting ghost towns inhabited by rattlesnakes and owls, and a confusing network of abandoned roads and trails. The unprepared can be cruelly tormented by poison ivy and chigger bites and mosquitoes.

But it is worth the time and trouble. With its trees hundreds of years old, and its small streams passing banks of pure white sand, the Big

Thicket is one of the most extraordinary places in Texas. We ought to value it at least as highly as the Alamo, but we don't.

It is also a resting place that migrating birds, hungry and tired from crossing the Gulf of Mexico, will find it hard to do without. Bird lovers in New England, who have never heard of the Big Thicket, will have fewer birds to love when the old forest is gone.

People who have struggled for decades to preserve a little piece of the region are hoping to save a hundred thousand acres from the developers and lumber companies as the Big Thicket National Park. But the process of creating a national park is slow. Bulldozers act faster than legislators do. At present there is no knowing how much, if anything, will be saved.

Dr. Claude McLeod estimates that if we chop the Big Thicket down completely it would need a thousand years to grow back to its original splendor and regain its ecological balance. But he adds: "Indeed, it is very unlikely that such a forest could be developed again."[5]

Though East Texas is distinctly hilly, it also has wide riverbottoms full of sloughs and bayous, where brown water stands motionless under a thick tangle of trees and vines. One of the prettiest bits of highway in the state is a mile or so between Marshall and Henderson, where Highway 43 crosses the floodplain of the Sabine River. The road is built on a long embankment and shaded by trees. The woods on each side stand in water. The Sabine, where you cross it in the middle of this stretch, is brown, majestic, and slow.

East Texans love their moody rivers, so different from the playful streams of the Balcones Escarpment. To strangers the forest rivers sometimes seem sluggish and dull. After heavy rains they rise and roll with frightening power, and spread far out of their banks.

The banks are mud, not always bound with roots, and you wonder why the water doesn't cut them away. The answer is, it does. The East Texas rivers are little Mississippis, constantly changing their courses and leaving old bends of the stream to one side as oxbow lakes. They make big swampy areas defended by mosquitoes and water moccasins and mud.

The rivers have been tamed considerably by dams. Stretches of the Neches, the Sabine, the Trinity have been converted to huge artificial lakes, and the lesser rivers have made smaller ones. East Texas, having more rain, is also better supplied with lakes than any other section of the state.

"Impoundments," wildlife experts call the artificial lakes, with distaste. But the reservoirs make money for the people on their shores. Some of them are useful in flood control, some generate power, they attract campers and fishermen, and they reflect sunsets beautifully.

For about a dozen years after they are built, the fishing in them is superb. Then it declines. The reasons for this are complicated and probably not completely known. They have to do with a disturbed balance between game fish and the "trash" fish they feed on—too many of the latter—and with the fact that the game fish can't get past the dams to spawn where instinct tells them to.

The lakes have attracted seagulls, which are as comfortable with fresh water as with salt. In many of them, large areas have been left filled with dead trees, their gray branches lifted out of the water as if in despair. Bulldozing trees out of a prospective lake bottom is expensive, and anyway the underwater branches protect many fishes, which need shelter and hiding places as much as birds do.

Most trees don't decay under water, and so remain standing on lake bottoms for decades. They might remain for centuries, except that artificial lakes tend to fill with silt and become swamps in less than a hundred years. Someone has tried cutting off the tops of the trees a few feet below water level, so that water skiers can ski above while fish find shelter below. But this too is expensive, and it isn't often done.

The big impoundments cover many square miles of bottomland where all sorts of wild things, both animal and vegetable, once lived. All of this lively tangle dies when the flood gates close and the water spreads. And the shores of the artificial lakes rarely become stable habitat, either watery or dry.

The lakes lap against upland trees and shrubs which aren't adapted to wet conditions, and they die. But few water-loving forms take their places, because the water level keeps going up and down according to rain and the need for electric power. Some of the smaller lakes, in fact, are drained every year, down to their original streambeds.

In the 1920s a woman tossed a bit of water hyacinth into a Florida stream. She had brought it from South America, liked its pretty blooms, and hoped it would grow in Florida. It did. From that one plant the water hyacinth spread until it choked the waterways of Florida with thick floating rafts of green. Then it moved westward through the Gulf states and has now reached the lakes of Central Texas (San Marcos, New Braunfels). It gives water an unpleasant taste, plugs the flow of small streams, makes waterways impassable to boats, and takes for its own growth millions of gallons of water that might otherwise irrigate crops or supply cities.

Chemical sprays (and lately a weevil which attacks it) have cleared the floating hyacinth from 25,000 acres of Texas waterways. But you can see it drifting about the East Texas lakes, sometimes as a single pretty plant, sometimes as a little floating garden, sometimes as huge rafts lining

Bluebonnets, Indian paintbrush, sneezeweed, and prairie grass
east of Navasota. (The Prairies and Cross Timbers)

A prairie beyond trees south of Austin.
(The Prairies and Cross Timbers)

Edge of a prairie woodland east of Roundtop.
(The Prairies and Cross Timbers)

A prairie stream north of Decatur.
(The Prairies and Cross Timbers)

Prairie phlox, white flowers, and grasses
east of Roundtop. (The Prairies and Cross Timbers)

Autumn oaks east of Luling. (The Prairies and Cross Timbers)

Prairie, oaks, and yaupon thickets east of Luling.
(The Prairies and Cross Timbers)

Wild little barley, speargrass, and great mullein
southwest of Elgin. (The Prairies and Cross Timbers)

Puff balls on a rotting log south of Silsbee.
(The East Texas Forests)

Maple, cypress, and water tupelo on Wolf Creek west of Jasper. (The East Texas Forests)

A palmetto swamp west of Conroe. (The East Texas Forests)

[1 7 1]

RIGHT: Grass lake and forest north of Beaumont.
(The East Texas Forests)

Red shelf fungi, needles, and leaves south
of Silsbee. (The East Texas Forests)

Cypress on Caddo Lake
northeast of Marshall.
(The East Texas Forests)

[175]

A bog orchid, pitcher plants, and ferns
south of Woodville. (The East Texas Forests)

miles of the leeward shore. It can be killed (at great expense) but it comes back rapidly. It will probably be with us from now on.

The big impoundments have helped the southern bald eagle, which is an endangered species. This bird lives in East Texas, and lately has been increasing in numbers. The lakes have meant more ducks and nutrias for the eagles to eat, and these are less poisonous for the eagles than fish, which are loaded with chemical pesticides.

The osprey, a big hawk which merely passes through Texas in migration, is helped by the lakes just as the eagles are: they can vary their dangerous fish diet with nutrias and ducks.

The nutria itself, like the water hyacinth, was introduced from South America and is now all too plentiful. The animal's true name is coypu. Only the fur should be called nutria. But if you tell most people that many thousands of wild coypus live in Texas, growing as large as twenty pounds, they won't believe you.

The nutria is a rodent almost the size of a beaver, with long orange incisors and a ratlike tail. The female's mammae are on her back instead of on her belly. Nutrias eat water plants, and do a good job of cleaning out a pond choked with vegetation. People introduce them into ponds especially to do this. But then they also multiply fast, eat all the available food, crowd out ducks and geese, and move on to places where they aren't wanted.

East Texas, with water everywhere, has a swarming nutria population. It thins out westward across the state with diminishing rainfall, to the Trans-Pecos and the Staked Plain which have virtually no nutrias. They are nocturnal animals. Unless you go looking for them, you may never see one except for an occasional specimen run over on the highway as it moved from one pond or bayou to another.

Texas is tilted and stairstepped downward from the Panhandle to the Gulf of Mexico. It is a land of rivers. The only natural lake of any interest in the entire state is Caddo Lake, and half of it lies in Louisiana. Nature made it, man drained it, then man remade it with a dam.[6]

By a curious series of events the lake became navigable, and the town of Jefferson, in northeast Texas, on a minor stream called Big Cypress Bayou, was for several decades an important river port, connected by steamboat to New Orleans and St. Louis.

It happened this way: to begin with, Big Cypress Bayou flowed quite normally from Texas into Louisiana, where it emptied into the Red River —the same Red River whose Prairie Dog Town Fork, far to the west in the Texas Panhandle, made Palo Duro Canyon.

In primitive America, rivers passing through heavily wooded country sometimes became clogged with dead trees and mud for hundreds of miles. These vast natural logjams slowed the flow of water or stopped it altogether. They were called *rafts* though they didn't float or move. They made the rivers back up, spread out of their banks, and form swamps, bayous, and lakes in the surrounding lowlands. The Colorado River once had such a raft, and so did the Trinity.

In Louisiana, the Great Red River Raft choked the river for a hundred miles. It plugged the mouth of Big Cypress Bayou, among many others, and in a wide valley among the hills formed Caddo Lake. This may have happened as recently as four hundred years ago, for the lake is not old in a geological sense. But it was there when the first white men arrived.

In the 1830s a man named Henry Shreve started to clear the Red River raft, in Louisiana, starting at the lower end, sawing and blasting the snags loose so that they floated on down. The work was done from specially equipped river boats, and it took years. At a certain spot Captain Shreve stopped work and founded Shreveport. That city is still the head of navigation on the Red River.

At that point the situation on Caddo Lake changed. The lake still existed, because above Shreveport the Red River raft was still in place, plugging the mouth of Big Cypress Bayou. But the lake overflowed through a series of connecting bayous and channels that wound on down to Shreveport.

This overflow did not empty Caddo Lake, which received water constantly from many sources. But the channels it flowed through were wide and deep enough to carry steamboats, which were flat-bottomed and shallow-drafted anyway. Soon some enterprising captain discovered that he could leave the Red River at Shreveport, and wind through swamps and forests into Caddo Lake, up the lake, and then along Big Cypress Bayou to Jefferson, Texas.

Jefferson became a rich river port, second in Texas only to the ocean port of Indianola. Its population reached thirty thousand. Many a pioneer family first stepped ashore in the Republic of Texas at Jefferson, having come comfortably by water instead of roughly by wagon. Fine furnishings, brought by river from New Orleans, filled the handsome houses of merchants and steamboat captains.

For nearly forty years Jefferson's prosperity held. Then in 1873 the U.S. Army Corps of Engineers started removing the Great Red River Raft above Shreveport. This eventually unplugged the mouth of Big Cypress Bayou, and most of Caddo Lake drained away. There was no longer water enough to carry steamboats beyond Shreveport.

Jefferson declined. It has had mild ups and downs in the past century, and now, with about three thousand inhabitants and dozens of fine nineteenth-century buildings, is one of the handsomest old towns in the East Texas woodlands.

In 1914 a dam recreated Caddo Lake on a smaller scale, and a new dam replaced that one in 1971. You may now, therefore, regard Caddo Lake as either natural or artificial. It's a little of both. But however artificial the dam, the lake has a lovely, natural quality that all other Texas lakes lack. There are floating islands with trees and underbrush, and swampy regions inaccessible to man.

And there's such a maze of channels winding among the cypress trees that it's easy to get lost. Even experienced natives have nosed their boats into obscure backwaters of the lake and then had trouble finding the small, vine-hidden channel that would let them out again. The Texas Parks and Wildlife Department has therefore laid out "boat roads" with numbered posts protruding from the water, ugly but helpful. People with maps can follow the numbered routes as if they were highways.

Among the remote swamps, too wet for walking and too shallow for boats, birds and fish breed undisturbed by man. Caddo Lake needs no stocking from fish hatcheries. Along with the plentiful game fish, there are cottonmouth moccasins, alligator gars up to six feet long, and huge alligator snapping turtles.

On shore, you may wish you could identify birds by their songs alone, as the experts do. In a given period you'll hear ten birds for every one you see. They are hidden in the heavy forest of pines and hardwoods, vines and Spanish moss.

Most of Caddo Lake's shores are private property. Marinas and commercial campgrounds are plentiful, but this ragged development of the shore doesn't affect the wildness that survives out among the cypress islands.

Caddo Lake State Park has campgrounds too, and a visitor center whose fresh and ingenious exhibits give some idea of the fine variety of life around the lake. To explore some of it in a canoe, perhaps camping on tiny islands, you had better go in winter when mosquitoes are few. There is often mild, sunny weather even in January.

Opossums are found over most of Texas, but are probably thickest in the eastern woods. Possum and sweet potatoes is an old Southern dish, now more of a novelty than a staple even for the backwoods poor. Possum folklore and possum recipes exist by the bookful.

As North America's only marsupial and most primitive mammal, the opossum has fascinated Anglo-Saxons since the first Englishman landed in Virginia and examined one. There are endless theories about how newborn opossums (hardly more than fetuses, thirteen days old, and so small that a teaspoon will hold a dozen) get into their mother's pouch, and what they do after they get there.

Most people believed that the mother picked up each new infant as it was born and put it in the pouch herself, and perhaps helped it find a nipple. Not until the 1920s did careful observation show that this is not what happens at all.

Newborn opossums weigh 2½ grains, which means that it would take 175 of them to weigh an ounce. Many of their organs are still undeveloped. They are blind and deaf, for example. But a newborn opossum does have good front feet, with claws, and a tiny, muscular tongue. These are the tools it needs.

With the feet it pulls itself over a short stretch of its mother's furry abdomen and enters her fur-lined pouch. There it finds a nipple, attaches itself, and settles in for another fifty to sixty days of development before it is ready to let go the nipple and climb out into the world.

The mother possum has thirteen nipples, but sometimes gives birth to fourteen or more young. Then the last infants to arrive, finding all nipples taken, starve.

How does the tiny and virtually brainless newborn creature know which way its mother's pouch lies? When someone finally watched the birth process carefully enough, the world learned that it doesn't know. With nothing but two clawed forelegs usable, the only way the baby can travel is uphill. And the mother props herself somewhat upright in giving birth, in what for humans would be a sitting position. Thus each new infant, when it appears, automatically starts the three-inch journey uphill along its mother's belly from the birth canal to the pouch.

Once it enters the pouch and fastens to a nipple, the nipple slowly stretches and becomes a tube, a lifeline which allows each blind baby to squirm around among its brothers and sisters. This tube has given rise to some strange theories—that it extends all the way down to the baby's stomach; that the end of the nipple and the baby's mouth grow together; that the mother *pumps* her milk through the thirteen tubes so that the little ones don't have to suck.

All that really happens is that the nipple often swells a little in the baby's mouth, making a ball-and-socket joint that is not easily disconnected.

Once out of the pouch, young lightweight possums can wind their tails around branches and hang by them longer than their heavier elders can. But the prehensile tail is useful to all possums for holding onto limbs in risky climbs, and for carrying bunches of leaves to line dens with.

Carl Hartman, a biologist who studied opossums for forty years, says in his book *Possums* that the opossum is probably the stupidest of all mammals.[7] Opossums hear and smell extremely well but their eyesight is poor.

You can wave your hand in front of one's face and it won't react. But if you touch one of its whiskers, it will snap your hand before you can move it away.

Opossums do kill chickens, as charged, but not many. They eat a little of everything: baby birds, insects, crayfish, rats, mice, young rabbits, fruits, and vegetables. They are mostly nocturnal, though they see as poorly in the dark as in the daylight.

I once lifted the hood of my pickup truck and saw a pink, triangular, hissing mouth so wide open that I couldn't see the animal behind it. For a startled moment I thought I was facing a gigantic snake. It was a large possum instead. Apparently it had spent the night snuggled against the truck's slowly cooling engine.

Opossums are conveniently rainproof. Under the sparse outer hairs is a dense, oily underfur that keeps water out. Opossums like to live near water if possible, and mother opossums can swim streams with their marsupial pouches so tightly closed that the thirteen babies attached to the tubes inside don't get wet. And they can and do play possum—that is, pretend to be dead when threatened—more convincingly than any human actor can.

Gray squirrels and flying squirrels belong to the East Texas forests. You seldom find them in the rest of the state. (The fox squirrel, the little cinnamon-colored panhandler of parks and courthouse lawns, ranges over much of Texas in wooded creek bottoms.)

Gray squirrels are stylish animals, with snow-white bibs and bellies, and white bands edging their luxuriant tails. Though they weigh only a pound (to the fox squirrel's two), hunters favor them for their superior flavor.

Flying squirrels weigh less than three ounces. They "fly" somewhat as Frisbees do. Actually they glide, always from higher to lower. They can't gain altitude except minimally, at the end of a long downward swoop.

What makes flying squirrels glide instead of merely fall is a fold of loose skin that runs from foreleg to hind leg on each side. The animal leaps, spreads out all four legs, and becomes, like a sailing newspaper, a lightweight rectangle with a large surface area. It lands gently on whatever lies below. It can even guide itself a little by shifting its legs and tail.

It would be interesting to watch a young flying squirrel about to leap into space for the very first time. Does it hesitate, uneasy, urged on by parents? A young bird can flutter along a limb, or from twig to twig, learning to fly by degrees. Presumably a young flying squirrel must risk everything and make a real leap the first time; otherwise the aerodynamics involved wouldn't work.

I know of no one who has watched a flying squirrel learn its trade, no doubt because the tiny creatures are almost totally nocturnal. (They have the outsize eyes nearly all night-loving animals have.) This is also why relatively few people have seen a flying squirrel at all.

The favorite food of all squirrels is pecans, when they can get them. Often they have to settle for acorns, various buds and berries, some insects, and a few small, tender frogs. These are all found in East Texas stream bottoms. But as this sort of country gives way to lakes and summer homes, the numbers of both gray squirrels and flying squirrels keep shrinking.

The gray squirrel, in addition, is over-hunted. Flying squirrels are not, being too small to make a meal. They're just a toothful, as a woman once said of the sparrows she ate in Berlin toward the end of World War II.

Along their western border the Piney Woods and the Big Thicket change into the Post Oak Belt. It is a kind of transition zone, and a very pretty one, that runs from Texarkana down to points southeast of San Antonio. It is so irregular that not a single county lies entirely within it, though Leon County comes close. Patches of pine trees from the east grow there, and two big islands of Blackland Prairie invade it from the west.

Post oaks are neither large nor beautiful compared with, for example, beeches or live oaks. They make fence posts and railroad ties and firewood, and have other pedestrian uses. But the Post Oak Belt, some nine million acres of it, is nevertheless an appealing mixture of grasslands and open, airy woods.

The early white settlers liked it. The grass could be plowed at once, needing no clearing, and the woods supplied building material. This was a double advantage that neither the plains nor the forests could offer. The Post Oak country became a region of small farms and stayed that way until recently.

Now it is cattle country, like nearly every other part of Texas. The landowners, at great cost, are trying to root out the brush—yaupon, greenbriar, mesquite—that came in when the rich native grasses were eaten away. Some of them are fairly successful. And there are still small farms, their sandy soils still growing fine melons and sweet potatoes.

The lower end of the Post Oak country, where it frays out into prairie, is the kingdom of the Texas phlox. It's a wildflower that comes in several colors—pink, blue, white, yellow—and it has a curious history.[8] More than a hundred years ago a Scottish botanist named Thomas Drummond collected phlox seeds in Texas and sent them to Edinburgh. From there plants were distributed over Europe and finally to Boston and New York.

Phlox became a rage. New England gardeners pampered it and prized it as a fabulous European import. This went on for several years before they learned that their phlox was actually a simple native of the uncouth Republic of Texas. Hybridized and grown in flower beds, as it now is over much of the world, phlox is rather genteel and dull. Growing wild on hillsides in the Post Oak country, and also on the Gulf Coast, it is lively and cheerful.

Near Palestine, the Gus Engeling Wildlife Management Area keeps eleven thousand acres of Post Oak savannah more or less in its natural state. There's a surprising amount of water—marshes, ponds, streams—and many waterfowl make use of it. Most visitors are surprised to find alligators in the Engeling preserve, far from the southern bayous. But alligators once ranged as far northwest as Waco, and one report claims they were found on the Leon River near Hamilton. There are also mink and beaver around the Engeling ponds, and bobcats and foxes in the uplands.

The Post Oak savannah is rather dignified country, perhaps at its handsomest around the village of Round Top, Texas, which has survived with little change from the nineteenth-century. Nearby is Winedale, a museum of early-day houses and barns which belongs to the University of Texas. The buildings are real, not modern reproductions.

The showpiece is an old stagecoach stop called the Winedale Inn. Its vegetable garden and peach orchard are in working order, its detached kitchen is equipped to cook an 1880s meal. The land nearby is sown in native grasses, or being planted with native trees and shrubs that are near extinction. A huge beam in one of the antique barns is completely original and unreproduceable. There is no cedar tree left in the Post Oak country to provide another beam like it, and no craftsman left who could shape it and build it into the barn with the same skill.

Most of Texas's geographic areas are homogeneous. But the long, thin Post Oak Belt reaches over so much country that its various parts have little in common except sandy soil and post oaks. The northern counties, bordering the Red River, don't much resemble the southern ones, 380 miles southwest near the Coastal Plain.

There are other trees than post oaks, of course. The blackjack oak, the post oak's equally homely cousin, is plentiful. In stream bottoms, elms and pecans grow tall. (The Dutch elm disease is approaching Texas, but hasn't arrived yet.) But then riverbottoms are not true Post Oak country. They are low and wet and usually filled with soil washed in from some other region. And this is true of all the physiographic regions of Texas, for the major rivers cut across them, creating special environments on their floodplains.

One of the best-known bits of the Post Oak Belt is the area of "lost" loblolly pines in Bastrop County. They are nearly 150 miles southwest of the Piney Woods, where they are considered to belong. Bastrop State Park is among these pines, linked by a quiet park road to Buescher State Park at Smithville, which has a few lost pines too.

A smaller and stranger region is the old Ottine Swamp, now called Palmetto State Park.[9] This is a few hundred acres of low, wet ground in Gonzales County, beside the San Marcos River. It resembles a patch of exuberant jungle, escaped from the tropics and surrounded by austere Post Oak country.

Dwarf palmettos grow fiercely here, far from the Gulf Coast riverbottoms which are their natural range. The park is named for them. The larger mud volcanoes—thirty feet across and five feet high—were active until a few decades ago. Some small ones, called "mud boils," still perform occasionally. They don't actually boil, of course. The mud is not even hot. What makes it bulge upward and burst with a *blop!* (or sometimes with a sigh) is gas rising from below.

Under the swamp are complicated faults and fractures which allow the gas and water to rise to the surface. And far more notable than the mud boils is the variety of living things that are packed into this small area. Only the wet brushlands along the Rio Grande, or the coastal marshes, support so many different plants and animals.

Orchids, hibiscus, and several ferns live in the shade of trees which don't exist in the true Post Oak lands. Wild iris, in several colors, stands three or four feet tall.

Walking through the park, you must stick to the trails. Off them you're in mud, or water, or tangled underbrush. Birds swarm into the thickets, as do butterflies. Hawks perch in the trees, tearing rabbits apart. There is so much going on that you can sit on a log with a pair of binoculars and see more of the natural world in an hour than you could in a week on the open prairie.

And open prairie is near. Strips of the Blackland Prairie lie on two sides of Palmetto State Park, and forty miles to the southeast the Gulf Coastal Plain, smooth and almost treeless, tilts like a long launching ramp into the Gulf of Mexico.

7 | THE GULF COAST

Heavily populated and polluted though it is, the Gulf Coast throbs with the energy of nature. The sun shines, the wind blows in from the sea, birds are everywhere. On the little ferry ride to Port Aransas, dolphins play around the boat.

Mud flats, marshes, and scrub lie between towns and among industrial installations. Shallow bays and inlets stretch for miles, rarely more than six feet and often only a few inches deep, and the big historic bays (Galveston, Matagorda, Corpus Christi) in turn are indented by little bays around their shores. A mile or two off the mainland, the long barrier islands set their dunes against the sea.

There is some uncertainty about how these long sandy islands got built. They are not peculiar to Texas. Atlantic City and Miami Beach are on similar islands, and North Carolina has a long string of them.

Water can't raise sand or gravel above its own level. Any sandbar you see, whether in a river or in the sea, was built by water high enough to cover it, and exposed when the water went down. The Gulf can raise its own level by a good many feet, when storms push water against the shore.

Galveston Island and the other islands probably first appeared as long sandbars, or collections of them, emerging after a storm. After that, waves deposited more sand along their edges, and the wind carried the sand higher up the strand. About a quarter of a million years ago the sketchy sandbars became the islands we see today, complete with soil and trees.

The storms which first lifted the coastal islands out of the sea were probably hurricanes. They come ashore from the Gulf almost every year, but really disastrous ones occur only four or five times a century. The great Galveston Flood in 1900, with six to eight thousand persons killed, is still the worst natural disaster in United States history, and it was caused by a hurricane which washed sea water over the island.

The old harbor town of Indianola was three-fourths destroyed by a hurricane in 1875 and completely destroyed by another one ten years later.[1] It was for years the leading seaport of Texas, the place where Near Eastern camels, German settlers, Anglo-Saxon colonists, and shiploads of manufactured goods came ashore, but its surviving citizens had had enough. Indianola was never rebuilt. Today a paved road leads down from Port Lavaca, and ends at a few commemorative markers and oleander bushes along an empty, windy shore.

Many obscure little coastal towns have been wiped out by hurricanes. Some were rebuilt, some not. Austwell, Texas, on the road which leads to the Aransas National Wildlife Refuge, is a small living fragment of a larger town that was heavily damaged in 1942. Some of the ruins are visible still.

But though much has been washed away from the Texas shore, much remains. A number of old-fashioned seaside hotels, of white-painted wood, with long front porches and the Gulf breeze sweeping into the rooms through broad windows, are still in operation. One of the sprucest specimens is the Luther Hotel at Palacios, built in 1903 and still first-class.

Construction near the Gulf is usually either solid and hurricane-proof or cheap, flimsy stuff that can be quickly replaced. Port Aransas, for example, is basically a fishing village of expendable wooden shacks clustered around a few super-solid structures like the Coast Guard headquarters (on massive concrete legs) and the University of Texas's big Marine Science Institute.

The Gulf of Mexico, that restless sea, has risen and swept in over Texas many times in the geologic past. It is rising now, as indicated by submerged valleys out in the Gulf, made by flowing rivers but now under salt water; and by long estuaries in our present rivers where the tide moves in from the sea.

No one knows how far the Gulf will reach in over Texas before it recedes again, but then no one cares, either. The process is so slow that the human race may be extinct before it is even well under way. The last deep invasion of the sea into Texas was about 40 million years ago, long before man existed.

When the deluge does come, some quite recent phenomena may still be around to be drowned. Oleanders, for example—poisonous but considered pretty, introduced into Texas from the Near East. Oleander fanciers along the Gulf like to collect bushes bearing the various shades of peach and pink flowers. To me their chief interest is that even goats will not eat them. In some of the man-made deserts of Jordan and Iraq, the only plants left alive on the dusty, goat-bitten riverbanks are oleander bushes in cheerful, poisonous bloom. They may survive in Texas for a long time.

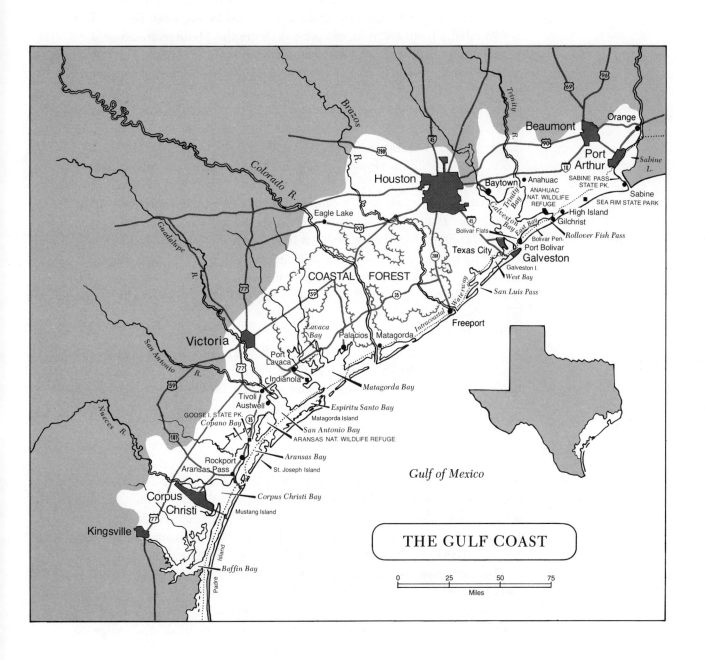

THE GULF COAST

And the rising Gulf may drown the little corkwood trees that grow in Texas only near the mouth of the Brazos River. Corkwoods, unlike oleanders, are natives to the state. Their light wood (the lightest in the U.S.) is not cork, but can be used like cork as floats for fishing nets. Real cork is not wood at all, but the bark of cork oaks from the Mediterranean area.

The deluge will drown Green Lake, a drab body of water near Tivoli, notable mostly as the biggest fresh-water lake in the state that was made naturally, by overflow from the Guadalupe River. It is ten thousand acres broad and six feet deep, and sometimes it drops to eighteen inches. In 1918 it got so dry that a man crossed it on horseback. Oddly, this thin sheet of fresh water is within a rifle shot of the salty Gulf of Mexico.

Though the Gulf is slowly moving in upon us, there are places where the land is building rapidly out into the Gulf. These are river mouths. The Trinity River, where it empties into salt water east of Houston, has added more than seven thousand acres to its delta since 1900.

But the biggest pileup of soil has been made by the Colorado. A lock tender on the Intracoastal Canal at Matagorda told me that his father, as a boy, used to take a boat from the town out to points along the Matagorda Peninsula, a matter of six or seven miles. Now one travels the whole distance by paved road, on a piece of land several miles wide built by the Colorado out of inland topsoil.

The river itself, still heavy with silt, flows beside the highway in a straight channel dredged out for it through the land it built. This new land—scrubby pasture—represents not only the loss of good oyster beds and marshes, which it now covers, but also the loss of soil from farms and ranches all over the Colorado River watershed.

Karankawa Indians once lived on Galveston Island, and on down the Texas shore as far as Corpus Christi.[2] We think of them chiefly as stinking naked cannibals more primitive than any other tribes in Texas. Actually we have few hard facts about the Karankawas, but many harsh accusations based on hearsay from people who wanted them exterminated so they could move in. There is no proof that they were cannibals.

The Karankawas inhabited the offshore islands or peninsulas—Galveston, Matagorda, San José—and a thin strip of the mainland. More advanced tribes kept them from going very far in from the sea. They moved about their watery homeland in dugout canoes too small and crude to allow them any mastery of the deep ocean. The Gulf marshes then as now grew billions of mosquitoes, and it may be that the Karankawa reputation for smelling bad came merely from their insect repellents— probably alligator grease or rancid shark oil.

Karankawa men were superb physical specimens and wore no clothes.

The women dressed in animal skins and Spanish moss. The clans wandered over their territory, eating whatever was in season—oysters, blackberries, mussels, ducks, deer. The men hunted with bows as tall as themselves—six feet or more—and built traps in the shallow bays to catch fish.

The Karankawas made portable huts of poles and skins, much cruder than the teepees of the Plains Indians. They made fairly good clay pots and may have cooked some of their food, though they ate much of it raw. They knew how to get mildly drunk, not on alcohol but probably from a vision-inducing bean brewed into a tea.

The Karankawas' life was hard, partly because they were such poor boat-builders that they couldn't harvest much of the riches of the Gulf of Mexico. Put ashore in Karankawa country, the seagoing Tahitians would probably have established a much more prosperous society.

Yet the Karankawas seem to have been content and even happy, and they treated the first white men they ever saw—Cabeza de Vaca and his shipwrecked companions, in 1528—with kindness. Cabeza de Vaca reported that the Karankawas seemed fonder and more indulgent of their children than any other people he had known.

When badly treated by the whites, as they usually were, the Karankawas were pitiless. They killed nearly all of La Salle's men in 1685, and they rarely got along with the Spaniards. What they seem to have wanted was to be left in peace, unplundered and unchristianized, to live their own rough way with hurricanes and mosquitoes.

They never grasped the idea that their islands had somehow become the property of the Spanish and American settlers, and the white man's whiskey led them to acts of madness and violence. Many white men regarded them as a kind of wildlife and killed them casually.

In the 1840s the last of the Karankawas were transported into the Mexican state of Tamaulipas, and in 1855 only six or eight survived there. It is just possible that small amounts of Karankawa blood still flow in the veins of a few Texans or Tamaulipans, but their culture, such as it was, is totally gone. Which is too bad; they might have had something to teach us—about predicting hurricanes, or making useful drugs out of Gulf Coast plants, or raising children.

Certainly they could have taught us fortitude. They fitted themselves into a violent environment and lived cheerfully under threat of disasters. Very few of us, put naked on today's Gulf shore to live as the Karankawas did, would survive more than a month or two.

The two big national wildlife refuges on the Gulf Coastal Plain (Aransas and Anahuac) are radically different. One is plush, the other rough, and both are valuable. The Aransas Refuge, where the whooping cranes spend half the year (October to April) has elaborate facilities and paved roads. The birds and animals flourishing in these 55,000 acres owe their protected existence to the whooping cranes. Without them, the refuge would probably not exist at all.[3]

Small fields of grain are specially planted for the cranes. A sixty-acre feeding pond is enriched with sea water and pumped-in marine organisms, and other birds benefit from these procedures too.

The big new observation tower, with its ramps and telescopes and the words of the taped lecture blowing away in the wind, overlooks an area where a single pair of whooping cranes lives, sometimes with a chick. Visitors may arrive when the family is away for the day, feeding somewhere else. The other cranes defend territories in remote parts of the big refuge and are much harder to observe, except from commercial excursion boats run for that purpose.

Ornithologists are watching them, though, unobtrusively doing what they can to help the birds survive. They are also watched at their summer breeding grounds in Canada. And in the spring and fall, when the cranes make their 2,600-mile migration, newspapers and broadcasting stations along the route urge people not to shoot any large white bird, lest it be the largest and rarest white bird of all, a whooping crane. A whooper's wingspread is 7½ feet, and there are only about sixty of them left on earth.

Even in the best of times, there were probably never more than two thousand. Each pair of cranes stakes out a territory of several hundred acres, which other birds and animals are allowed to use but not other whooping cranes. This highly special habitat of mud flats and shallow bays was never overly plentiful, and now it is scarce indeed. A chief reason for the small crane population is that there is no place for a large number to live.

Besides the migrating cranes, there is the captive flock.[4] Those in the New Orleans and San Antonio zoos are chiefly captured cripples. The enduring Josephine, who was a captive for 24 years, hatched four chicks that died and four that lived, and in many years did not nest at all or laid eggs that didn't hatch. Her mate was a cripple named Crip, and it is their offspring that now live in New Orleans's Audubon Park Zoo. After Josephine's death, Crip was moved to San Antonio and is now the only crane there.

Most of the captive flock—seventeen birds—is at the Patuxent Wildlife Research Center in Maryland. All but two of them were hatched by incubators from eggs taken from the whooping cranes' nests near Great Slave Lake in northern Canada. Stealing whooping cranes' eggs may sound like a risky and reprehensible business, but as the Canadian and American wildlife men did it, it wasn't. It worked.

Biologists had noted that when two eggs hatched in a single nest, one chick almost invariably died. Therefore they took eggs only from nests containing two, leaving one for the birds to brood themselves. The results were excellent—a better-than-usual crop of young cranes hatched in the wild, plus fifteen incubator babies at Patuxent.

The entire experiment had been rehearsed on sandhill cranes before it was tried on the whooping cranes, and the egg-taking was done over a five-year period between 1967 and 1971. Some of the incubator chicks are now of breeding age themselves.

Many people make the long drive to Aransas expressly to see the whooping cranes. Some see one and leave immediately, some see none and feel cheated, some sight a white pelican through binoculars, call it a crane, and hurry on. But there is a great deal more to this place than that handful of majestic and possibly doomed birds.

Twenty miles of shell roads reach beyond the pavements, winding through meadows and oak thickets, past marshes and fresh-water ponds. You may have to slow down for wild turkeys and stop for a family of javelinas. Deer, now little threatened by predators, appear by tens and twenties. Aransas produces so many that hundreds have been captured there and taken to repopulate other parts of the state.

Three walking trails have been built through different habitats: woods, tidal flats, brush. The refuge checklist contains 328 species of birds (probably no one person has seen them all) and 45 mammals, including mountain lions in the brush and dolphins in the shallow bays.

The Anahuac Refuge, fifty miles from Houston, is like another country. The visitor center is an open shed where you may register and pick up a pamphlet or two. The roads are rough, sometimes closed by barriers, and occasionally too wet to drive. The administrative staff is in the town of Anahuac, miles away.

All you see is ten thousand acres of marshland and prairie and salt water, lying as flat as a tabletop under the sky. Only people who really want to see wildlife bother to go there, and the absence of mere vacationers is good for the animals. Lying in the middle of the coastal rice belt, Anahuac is run chiefly as a winter feeding ground for ducks and geese. But the population of other birds is huge, and there are minks, otters, alligators, and red wolves. In winter, a staff man guides people once a week to see rare yellow rails.

Anahuac is the center and safest territory of the world's small remaining population of red wolves. They are bigger and handsomer than coyotes, as wolves ought to be, and they aren't red but yellowish brown or gray. They once ranged through most of the South and into Illinois. Now their territory has shrunk to a few coastal counties in Texas (from Brazoria County eastward) and Cameron Parish in Louisiana.[5]

Red wolves are long-legged, rangy animals, hunting at night over thirty-five square miles or more of territory. They mate for life, establish dens in the low sandy mounds of the coastal prairie, and raise litters of three or four pups. They eat nutrias, rabbits, rats, and muskrats—not a bad diet, from the rancher's or farmer's point of view.

But many farmers like to shoot red wolves anyway. Now so few of them remain that when one of them dies, its surviving mate breeds with a coyote. The ever-prospering coyotes, willing to live almost anywhere and eat almost anything, have moved into the red-wolf country and thus many hybrids—part coyote, part wolf—are seen among the wolves.

Genetic pollution may end the red wolf species. The end is hastened, too, by the steady loss of wolf habitat to farming and industry, and by the tendency of duck and goose hunters to shoot red wolves that come within range.

It is odd that red wolves should survive in the heavily populated Houston-Galveston-Beaumont area. They were forest animals until man drove them out onto the coastal prairies. There, mosquitoes have infected them with a number of diseases. State and federal agencies are trying to stop the hybridization and help the species get back to "secure population levels." The prospects are not very good.

Alligators, another endangered species, are recovering slightly under federal protection. They can be seen as far down the coast as the Aransas Refuge, and eastward to Florida. Anahuac is a favored spot for them, and gives them some special protection.

It is one thing to see an alligator safely enclosed in a zoo or an "alligator farm" and something much more exciting to see one in the wild. Alligators have been known to attack humans, especially in water. But far more often they run away.

In recent years scientists have found that much of what people "know" about alligators is nonsense. For example, they do not deliver mighty blows with their tails when fighting. They use their tails merely to swim. Their teeth are what you must be wary of. It is not just the males that bellow; females do too. Alligators don't lie torpidly in the hot sun all day because if they did they would die. Their nests don't contain hundreds of eggs, but usually about thirty.

The big alligator in the roadside exhibit is not "a thousand years old." Alligators grow senile, lose their teeth, and die before fifty. Nobody, just glancing at an alligator, can tell whether it is male or female. Only by seeing alligators mate, or watching one lay eggs, or giving it a detailed physical examination, can a scientist tell male from female—except that females rarely grow longer than ten feet while males may reach seventeen feet.

A baby alligator, freshly hatched, is about 8½ inches long, decidedly aggressive, and able to take care of itself, although frogs and birds, notably the great blue heron, do eat them. Some privileged investigators have heard infant alligators cry out while still in the unbroken egg. It's a sound like hiccupping, they say.

What alligators eat is partly determined by their size. Only a big one would tackle a dog or a hog. Their general diet includes fishes, frogs, snakes, turtles, ducks, rats, nutrias, rabbits, and muskrats. Large alligators do not eat small ones.

Alligators of any size eat very little, compared with warm-blooded animals. This is partly because they don't have to use any calories maintaining body heat, and partly because their metabolic processes are relatively slow. An experiment showed that the amount of food a ninety-five-pound dog ate in a year would keep seven hundred pounds of alligators alive and healthy. (The experiment involved one dog and seven small alligators each weighing about one hundred pounds.) The alligator's impressive teeth are for capturing food, not for chewing it. It swallows its food whole or in large bitten-off chunks and breaks it down with powerful digestive juices. Surprising objects of metal, plastic, rubber, and wood, which the juices wouldn't digest, have been found in alligators' stomachs.

Alligators and crocodiles have been living on the earth for 200 million years.[6] They were contemporaries of the dinosaurs, and while dinosaurs dropped out of the earthly picture long ago, there are still alligators or crocodiles on every continent but Europe.

Alligators once lived in Texas near present-day Dallas, Waco, and Austin, and all the way down the coast from Louisiana to the Rio Grande. Today their range is hugely shrunk, and still shrinking. Many people are concerned that their long history will soon end, that commercial hunting and damage to wild habitat will bring extinction to all crocodilians early in the twenty-first century.

Everything about the Gulf Coast (except most of man's activities there) tends to make it matchless bird country. It is far enough south to be a wintering place for ducks and geese. It has woods and fields for songbirds as well as beaches and bays for shorebirds. It is a resting place for birds that have crossed the Gulf of Mexico on their spring migrations, both for those that will nest in Texas and those that will move on north.[7]

In 1971, the Christmas bird count at Freeport—on the coast, of course—produced 226 species seen within a fifteen-mile circle in a single day.

This is a record for the entire United States and for the whole history of the Audubon Christmas count, which began in 1900. Many specialists believe that it will never be equaled. Texas has its own bird book, Roger Tory Peterson's *Field Guide to the Birds of Texas*, produced because Texas is, in Dr. Peterson's phrase, "the Number One bird state."

Each spring, motels along the coast fill up with people who have come from all over the United States to see birds. Certain spots are renowned for certain species. High Island has warblers, San Luis Pass has nesting black skimmers, and the Bolivar ferry slip has magnificent frigate birds.

Brown pelicans were plentiful along the Texas shore until DDT killed them off. I remember them at Rockport, plain and solemn and very large, flapping along in formation parallel to the shore. They seemed to work hard at flying, like bulldozers that had taken to the air, and they crash-dived for fish as if they had been shot down.

But though they looked clumsy they were very efficient, and they lived at the top of a food chain where they got high concentrations of DDT. A few years of it finished them off.

A friend of mine, a doctor, used to find pelicans helpless and quivering along the beaches and highways. Dissected, they showed no diseases in their muscles or internal organs. The chemical attacked their central nervous systems and simply left them unable to eat, walk, or fly. Fortunately, brown pelicans survive in Mexico and South America, at least for the time being.

Besides the rarities and the complicated subtribes of gulls and sandpipers, the coast has birds which are not subtle problems in identification but just good to look at: marsh hawks, patrolling low on long wings over the grass flats; loons whose mad laughter you hope to hear in Texas but rarely do; white pelicans with wings that spread nine feet; roseate spoonbills in their fine pink feathers; and my favorite, the magnificent frigate bird.

A few frigate birds turn up each year on the Texas shore, leaving an impression of strangeness and beauty. Their wingspread is 7½ feet, so they are visible at great distances. And their wings are curiously shaped, bent in a way which makes them a kind of romantic ideal of what a bird's wing should be.

For all their wingspan, frigate birds weigh only three or four pounds. They can't swim, or take off from the water. Flight and soaring are their specialties. They pluck fish out of the Gulf while flying, and steal food from seagulls in midair. They consist almost entirely of lifting surfaces.

William Beebe, on the Galapagos Islands in the 1920s, walked among frigate birds which, like nearly all the Galapagos animals, had seen so little of man that they were not afraid of him. He touched one. "Taking the tip of one great wing in my hand I raised it up as high as I could

reach," Beebe wrote. "The bird spread the other and, lightly as thistle-down, lifted and drifted away."[8]

Of all the encounters with wild animals I have read about, that is the one I would like most to have had myself.

Trees sculptured by the wind can be found anywhere along the Texas shore, provided trees can be found at all. Around Rockport, they seem most numerous and most strange, their long horizontal branches reaching inland as if they were streamers blown in the wind.

Unquestionably these are deformed trees, but they are deformed so dramatically that they are more interesting than ordinary trees. Their strange shapes suggest the movements of modern dancers. Yearning, submission, endurance, resistance, streamlining, come to mind, according to who is looking.

The deformation is not all done by the wind. Salt spray is a factor too.[9] Blown inland from waves crashing on the beaches, it "burns" the Gulf side of a tree with salt and stunts its growth, so that branches on that side are short and stubby. The downwind branches are protected, and may even grow longer than normal in compensation for the stunted limbs to windward. The main trunk of the tree leans inland, a result of the wind alone when the tree was small and flexible enough to be bent like a stem of grass.

There is still another curious effect. Clumps of trees, notably live-oak mottes, have upper surfaces that look as if they had been clipped—not in straight lines but in smooth, curving contours, like the upper surface of a muffin or a haystack. They look as if no twig dared grow beyond the general contour and thus expose itself to stronger wind.

And this may be exactly the case. A steady prevailing wind, even without salt spray, can stunt growth by rapid evaporation and drying. So the twigs and leaves, using each other for protection like sheep in a storm, grow slowly and evenly outward into the threatening wind.

Other plants are threatened too. Anything growing near the shore is frequently sprayed with salt, which some plants tolerate better than others. The result can be changing bands of vegetation as you move inland from a beach, each band less tolerant of spray than the one before.

Storm winds can carry salt spray several miles inland, and damage plants far from the Gulf. Usually, though, storms bring rain to wash the salt off, and all is well. Really spectacular tree sculpture by wind and spray is nearly always within a hundred yards or so of the sea.

The Gulf shore is the kingdom of the live oaks, which in many people's minds are the royalty among trees. Not everyone's yard is big enough for a full-grown live oak. Its long, heavy branches reach out horizontally in all directions, finally dipping to touch the ground and perhaps take root.

Such a tree makes a leafy canopy, 150 feet across, permeable by breezes and birds. You can give a cocktail party for fifty people under one, and in good weather no more satisfactory setting could be devised. Or you can lie under one alone and study the pattern of black gnarled limbs and green leaves against the blue sky.

Ferns and moss grow on their branches. An old live oak in fact becomes an ecological system in itself, with birds, squirrels, frogs, insects, and plants all living in its branches.

The biggest of all live oaks (and the state's biggest tree of any kind) is at Goose Island State Park, near Rockport. It is thought to be about two thousand years old. Like many "champion" trees, it is not necessarily the handsomest of its species. Making it a public monument, equipping it with a parking area and a protective fence, have given it the air of an old captive. Even so, as the oldest living thing in Texas it deserves a visit of respect.

On the sea-damp coast, where trees bear Spanish moss, live oaks look more dignified in these gray robes than any other tree. On rare occasions streamers of Spanish moss can grow twelve feet long. This curious plant does more to set the mood of the country it grows in than any other. Developers around Houston charge more for lots with moss-hung trees than for similar lots without, because many people associate moss with elegant Southern plantation homes.

Some Indians called Spanish moss "tree hair." Each clump is made of many tangled plants, and each plant has one tiny yellow flower in the spring. Like its Hill Country cousin ball moss, Spanish moss is an epiphyte, taking no nourishment from the thing it grows on, whether an oak tree or a telephone wire. It feeds on dust particles and rain. Getting little nourishment this way, it grows slowly.

Birds and squirrels use it in their nests. And so, in a sense, did people until recently. They used to stuff mattresses and sofas with it, and put it as a binder in the mud chimneys of early East Texas houses. There were even Spanish-moss gins in the Texas coastal counties, which cleaned and baled the moss for packing material and padding. But foam rubber and plastics replaced Spanish moss for most of its uses, and the little industry faded.

Inland the Coastal Plain is flat, and of course tilted a little toward the sea. Geologists call it featureless, meaning that it has no mountains or interesting rocks. Tourists call it monotonous. But its heavy, rich soil grows rice and cotton, and there is oil underground.

And beef above ground, for the natural growth on most of the plain is grass. It is rather coarse grass, but the plentiful rain makes it lush and the soil makes it nutritious. It supports more cows per square mile than any other grass in Texas. So many, in fact, that Harris County, which would seem to have room only for the city of Houston, has often been the leading cattle-producing county of the state.

The Coastal Plain was once the home of millions of prairie chickens. They were, and are, big, tasty gamebirds, and it was easier for the settlers to shoot them than to raise domestic chickens. But they shot too many, and prairie chickens are endangered birds now, surviving chiefly on a refuge maintained near Eagle Lake by the World Wildlife Fund.

Grass is all to prairie chickens. They have no use for trees. They nest in grass, hide in it, eat it, and eat its seeds and the insects that live in it. In turn, armadillos eat them, or their eggs, and so do coyotes. If the birds range outside the refuge, they get shot.

They are multiplying well on the protected ground, and their mating ceremonies in February are a spectacle. A few privileged persons are allowed to drive up in cars to watch. Both cocks and hens are so intent on the ritual that they pay no attention to the visitors.

The males inflate large orange air sacs on each side of their necks and strut, dance, and fight over the females. They also make a strange booming sound, like that of no other bird.

There are woodlands as well as grasslands on the Coastal Plain, usually along the big rivers like the Brazos and the Colorado, where they cross the plain in remarkably straight courses toward the Gulf. Brazoria County and its neighbors are handsomely furnished with live oaks, pecans, sycamores, and willows, enough to make up what the Texas Forest Service classifies as the Coastal Forests.[10] In open spaces among the trees are dwarf palmettos, trunkless, their long-stemmed fan-shaped leaves springing out of the ground like little green fountains. Cattlemen would rather have grass in their place. But, like mesquite, dwarf palmettos are hard to get rid of.

The official pest plants of the Coastal Plain are not the palmettos but the wild rose, huisache, live oak, and retama. None of them is a major problem, as mesquite and creosote bush are in other areas.

Some of the most attractive trees and bushes in Texas are also the most aggressive and troublesome. The retama, with its heavy golden bloom and strange long leaves, is a far handsomer tree than its cousin the pink mimosa, which everybody seems to want on his front lawn. The retama even has handsome seed pods which narrow down to a wasp waist between beans. Some people do plant it instead of the mimosa, but the retama's real home remains in the wild.

A very large untapped supply of geothermal energy has been found under the Texas coastline, stretching all the way from Louisiana to Corpus

Christi. It consists simply of hot water. But there is a great deal of it, and it's so hot (about 320 degrees Fahrenheit) that it would be steam if it were not stored under great pressure, more than two miles below the surface.

Eventually it will be tapped through drilled holes and its heat used to run steam engines, generate electricity, warm houses. It is fresh water, not salt, so it may be possible to drink it and irrigate farms with it after the heat has been exhausted.

It will be a pollution-free source of energy, but not without problems of its own. The water is contained in beds of sand, and as more and more of it is pumped out (or perhaps forced out by its own pressure) the Gulf Coast may sink, perhaps well below sea level. Various areas around Houston have sunk several feet in the last fifteen years, merely from the removal of well water near the surface.

To prevent such sinking, it may be necessary to pump cold water in to replace the hot. Sea water might do. We are still such beginners at the use of geothermal energy that we are not sure what all the problems are, much less the solutions.

Bolivar Peninsula is a pleasantly backwaterish place, lightly populated and still supplied with acres of blackberry brambles and miles of dunes and open beach. It resembles the long barrier islands exactly—the Gulf on one side with sand, East Bay on the other with mud flats and marshes —except that its eastern end is connected with the mainland.

You reach it from Galveston by Bolivar Ferry, a brisk free service whose three-mile ride is so closely escorted by gulls and terns that with binoculars you can examine them feather by feather and eye to eye. Bolivar Flats, near the ferry terminal, is the best place to see shorebirds on the whole peninsula.

The Intracoastal Waterway has been cut into the peninsula on the inland side, through land so flat that the barges and pushboats, seen from a distance, seem to be moving on rollers across pastures of salt grass. Windmills are mounted just three or four feet above ground level, for there's plenty of wind here. The stubby towers are braced with guy wires against hurricanes. Houses are built on stilts, to be above the sea when the wind pushes it over the peninsula.

Cattle egrets accompany the grazing cattle. Yucca and prickly pear live somewhat incongruously beside dwarf palmettos. Trees are rare and stunted, and the Bolivar sand dunes, rarely more than ten feet high, seem stunted too, compared with the lordly fifty-foot dunes of Padre Island.

The peninsula has been severed from the mainland at a point where it narrows to two hundred yards. The cut is called the Rollover Fish Pass. It is a short canal dug to let sea water and ocean fish into the shallow bay.

The name Rollover was given to the place long ago by smugglers. They used to land barrels of illegal liquor and other cargo from ships, roll them across the narrow neck of land, and load them on small boats for the mainland. Now the village of Gilchrist thrives here on amateur and professional fishing, and the tides push Gulf water into East Bay and suck it out again.

Near the base of the peninsula sits High Island, a large mound whose forty-five-foot elevation above sea level makes it visible for miles across the flats. The bulge of High Island is caused by a salt dome beneath it, one of those big plugs of salt that extend downward for thousands of feet from the surface and are nearly always associated with underground oil. Louisiana more than Texas has the habit of calling these bulges islands. They are not surrounded by water but merely rise above marshes or pastures as islands do above the sea.

High Island holds a small town of the same name, and patches of woods whose live oaks and brush thickets become, as one man told me, "the world capital of warblers" during spring migrations. If bad weather pins the birds down for a few days, the warblers and other songbirds, continuing to pour in from their Gulf crossing, get so thick in High Island's trees that ornithologists turn dizzy. The birds concentrate here chiefly because High Island has the only woods for many miles. The surrounding flat land contains brackish water too near the surface for trees to grow.

Beyond High Island, and on for thirty miles east to the Louisiana border, the Texas mainland fronts the Gulf. Except for this short stretch and a shorter one around Freeport, all the rest of the state's long coastline has barrier islands or peninsulas parallel to the shore.

Dunes and beaches lie on the seaward side of the highway here, with marshes, mud flats and salt pastures inland. There are very few human inhabitants anywhere.

Until recently, most people thought marshes were dismal wastelands, full of mosquitoes and snakes, useless except as places to dump sewage and corrosive chemicals and situate the city dumps. Marshes are indeed full of mosquitoes and snakes, but also full of other things which put them among the most valuable lands we have.

Biomass is a word used in connection with marshes nowadays. This sounds modern, like *megaton* and *overkill*, and it is indeed a new word, chiefly the property of biologists. What it means is, the total mass of living material, both animal and vegetable, that a given area produces.

It happens that marshes produce the greatest biomass of any environment on earth. Counting everything from gnats to red wolves, from tiny seeds to eight-foot stems of salt grass, the tonnage of life is higher in good salt marshes than in the densest forest. This seems appropriate as well as inevitable, since a salt marsh is a place where the land and the sea meet and mingle, and forms from both worlds live there.

Some parts of marshes stick up above even the highest tide. Some parts are always under water. Still others get a regular bath of sea water every day and then are exposed to the air, and there are plants and animals which find that arrangement just right. A marsh is not just one environment but several, each with its own snugly adapted population of worms and weeds, fish and fowl.

Besides the various combinations of wet and dry, there are those of salt and fresh. River water meets sea water in marshes, and they mix in varying proportions. Many plants and animals have to have the mixture just right, which means that they can live only in that part of the marsh where it *is* just right.

Marshes serve as a kind of compost heap, among other duties. The things that live in them die, and then decay, and floods and tides wash this rich biological soup out into the bays where it enters the food chains of virtually everything that lives in the sea.

Waterfowl, highly visible and present in the thousands, are the most noticeable animal life in marshes. There are also raccoons, rabbits, rats, otters, minks, nutrias, frogs, hawks, and owls, plus songbirds and occasional visiting deer. Also snakes and billions of insects, shrimps and crabs, and in the water of marshes the eggs and young of many ocean-going fishes.

For marshes, we have recently learned, are safe, sun-warmed, nutrient-rich nurseries for a long list of fish and shellfish, from shrimp to tarpon, that later will spend their adult lives in the harsher environment of the sea. If our marshlands are destroyed, much of our oceans' fish production will stop.

Texas, with nearly every kind of land except tundra and tropical rain forest, is blessed with thousands of acres of marshlands along the Gulf shore. They rarely occur directly on the Gulf, but on the inland sides of the barrier islands and on the mainland where it sinks down to sea level among sloughs and sluggish rivers. Between Galveston and the Louisiana border, the marshes reach inland for miles.

But while we have plentiful marshlands, we don't yet have the sense to stop destroying them. They are disappearing at a great rate. People pump mud from bay bottoms into a piece of marshland, and presently have salable real estate. We still dump everything from wastepaper to corrosive chemicals into our marshes, and we dredge and repeatedly re-dredge the Intracoastal Waterway across them.

Dredging bays and filling marshes are activities which stir up mud, and muddy water blocks out sunlight. Thus the number of plants and animals that can live in the bays is reduced, sometimes almost to zero. And of course a filled-in marsh is no longer a marsh at all.

But oddly enough, the most serious present threat to our marshes and bays comes from far up the rivers. It is dams. What dams do is store fresh water and withhold it from the sea. To the sea itself this makes little difference, but marshes and bays are very special environments where salt water is tempered with fresh. If too much fresh water is withheld, the ecological balance of the bays is thrown out of kilter, and their productivity cut.

Thus one price we pay for more than two hundred large artificial lakes in Texas is less of almost everything valuable in the Gulf: shrimp, oysters, crabs, gafftopsails, flounders, and even big-game fish like tarpon. They all, at one time or another in their life cycles, must live in the marshes or bays, where salt and fresh water are mixed. The less of this mixture there is, the fewer of them there are.

Originally, Texas and Louisiana had miles of the finest oyster reefs in the Gulf. Damming the rivers, plus dredging, filling, and pollution, have reduced them considerably. Oysters can't live at any period in their lives either in salt water or in fresh. They must have a mixture of the two. Moreover, oysters can't move around. If the water they live in grows too salty, they can't escape. They die.

The annual haul of shrimp is holding steady, largely because equipment of advanced design is catching an ever-larger percentage of an ever-smaller total production. Nowadays, virtually every shrimp that makes it to adulthood in the Gulf is hauled out and sold. The biggest shrimp trawlers moved years ago to South American waters. The Gulf was no longer profitable for them.

Exploring marshland is not always easy or comfortable. The best place for most people to see marshes is the new Sea Rim State Park, a few miles southwestward along the shore from Port Arthur and the small town of Sabine.

Sea Rim's fifteen thousand acres are nearly all marsh, with canoe trails leading to camping platforms in the salt grass. Only eight acres are occupied by the shelters and hot showers that most Texans now demand when roughing it. There are more than three miles of beach.

A series of exhibits at the visitor center shows what lives in marshes, and why these lands are of such immense value, reflecting the changing attitude of the Texas Parks and Wildlife Department—away from the kind of recreation which paves the land and drives out wildlife, and toward some conservation of the natural world and its inhabitants. But the Parks and Wildlife Department still regards wild things primarily as something to be protected today so there will be some left to shoot tomorrow. Most

state parks are small and full of people, and have signs that say: No
Firearms. No Hunting. On Sea Rim's vast acreage hunters are allowed,
with certain restrictions, to shoot waterfowl and nutria.

The nutrias are indeed getting out of hand, but the official rationaliza-
tion for permitting hunters to shoot ducks and geese is that most of the
waterfowl in the Sea Rim area would flock into the park for safety if
hunting were banned there, with resultant overcrowding and disease. Yet
nothing of the sort has happened in our huge federal wildlife refuges at
Aransas and Anahuac and Laguna Atascosa.

Almost every Texan who grew up inland can remember his first
glimpse of the Gulf of Mexico, which was often his first look at any sea.
Mine was at Galveston, at age fifteen, on a winter day when the Gulf was
gray and flat. Gulls, brown pelicans, and two far-away freighters were its
only ornaments. It looked dull. Later I was reintroduced to this little
ocean in a more interesting way.

I had sailed from New Orleans on a freighter, at midnight. The ship
slid so smoothly down the Mississippi that we had no sense of movement
at all, except for the passing of a gas flare or a navigation light in the
damp, warm blackness on either side. On deck, we shut off a radio and
listened to shrieks and croaks and the cries of small captured animals. It
was easy to believe that the banks on either side were jungle.

At dawn I was awakened by the movement of my bunk. The ship had
come out of the Mississippi and was being rocked like a big, slow cradle
in the Gulf of Mexico. Through a porthole I gazed at dull light over mud-
colored water, and a low, mud-colored uninhabited shore.

It must have looked just that way to Spanish sailors three hundred
years earlier, prudently following the coast from Mexico to Cuba in ships
loaded with gold. In fact their name for the Mississippi Delta was Cabo de
Lodo: Mud Cape.

We may tend to think of the Gulf of Mexico as a smallish backwater,
not really like the ocean. But it is precisely like the ocean; it *is* the ocean
on a diminished scale, a tropical sea that has a few stray whales and
occasional waterspouts but no icebergs.[11]

Troughs and trenches and submarine canyons cut across the floor of
the Gulf, not all of them fully mapped. Underwater mountains lie about
one hundred miles east of the mouth of the Rio Grande. One peak rises
2,700 feet above the ocean floor, and the other 3,800 feet. But both are
many fathoms beneath the surface. No ship will ever strike them.

What the Gulf conspicuously lacks is oceanic islands. The long barrier
islands of the Texas shore are merely banks of sand and shell, big sandbars piled up by wind and water. The Gulf's only true islands are the

waterless Dry Tortugas, off Florida, and seven small atolls off Yucatán. These are mere specks around its rim.

The center regions lie unobstructed, which is good for shipping but bad in other ways. It means that offshore birds—birds so closely linked to the open sea that they are rarely even seen on the mainland—are few in number. Shearwaters, petrels, gannets, and phalaropes are such birds, and there might be far more of them in the Gulf if there were offshore islands for them to nest on.

The Gulf Stream makes a big clockwise loop around the Gulf, then pours out into the Atlantic Ocean. There are also countercurrents going the other way, notably one which moves westward along the U.S. shoreline and carries the sediments of the Mississippi along the Texas coast as far as Galveston. Almost no mud from the Mississippi goes eastward or straight out into the Gulf. Seventy miles out to sea from the river's delta, the ocean water is as transparent as any on earth, except when mixed with crude oil.

Travelers on the Gulf are struck by the sudden changes in the color of its water. A precise line may divide opaque green water from water of a deep, clear blue in which you can see your hooked fish flashing its silver belly far below. These color changes indicate the currents, often traveling in opposite directions and at different speeds, like trains on parallel tracks. The line between the two colors of water may be marked by a long windrow of seaweed. This is the sargassum weed which gave the Sargasso Sea its name.

All plants which float free in the ocean are microscopic in size except one—the sargassum weed. It lives in tropical waters around the world, keeping afloat by means of air bladders and supporting a special, highly-adapted group of small animals which eat it, cling to it, hide in it, nest in it, or depend on it for shade. Some of them can't swim. If they lose their foothold on the sargassum they are like a man falling out of a dirigible. They drop to the ocean floor and die.

At times the Gulf of Mexico is second only to the Sargasso Sea itself in the amount of weed it contains. There have been periods after severe storms when sargassum weed buried the beaches of Texas two feet deep for hundreds of miles, making the shore impassable and giving it a putrid smell for weeks.

On the Gulf Coast Texas dips down gently and disappears under the sea. We have no dramatic rocky headlands like those of California, no high cliffs beaten by waves. The timid swimmer need never fear, as he wades out from a Texas beach, that he will suddenly step off into frightening depths. The easy slope of the dry land continues under the Gulf water as the Continental Shelf, smooth near the shore but rough, like hilly country, thirty miles out. Then, at 100 fathoms (600 feet) the slope grows much steeper and plunges down toward the true ocean floor. Off Port Arthur this 100-fathom line is 125 miles out in the Gulf. Off Port Isabel, at the mouth of the Rio Grande, it is only 50 miles out.

Thirty species of sharks live in the Gulf. Some of them are very good to eat.[12] They range in size from the Bottlenose, which is two feet long at maturity, to the Great White Shark, which may grow to weigh eight thousand pounds.

The octopuses of the Texas shore cover only about a foot with their arms outspread. No one seems interested in them as food. People who seine them up just leave them on the sand to die.

Bottlenose dolphins live near the shore, pleasing everybody who sees them except commercial shrimp fishermen. They tear holes in the shrimp nets to get at the piled-up shrimp within. The fishermen say that the dolphins can tell, from the changed, laboring tone of the boat's engine, when the big nets have been lowered, and they gather from miles around to feed.

Dolphins are rarely found even five miles out at sea. Where we used to see fifteen or twenty playing off a Texas beach, or jauntily escorting the Port Bolivar ferry boats, we now see two or three, or none. Their top speed is only about twenty miles an hour, not fifty as many people believe.

Manatees, those strange, sluggish, harmless grazers on underwater grass, are sometimes seen in Texas rivers and bays. They once lived in huge herds along the shores of Yucatán, weighing eight or nine hundred pounds each and supplying Spanish ships with meat "as white as the finest veal." Their hides made long, supple whips for use on West Indian slaves.

Manatees are extremely sensitive to cold. The Texas bays in winter are too chilly for them. They migrate south, probably following the shorelines so they can feed on submarine pastures of seaweed.

Sea turtles are being crowded out of the Gulf of Mexico by overfishing and man's use of the beaches where they formerly nested. Five of the world's nine species now turn up sparsely on Texas shores, including the giant leatherback turtle, which is six or seven feet long. A few leatherbacks are cruising the Gulf equipped with radio transmitters to help marine biologists learn where they go on their long migrations and how they navigate.

Before tarpon became rare, the place now called Port Aransas was named Tarpon, Texas. Theodore Roosevelt, who seems to have gone everywhere and done everything, once fished for tarpon there.

Tarpon are edible, but just barely. Sports fishermen love them because they are big (up to 350 pounds) and fight hard. They are also beautiful, with huge scales that glitter like polished silver and make good trophy pictures. But now only two or three a year are caught at Port Aransas.

Tarpon keep near the shore and even swim up rivers. Other big-game fish, in the open Gulf, are being caught too freely by Japanese fishing fleets. The Japanese fish for yellow-fin tuna. They catch them by a method called long-line fishing, cook and can them in factory ships, and eventually ship them from Japan to the United States. It is possible that the tuna you buy in Corpus Christi was caught a hundred miles out in the Gulf but reached you by way of Yokohama.

Long-line fishing involves a kind of enormous seagoing trotline, as much as five miles long, suspended from floats and patrolled by boats. To the long line hundreds of short lines are attached, with baited hooks. They hang down to the proper depth, and the tuna they catch weigh one hundred pounds or so. Blue marlin, wahoo, sailfish, and other big-game fish take the baits too, with the result that their numbers are declining steadily in the Gulf.

The water temperature off Texas ranges from 52 degrees in winter to 85 in August. In summer, when it's around 100 degrees on shore, the difference in temperatures (and thus air pressure) between sea and land produces the fresh sea breeze that makes life along the Texas coast pleasant. A meteorologist states flatly that it is "an onshore breeze of about 12 knots" and that "it blows from 11 A.M. to 8 P.M." When I lived on the beach at Galveston it did not seem to me so exactly on schedule, but it did die down after dark when the land began to cool.

Most of the Gulf's rain falls in July, August, and September, the same rainy months that the Trans-Pecos deserts have. And while the deserts have dust devils, the Gulf has waterspouts. They form when a funnel of spinning air dips down from a thunderstorm and sets the sea to whirling.

A good waterspout may reach several hundred feet into the air and last half an hour. They are harmless, being little more than spinning spray. On shore they disintegrate rapidly, and even a big one could damage only some old shed ready to collapse anyway.

You may also see, along the Texas shore, breaking waves glowing with an eerie greenish light, or small luminous whirlpools. A friend once phoned me at 3 A.M. and urged me to go to Galveston beach. I did, and found sheets of glowing green water rolling up the sand and fading out, replaced by other sheets as each phosphorescent wave came in. In the moonless night I could see waves glowing half a mile down the shore. The sea's luminescence is caused by millions of tiny light-producing organisms.

The Gulf's tides are mild, rarely more than a foot or two. Some places have two of these little high tides and two little lows a day, others only one.

The most interesting Gulf tides are the lowest ones, coming, as the highest tides do, when the moon is new or full. Then you can walk out in the darkness on a band of clean sand as wide as a football field that a few hours earlier was sea bottom. You hear waves breaking two hundred yards farther out than usual, and find small crabs and fishes in tide pools filled with an inch or two of water. The farther out you go toward the retreated sea the more kinds of marine organisms your flashlight will find.

Along the southernmost hundred miles of the Texas coastline, these tide flats are essentially the same as those off Galveston or Freeport. But the land they adjoin is Padre Island, the longest island for its width on the surface of the earth. And inland from Padre lies a land of big deer and big ranches, the brushy Rio Grande Plain.

8 | THE RIO GRANDE PLAIN

Texas reaches a long way south into the subtropics, with a dry, rocky region called the Rio Grande Plain. Three of the Plain's boundaries are exact and traceable—the Balcones Escarpment, the Rio Grande River, and the Gulf of Mexico. The northeastern one is not. Instead there's a transition zone where the Rio Grande brush thins and dies away into relatively treeless coastal plain of a different character.

You can call the San Antonio River the northeastern boundary, or you can choose a line—perhaps the highway—between San Antonio and Corpus Christi. In any case, the farther you go south toward the Rio Grande, the stronger the residues of Spain and Mexico—Spanish place names, Spanish slang, Mexican food. And lots of Spanish-speaking people.

Northers that freeze the Panhandle solid are mild cold snaps when they reach the Rio Grande Plain, and most of them never get there at all. Spring comes in late February, with wildflowers blooming in the pastures to join the poinsettia and bougainvillea that have bloomed through the winter in gardens. Summers are hot, as you would expect in a place 27 degrees north of the Equator.

In 1836 Texas won independence from Mexico, and the Rio Grande became the boundary between the two countries. Some Mexican ranchers then found themselves unwilling and unpopular residents of the Republic of Texas. They withdrew below the Rio Grande, abandoning thousands of head of cattle which went wild in the unfenced country. The fittest survived and in a few generations had become Texas longhorns.[1]

They not only survived, they multiplied. Texans began to round them up on the Rio Grande Plain and drive them to New Orleans for sale. Then they started ranching. Thus the American Cattle Kingdom had its beginnings here, in south Texas, when Anglo-Saxons adopted the Spanish technique of working cattle on horseback, something they had never done before. In just a few years the practice spread all the way up the Great Plains into Canada—unfenced range, branded cattle, cow ponies, trail drives, lariats, chuck wagons, cowboys, and sometimes enormous profits.

The Cattle Kingdom became a phenomenon of the Great Plains. But this southern plain where it all began is not a part of the Great Plains at all. They stop at the Balcones Escarpment. The Rio Grande Plain is part of the continent's coastal plain—low in elevation, swept by Gulf winds, with rivers meandering sluggishly to the sea.

Its geological underpinnings are exactly the same as those of the Piney Woods and the Post Oak Belt and the plain on which Houston lies. But what a difference on the surface! For the Rio Grande Plain, except for a few large, well-known clearings, is the Brush Country, the land of thorns.

One of the cleared spots, around Crystal City and Carrizo Springs, is called the Winter Garden. It is famous for growing vegetables, mostly spinach, and Crystal City has a statue of Popeye, its patron saint. The dark-green leaves that lie wilting on miles of highway are spinach leaves blown from passing trucks.

Irrigated agriculture is possible because the Winter Garden sits on a geological formation called the Carrizo Sands, which hold huge amounts of underground water. Most of the brush country has no such resource, and has to make do with rainfall, which is sparse.

More than two hundred miles southeast of the Winter Garden is another large open space. The banks of the lower Rio Grande—actually its delta and its floodplain for many miles inland from the Gulf—are wide and flat and called simply the Valley, although it is not a valley at all, since no hills rise on either side. It too has been cleared of brush—almost totally—and grows fruits and vegetables.

Falfurrias, in Brooks County, is noted for sweet pastures and dairy products. South of Corpus Christi, along the coast, lie several of the largest ranches in Texas, including the King Ranch. Here the counties, and some of the towns, are named for the ranchers who own them.

For the rest, it's mostly brush. There are thousands of square miles of it, and they serve as a reservoir, though a steadily draining one, of wild animals. In the southernmost reaches are tropical plants and animals whose main abode is Mexico. Subtropical Texas is the only place in the United States where you can find them. Florida's tropical plants and animals are those of the Caribbean. Those in Texas belong to the continent.

The Mississippi River's delta sticks like a tongue into the Gulf. The Rio Grande's delta is a smooth breastlike bulge in the coastline, part Texas and part Mexico. The Rio Grande spent about a million years building it, with soil from six states (three Mexican, three American). The delta is as flat as Holland, but with palm trees instead of windmills. A place called Southmost, in a bend of the river below Brownsville, is the southernmost bit of Texas, 168 miles above the Tropic of Cancer.

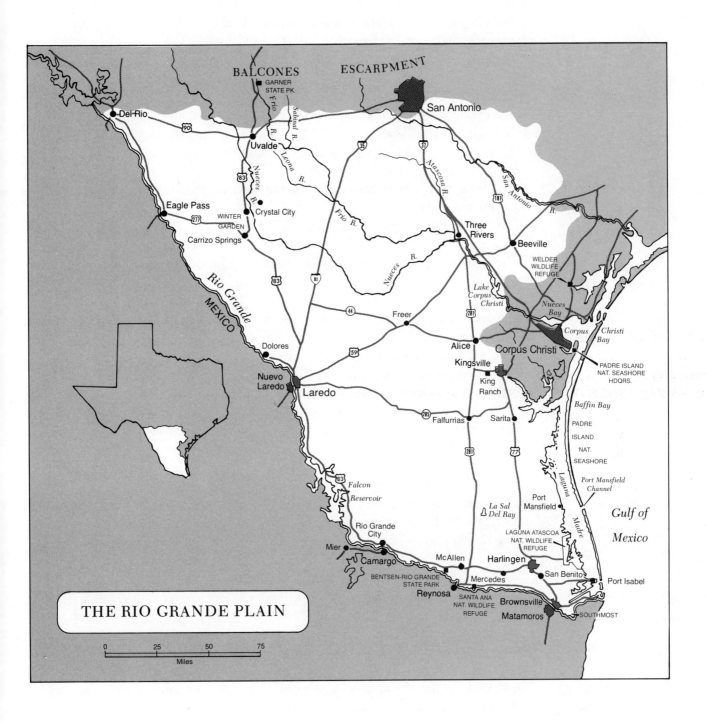

THE RIO GRANDE PLAIN

BALCONES **ESCARPMENT**

GARNER STATE PK.

Del Rio

San Antonio

Uvalde

Eagle Pass

WINTER
GARDEN

Crystal City

Carrizo Springs

Three
Rivers

Beeville

WELDER
WILDLIFE
REFUGE

Nueces
Bay

Lake
Corpus
Christi

Corpus Christi

Dolores

Freer

Alice

Corpus Christi
Bay

Nuevo
Laredo

Laredo

Kingsville

King
Ranch

PADRE ISLAND
NAT. SEASHORE
HDQRS.

Baffin Bay

PADRE

ISLAND

NAT.

SEASHORE

Falfurrias

Sarita

Falcon
Reservoir

La Sal
Del Ray

Port
Mansfield

Port Mansfield
Channel

Gulf of
Mexico

Rio Grande
City

Mier

Camargo

McAllen

Harlingen

San Benito

Port Isabel

LAGUNA ATASCOA
NAT. WILDLIFE
REFUGE

BENTSEN-RIO GRANDE
STATE PARK

Mercedes

Reynosa

SANTA ANA
NAT. WILDLIFE
REFUGE

Brownsville

Matamoros

SOUTHMOST

MEXICO

Rio Grande

Frio R.

Sabinal R.

Nueces R.

Leona R.

Atascosa R.

San Antonio R.

Nueces R.

Laguna Madre

0   25   50   75
Miles

The growing season here is about 340 days a year. (In the northern Panhandle it's 190 days.) Some years there is no frost at all. But every ten years or so, a hard freeze reaches down and kills all the crops, plus the orange and grapefruit trees.

Six inches of snow covered Brownsville in February, 1895, breaking the record of four inches set in 1866. But a mere trace is what usually falls, and often none at all.

The relation of Valley people to the Rio Grande is like that of Egyptians to the Nile. The river is all. It built the delta, and now it supplies the water that makes things grow. There isn't much rain, and the climate is so hot and dry that in any given period more water will evaporate out of a bucket or a lake than rain will put into it. This is true for every month of the year.

So the Valley people irrigate—massively, incessantly. Those thick pipes sticking up everywhere give access to the underground irrigation system. Many of the pipes are there to let air in or out of the system so the water will flow.

Because you can grow three crops a year here, the land is immensely valuable, and the Valley has been scraped clean of natural vegetation. What you see are rectangular fields, thousands of acres of brown dirt with nothing whatever growing in it but onions or carrots or peppers. Herbicides, insecticides, fertilizers, irrigation, chemicals to make fruit set early—these make the Valley a kind of laboratory, or food factory.

Much of the Valley is ruled off into a precise grid of straight farm roads, each square enclosing huge fields. Yards and barnyards are small; every possible foot of land is planted and set to making money.

No one stays in the Valley long without hearing the term *resaca,* a Spanish word with many different meanings. Probably it meant mudhole or slough when first used in the Valley; now it is the name for the ponds and lagoons that dot the countryside. Floodwater from the Rio Grande is stored in them, for use in dry times. Some of them are manmade. Some are oxbow lakes, old courses of the Rio Grande, which ravels out into shallow shifting channels as it approaches the sea.

The resacas in San Benito support water-skiers and are bordered by flower gardens. Others, far from towns, are surrounded by weeds and willows and offer a scrap of living space for birds and little animals—mice, moles, rabbits.

What grew in the Valley before those assembly-line rows of vegetables? Why brush, of course—a prickly, hot jungle full of fruits and seeds and cactus apples, swarming with wildlife.

A good part of the swarm was whitewing doves, tasty gamebirds an ounce or two heavier than mourning doves. The whitewing is *La Paloma* of the old Mexican song, and it figures in folk tales and superstitions. In the days of brush, the whitewings nested in it and raised millions of young. The accepted way to shoot them was to wait for a "feeding flight" to pass over, to fire into the swarm, and pick up as many dead and wounded as you could find. People outside the Valley have been shocked to see on their TV screens a country road solidly lined with pickup trucks, and whole families bearing shotguns, waiting to blast a freezerful of whitewings out of the sky.

There is less shock now, because there are so few whitewings. Removing the brush removed their nesting places. They *will* nest in mature grapefruit trees, but unenthusiastically, in small numbers. The World Wildlife Fund and the Texas Parks and Wildlife Department have established small refuge areas for them, about 1,700 acres altogether. But a short season of whitewing slaughter is allowed nearly every year. They will eventually cease to be gamebirds and end as rarities.

Palm trees are favored in the Valley. They stand straight and take up little space. Royal palms, California palms, cabbage palms have been imported. But one, the Texas palm, *Sabal texana,* got there on its own, probably carried up from the Caribbean as seeds. It is our only native palm tree.

In 1519 the big palm groves at the mouth of the Rio Grande led Alonso de Pineda to name this river the Rio de las Palmas, but the name didn't stick. The trees grew for about eighty miles up the river, and that was the extent of their natural range in Texas. *Sabal texana* is one of those Valley forms that mainly grow in Mexico. It is common down the Mexican coast as far as Vera Cruz.

You recognize *Sabal texana* by its straight trunk and the fact that its leaves stick out in all directions to make a big green sphere, as round as the head of a dandelion gone to seed. The fruit is a brown berry, edible but uninteresting, yet sometimes sold in the markets at Brownsville or Matamoros.

The old palm groves at Southmost have largely been bulldozed away to make farmland. Now *Sabal texana* is seen chiefly as a tame tree in the Valley's yards and city parks. Gardeners, impelled to take strange plants home and try them out, have got Texas palms to grow in Uvalde, San Antonio, and Austin. And I know of one that gets through the winters in Waco, four hundred miles north of the Valley.

Towns in the Valley are full of trees and vines and flowers. The countryside is a different matter; it is just one big truck garden and fruit orchard except for a state park and two wildlife refuges.

The Bentsen–Rio Grande State Park, on the banks of the river, goes in heavily for picnic grounds and campsites but also has a fine long nature trail through virgin brushland inhabited by beavers, badgers, birds, and the strange thorny trees and shrubs of the brush country—granjeno, huisache, catclaw, retama.

The Santa Ana National Wildlife Refuge, a few miles downstream, is bigger and wilder. It covers nearly two thousand acres, and in the spring it is a bright tangle of butterflies, wildflowers, birds, Spanish moss, trees, and vines. Animals are there too, but mostly hidden.

The tourist attraction at Santa Ana is the chachalacas, another Valley specialty ranging up from Mexico. These are birds, as big as half-grown turkeys and as meek as chickens. In the early morning they fly into the treetops and squawk. The rest of the time they would normally stay hidden in the brush, but the Santa Ana chachalacas are so regularly fed by tourists and studied by ornithologists that they will gather round your car expecting food.

Santa Ana has eleven miles of foot trails, and blinds to hide in for photographing—or just watching—hummingbirds and ducks. Several ponds are dotted about, and occasionally the river rises and covers everything with an enriching layer of mud.

A little graveyard lies in the Santa Ana refuge, a relic of another century. Near it grows an old, ill-shaped ebony tree that no one would admire if it were not the biggest ebony tree in Texas. Texas ebony is not ebony; it is another south Texas legume. (Real ebony grows in tropical Asia.) But its wood is dark and dense and would make fine furniture if it were not so often used for fence posts. "It's the only tree we've got down here that gives any real shade," a border patrolman told me. And he's right—most of the brush country trees have gauzy, minimal foliage that lets the sunlight through.

The Laguna Atascosa National Wildlife Refuge is wide, windy, watery, and flat, bordering the Gulf of Mexico. It covers nearly 46,000 acres. But unless you view it from an airplane or an observation tower you have no sense of its size. Brush and scrub grow higher than your head, and to climb its greatest elevation—a sand dune—would put you only four or five feet above sea level.

The place isn't pretty or scenic. It is all mud flats and brush and ponds. It is the only really big piece of the Valley which remains more or less in its natural state. And it's a refuge in more than the usual sense. Not only is it a place where the birds aren't shot or the animals trapped; outside its boundaries, in the endless brown fields full of row crops, they couldn't live at all.

Big numbers are characteristic of Laguna Atascosa. Thirty thousand geese in winter. Eighty percent of the continent's population of redhead ducks, making "rafts" in the Laguna Madre or sunning themselves on the mud flats.[2] The continent's Central Flyway narrows down like a funnel by this point, and Laguna Atascosa sits squarely upon it. As a result, more different species of birds have been spotted on this refuge than on any other in the nation.

At the same time, rarity is another specialty. Thirty-two threatened birds and animals are hanging on to American citizenship at Laguna Atascosa. (Some of them are doing better in Mexico.) The bald eagle and the peregrine falcon, both nearly extinct, turn up at Laguna Atascosa in winter. The green jay, a Mexican bird, can be seen there, but also lives in the Valley towns. And two pretty little wildcats, the jaguarundi and the ocelot, find Laguna Atascosa and the Santa Ana refuge the only good habitat left in the Valley.

It sounds ideal, but there are problems. Flood control and irrigation have withdrawn a lot of water from the refuge. In many years a number of the ponds are dry, and the grain crops, specially planted for migrating waterfowl, fail. Much of the water that does run into Laguna Atascosa is contaminated with agribusiness chemicals which kill both plants and animals.

When the Southwest belonged to Spain, the two big northern towns were San Antonio and Santa Fé. The Rio Grande Plain was part of a nearly empty Mexican province called Nuevo Santander. In 1749 the King of Spain sent a military man named José de Escandón from central Mexico, to establish settlements along the Rio Grande and govern the province. He was thorough, and most of the twenty-three towns he founded are still there. Laredo is one and Dolores another. On the Mexican side is a whole string of them—Mier, Reynosa, Camargo, and various villages and missions.

Most of the settlers lived on the south bank of the river but crossed over into what is now Texas to ranch and farm. Their cattle ranged out to the Nueces River.

José de Escandón was shrewd and grasping and had good connections in Spain. As governor of Nuevo Santander he grew rich, and still richer when the King granted him three million acres of land along the Rio Grande.[3]

His heirs eventually sold it. But the heirs of other big landowners didn't. There are wealthy bilingual families in south Texas today whose heritage is not recent Mexican but much older Spanish; who have been Americans since Texas joined the Union; and whose ranches and farms have been handed down through the generations since the 1750s.

In the last million years, the wind has moved sand by the cubic mile from the Gulf onto mainland Texas. Before Padre Island existed, currents piled sand up on the shores of Kenedy County and the wind blew it inland, coated with salt. Sand now covers Kenedy and Brooks Counties, and parts of several neighboring counties, to a depth of sixty feet.

In places the wind builds dunes. In others it carries all the sand away, making hollows called blowouts. But sand weathers into topsoil as inevitably as granite does, and the sand counties grow grass and prickly pear and the irrepressible mesquite. About fourteen large ranches occupy Kenedy County and almost nothing else. There is one town, Sarita, and a county population of 678, about two human beings per square mile.

The sand counties make an ecological barrier. Pecan trees and fox squirrels, among other things, lived north of the sand, along the Nueces River. But they were unable to get across the sand barrier, to the hospitable Rio Grande, without man's help. Once transplanted, they flourished.

South of the sand is flat, rich Willacy County, the only county in Texas with no flowing streams. Irrigation ditches, yes—Willacy County, or most of it, is part of the Valley and grows oranges and cotton. But no rivers, not even creeks. Such rain as falls—twenty-six inches a year—sinks into the porous, sandy soil. The residents seem to get along very well without streams, and so did I, for one day. Until it was pointed out to me, I didn't even notice that there weren't any. Then I missed them badly.

Salt water lies under the coastal counties. The sand blown inland was covered with salt. And so a few intensely salty lakes can be found, miles inland from the Gulf.

These lakes are actually strong solutions of brine, far saltier than the sea. Yet some fish and some plants live in them. La Sal del Rey (the King's Salt), a shallow lake of a few dozen acres, was once the property of the King of Spain and supplied salt to the people and cattle of a good part of northern Mexico. Its bottom was covered from shore to shore with salt deposits whose thickness was measured in feet. A visitor noted that no matter how much salt was removed one day, more had crystallized to replace it the next. That was in 1885. La Sal del Rey was still being mined commercially in the 1940s. Now its bottom is no longer a reef of salt crystals. But its shores are rimmed with white, and the cows and horses which graze around it go somewhere else to drink.

The Rio Grande Plain, somewhat unexpectedly, has the best spring wildflower displays in Texas. This comes not from abundance but from the mingling of bright colors—pink, blue, yellow, wine, white, and red all mixed together, making patchwork patterns that you wish you could roll up and take home. Spring spreads a vivid carpet in South Texas, on any bit of land that isn't brush.

But most of it *is* brush. Brush is a tangle of plants, most of them thorny: mesquite, catclaw acacia, huisache, granjeno, retama, black chaparral, prickly pear, yucca, rat-tail cactus, vines, grass.[4] The mixture varies according to place and may include many other plants. Brush grows in clumps up to twenty feet high, so thick and tangled that men and livestock can't get through. Only birds and small animals can.

Luckily, brush almost never covers the land in a solid mass. There are open glades and passages where grass grows and cattle can graze. Walking through them is like wandering in a maze; you can get hopelessly lost in brush in five minutes, and be unable to find your way out to the sound of trucks on a nearby highway.

Before the white man came, the Rio Grande Plain was grassland. But overgrazing thinned and killed the grass and gave the brush a chance, and in a generation or two it took over.

People find it hard to believe that this thick, thorny growth could have spread over millions of acres of grass in just a few decades, but men saw it happen in their own lifetimes.

A few years ago this was a vast rolling prairie, with no growth but a scattering of mesquite trees and isolated groves of live oak. The chaparral has now possessed every foot. . . . It is ruining our country for cattle. We cannot now see our cattle for 20 feet where we could formerly see them for miles.

—Nathaniel Taylor, *Two Thousand Miles in Texas on Horseback*, 1877

And researchers, checking old documents, found that early explorers on the Rio Grande Plain saw prairies and wooded stream bottoms but no brush.[5] The various plants which now form the brush were present, but in small numbers. Only after the grass was overgrazed by cattle did the brush spread and thicken.

For wild animals and hunters, brush is not all bad. The biggest deer in Texas grow in it, since deer are browsing animals—eaters of twigs and leaves in preference to grass—and brush has plenty of both. It also offers unlimited places to hide, and deer like that.

A fourth of all the plants that make up brush are legumes, members of the pea family which bear their seeds in pods. Not just vines, but bushes and trees—mimosas, acacias, mesquites, locusts, and paloverdes are all legumes. Their seeds feed birds and animals. Small creatures live nimbly among the thorns, unscratched and safe from predators.

There are also fruits and berries. Javelina, wild turkey, quail, coyotes, doves, rattlesnakes, rabbits, roadrunners, lizards, butterflies, turtles, mice—all live well in the brush. It is not the grim, barren stuff it seems to tourists on the highways, but a lively community. The wind blows through it with a pleasant sound. A great many birds sing. Leaves shimmer, but the yuccas and the big masses of prickly pear—some as high as a man on horseback—are rigid and still.

Prickly pear is the favorite food of javelinas, the piglike animals also known as collared peccaries. This makes the brush their best Texas habitat. Once they were heavily hunted for their hides, which make good leather. Now they are classed as game and protected. Ranchers welcome them as destroyers of cactus, and in fact were cactus is plentiful the javelinas eat so much of the juicy stuff that they seldom need a drink of water.

Because of their long, sharp tusks, and their rooting, heads-down, piglike behavior, javelinas are feared as ill-tempered and vicious. People who like to shoot them encourage this fiction, pointing out that dogs fighting javelinas usually end up dead or maimed. It is the dogs, however, who pick the fights.

Left alone, javelinas are harmless to other animals and good for the land they live on. Even a big javelina weighs only about fifty pounds. Besides prickly pear, they eat mesquite beans, sotol, acorns, and insects.

They travel in little herds of six or eight over a small home range, apparently interested in nothing but their young and getting plenty to eat. I have watched them from fifteen feet away, and the snuffling, rooting adult animals and squealing piglets seemed unaware that I was there. They did, however, work their way slowly out of sight into the brush.

Unlike javelinas, roadrunners appeal to everybody, though not everybody calls them roadrunners. Chaparral and paisano are two other names, and there are several more in Spanish.

Roadrunners probably don't think of themselves as comical, but to us they are. Scuttling across the road in front of a car, with their long necks stretched out and their long legs a blur of motion, they behave more like animated-cartoon characters than any other animal. They can fly across a ditch with a few wing-beats and a glide, and they can flutter up into a tree, and that's about the limit of their travel by air. What the roadrunner does best is run. Men in cars have clocked them at fifteen miles an hour, which would make roadrunners four-minute milers if they could hold this pace for a mile. And for all I know, they can.

People who shoot roadrunners say they eat songbirds and baby chickens. But biologists, opening roadrunners' stomachs, find mostly snails, worms, bees, spiders, crickets, grasshoppers, mice, lizards, tarantulas, and scorpions, occasionally a baby rabbit or a small snake, and almost never a sign of a bird.

A roadrunner will sometimes walk about for hours with the tail of a snake dangling from its mouth while the head is in its stomach being digested. It can't swallow the whole snake, so it feeds it in slowly, as room becomes available.

Rural people in Mexico and on the Rio Grande Plain sometimes keep pet roadrunners, hatching the eggs under domestic hens. The birds tame easily, live with the chickens, and are better than cats at killing rats and mice.[6]

They kill rattlesnakes too. Many people don't believe this, but hundreds have seen roadrunners do it. Their technique is to dart in and back, in and back, pecking each time at the top of the rattlesnake's head. When a few strong blows have opened his skull, he dies. The snake strikes at the roadrunner too, of course, but the bird spreads its wings and offers a wide target that is mostly feathers. And it can dodge too, for roadrunners move fast.

Tender, juicy grasshoppers are what roadrunners feed their young. The eggs hatch in the order in which they were laid, over a long period. When the parents are off the nest hunting food, a half-grown chick may be warming the eggs which are to become its younger brothers and sisters.

The system must work since roadrunners are steadily extending their range. They are adaptable, and almost any habitat contains the foods they like. They live throughout Texas and far beyond. But southern Texas and northern Mexico are their Old Country—the place where the roadrunner tribe began and where it is still most numerous.

For ranchers, brush is a disaster. Land that is 60 percent brush is only 40 percent grass or less, for the roots of the brushy plants extend under the grass and steal water and nutrients from it. Thousands of springs and hundreds of little streams have gone dry since the brush took over.

It is hard to work cattle in the brush. It is hard even to find them. "Brush-popping," as practiced by the cowboys, was riding through the open passages in the brush at full speed in pursuit of cows, ducking overhead limbs and being raked by thorns. Leather chaps, called "leggins" in south Texas, protected the riders' legs. They also wore gloves with high cuffs, long-sleeved jackets, and sombreros held on by thongs. Even in this armor, brush-popping was dangerous. Some cowboys brought in from the open prairie country never learned to do it.

The Rio Grande Plain turned to brush, but it went on being ranch country. It had started out that way, and it was unfit for anything else. Ranchers lived with the brush because they had to, and even grew rather proud of it.

In the 1930s, people began trying to clear brushland. They kept experimenting, and the techniques progressed from chaining, chopping, and

burning, to poisoning.[7] The currently preferred method is a costly procedure called root plowing, which means that a large machine goes over
the land, gouging deep into the soil and pulling brush out roots and
all—even full-grown trees. The debris is then bulldozed into piles and
burned.

Root-plowed land looks as if it had been bombed. But the machine
scatters grass seed behind it on the ripped-up earth, and if rain falls, the
landowner soon has a fresh green pasture. The problem is keeping it that
way. For the soil also contains millions of seeds and root fragments from
the brushy plants that were pulled out of it, and they sprout year after
year.

Reinfestation begins almost at once, with flimsy little mesquite seedlings and prickly pears consisting of just a pad or two. In many cases land
expensively cleared by root plowing has returned to brush again in seven
or eight years.

Still the fight against it grows bigger every year, and so do the ma-
chines that do the work. It is now common for several square miles of
land to be stripped of brush in one operation, which means stripped of its
wildlife too. Most of the animals that live in brush are unable to survive
on a prairie. So it seems that the Rio Grande Plain, whose ecology
changed drastically after 1850, may be going through another change
now.

The battle will continue for the next several decades. No one really
knows whether the brush or the root plows will win. Some men of the
Soil Conservation Service claim that there is now more brush than ever,
after forty years of efforts to get rid of it. Some biologists, on the other
hand, say that the whole ecological structure of the brush country, its
interlocked systems of plants and animals, will soon come crashing down.

Along the Rio Grande, all the way up to the Big Bend, an amusing
animal called the coatamundi lives in the brush or woods. Many Texans
don't know it exists. It is kin to raccoons and ringtails, but unlike them
prefers daylight. Its major range is the forests of Mexico and Central
America.

A full-grown coatamundi weighs eight or nine pounds. Half of its total
length is tail—a long furry stalk, faintly ringed, used in balancing. The
animal's coat is yellowish-brown. Its face is a mask, with white eye-rings
and a long white muzzle.

Coatis are almost as acrobatic as monkeys and spend a lot of their time
in trees. They travel in packs, in constant, silent, investigative movement.
In zoos they are cheerful and lively if they have the company of other
coatamundis, running tirelessly up and down dead tree trunks. In the
wild, searching for food, they seem more serious, less playful.

Captured young, they make mischievous and amusing pets. Vaqueros on the lonely ranches of Coahuila like to tame coatamundis. The one pack I ever came across on the Rio Grande let me get very near while they nosed among dead leaves. Then they raced into some bushes. Their long tails, sticking up above the bushes like buggy-whip antennae, gave their location away. But they kept going until even their tails disappeared.

The mesquite is a curse and a burden, and the Rio Grande Plain produces more of it, ton for ton, than oil, cattle, vegetables, or anything else.

Mesquite thorns can puncture the tires of a pickup truck. This seems like the final, intolerable insult to the rancher, who regards the mesquite as a punishment from on high. And that's exactly what it is. It did not become a pest until overgrazing brought on its disastrous spread.

If you crowd twenty cows into a three-acre pasture, they will eat all the grass and leave the ground bare. That's an extreme example of overgrazing. What has happened on the Texas grasslands is slower and more subtle. It is likely to involve just a few too many cows on each *square mile* of land. The damage is slight each year, and is spread over thousands of acres so that it accumulates slowly, unnoticed, over a lifetime or two.

The results of overgrazing are numerous and complicated and all bad. Cattle eat the tastiest and most nourishing grasses first, and on overstocked land will eat them to the ground and kill them. Then the less desirable grasses, which the cows passed over, will spread into the space once occupied by the better ones.

In dry years, on overgrazed land, bare patches of ground appear like worn places in a carpet. One of the functions of grass is to hold the world together—its roots bind the soil, its leaves break the impact of raindrops. Bare ground is easily eroded. The topsoil blows or washes away, and the land's ability to grow anything at all is lessened.

Grassland, if left alone, tends to remain grassland because trees can't get a start in the thick sod. The network of roots will not let a mesquite seed, for example, sink deep enough even to reach the soil. But Texas was overgrazed for so long that the Rio Grande Plain is brush country and much of the Edwards Plateau is scrub.

Ranchers know what overgrazing is and what it does. Yet many of them, perhaps a majority, still run too many cattle. They do it for various reasons. The chief one is that, for a few years at least, overgrazing works. The cattle thrive, while the land gradually loses its vitality. The pasture which supports fifty cows this year may support only forty-five ten years from now, and so on until it becomes little better than desert.

"But the grass is there," the rancher says. "It's a sin to waste it." Or there may be a drought. The rancher doesn't want to sell his cattle at a loss, so he keeps them on his land, gambling on rain. But it doesn't rain, and meanwhile the cows eat the grass so far down that it can't recover. The rain, when it comes, merely washes the soil away.

There are ways of getting good production out of ranchland without exhausting it, even allowing some of it to recover. These usually involve giving each piece of land an occasional rest from grazing—in the spring one year, in the summer the next, etc., so that in a four-year period the grass can carry on each season's processes unmolested.

It's also helpful to put cows, sheep, and goats together in one pasture. Cattle graze, goats browse, and sheep eat mostly forbs—that is, broad-leaved plants that are neither grass nor shrub. The right mixture of animals will eat a little of everything yet not enough of anything to do permanent damage. To earn the same amount of money with cows alone, the rancher would have to overgraze.

It all makes sense, but a rancher may balk because these procedures require additional fencing. Or he may hate goats or sheep. Or he may say, "Just let me get right with the bank, and then I'll try it." Millions of dollars have been made in the last hundred years by overgrazing. They are small change compared with the tens of millions that brush, erosion, root plowing, and diminished yields have cost.

Brush is interesting at close range. Some of it is even interesting through a magnifying glass. But merely driving across brush country is boring, and many counties of the Rio Grande Plain are just a patchwork of brush in various stages, landscapes marked only by fences and by deer blinds that look like privies set up on stilts.

The three brush counties along the Balcones Escarpment are more varied. One of them, Uvalde County, seems to me to have more character than any other county in Texas. Four good rivers—the Nueces, Leona, Frio, and Sabinal—gurgle down through their canyons in Uvalde County and out across the Rio Grande Plain. A component of the brush there is a thorny shrub called guajillo. Its white flowers yield Uvalde honey, commonly and seriously described as the best in the world.

Some groves of "lost" maple trees grow in the Sabinal canyon, a long way from their relatives in the East Texas woods. They are on private land and their autumn colors coincide with the deer season, so they are not heavily visited.

Garner State Park, on the clear, cold Frio River, has been elaborately developed for recreation and is overused. It is pleasant in winter, though, when the Frio is too cold to attract swimmers.

The town of Uvalde is heavily influenced by Mexico, and the older parts of it are good to look at. On the streets around the John Garner Museum (he was a Uvalde lawyer who became Vice-President of the United States in 1933), the big, brooding live-oak trees have assumed remarkable forms, like dancers stopped in some infinitely dignified dance. They seem sentient beings, in mysterious communication with each other. They are different from any other live oaks that I know.

A long way down the Nueces from Uvalde, in the blend-zone where the Rio Grande Plain fades into the coastal prairie, the Welder Wildlife Refuge sits quietly behind locked gates. The refuge is private but it can be visited—by appointment, on Thursdays at 2:55 P.M. Then the gates are unlocked for five minutes and the public is courteously let in. You'll see a lot of brush and cactus and live-oak mottes if you go, and some native birds and animals. Nothing spectacular. In fact, there's nothing wrong with not going at all. The fewer visitors a wildlife refuge has, the better refuge it is. Perhaps more important than visiting it is just to know and be glad that it's there.

The place covers 7,800 acres, a small part of a very big ranch that was set aside and is amply supported by oil royalties. It was created by the will of Robert H. Welder, a rancher and hunter who saw nature take a beating in Texas throughout his lifetime and decided to help out a little.

The Welder Refuge has laboratories for biology and photography, a small museum, offices, and living quarters for graduate students who do research there. Then there is all that living space afforded to animals that would be shot and plants that would be poisoned outside its boundaries. And though it hasn't done so thus far (it opened in 1961), the Welder Wildlife Refuge may yet inspire another super-rich Texan or two to make similar gestures of respect and thanks to the land that gave them their wealth.

It may also offer a clue to the future of brush. Aerial photographs taken from 1939 to 1960 show that brush increased steadily in those years all over the refuge. Yet throughout that period, a "vigorous brush-control program" was going on.[8] A less vigorous program, aimed at certain species in certain areas, has continued up to the present, and the brush still spreads.

The Rio Grande Plain slopes down very gently and disappears into the Gulf of Mexico. Then, a few miles offshore, along the whole ocean length of the plain, the barrier of Padre Island rises out of the water.

It once had a better name: La Isla Blanca, the White Island. Or sometimes the White Islands, because early explorers, sailing by, saw only the tops of the highest dunes and thought it an island chain.

The island *is* white, being nothing but sand and shell, and the Gulf clouds and most of its birds are white too. It was once owned by a

Matamoros priest, Padre Nicholas Balli, whose family received it as a grant from the King of Spain. When Mexico won independence from Spain in 1821, Father Nicholas was involved in some notable lawsuits over his title to the island. This led people to call it the Padre's island, and though it hasn't been his for more than a hundred years it's called approximately that still.

It runs unbroken for 113 miles, never more than two miles wide, from Corpus Christi to Port Isabel. In that whole distance no river of any size flows into the Gulf from the Texas mainland. If one did, its current would cut Padre Island in two.

Hurricanes have cut channels across the island, but the Gulf soon brings sand to fill them. The only present channel is the Mansfield Cut, opposite the mainland town of Port Mansfield. It was dredged out for shrimp boats and smaller craft, and has to be redredged regularly.

In essentials Padre is the same from end to end. On the Gulf side is a broad beach, crusted with shells. Then come the dunes, in places fifty feet high. They grow smaller inland, then there are low areas covered with grass, then mud flats, and finally the Laguna Madre, rarely more than six feet deep, separating the island from the mainland. Here and there in low places are freshwater ponds, replenished by rain.

The mood of Padre in its unspoiled stretches is of wildness and emptiness, of a primordial land incessantly beaten by the wind and sea. Everything is in motion—waves, birds, grasses, sand. When the wind is strong enough, plumes of sand like the snow plume from the top of Mount Everest trail westward from the biggest dunes. In places the shoreline has shifted westward 1,500 feet in the last hundred years. Before that no surveys were made or records kept.

About forty miles down from the northern end of Padre are Big Shell and Little Shell. These are deposits of small, clean shells which extend along the beach for miles. They were probably put there by an ocean current called the Devil's Elbow, which comes in from the Gulf at this point and then bends out to sea again. The Devil's Elbow also deposits mahogany logs, beans, whole trees, man-made rubbish from the Caribbean countries, and junk from ships.

Ships are rarely stranded off Padre nowadays. Their navigating devices are too good. The last really satisfactory shipwreck was that of the *Nicaragua*, a six-hundred-ton Mexican steamer that went aground one October night in 1912. Its rusting ruins, now about gone, lie a few miles north of the Mansfield Cut, still being beaten by the waves.

The older shipwrecks—those of Spanish galleons and pirate ships—yield treasure. Some very big finds have been made on Padre Island, or just offshore, but they take specialists, much equipment, and years of work. There are small treasures too, though, and the search for them has kept many men hopeful and happy.

Among them is Bill Mahan, who published a book about Padre Island in 1965. It contains this blunted, poetic line:

Of the ones who go to Padre, not all will find.[9]

But Mr. Mahan has found, many times. He says that the commonest treasure given up by the island is a single old coin buried in the sand; that the best surface clues to an ancient shipwreck are pieces of beeswax (which sailors used for waxing thread) and small lead plates (which covered ships' bottoms to discourage barnacles). Where the wind has uncovered these you may find treasure. And he adds that it is well to sleep in a floored tent, zipped shut to keep sand crabs from trying to pinch off the tenderest bits of your flesh for food.

The old sailing ships carried chickens, pigs, and horses, and these got shipwrecked on Padre too. Burros, especially, took to wild living on the island and thrived. They found good grass, and until man came there were no predators.

The burros' main problem was the lack of rocks to wear their hooves down; in the sand they grew long and splayed. The burros walked somewhat like cripples. Otherwise life on Padre was apparently ideal, and burros grew numerous. But as the nearby mainland was settled, people took to shooting them as a pastime, much as they shoot at bottles and cans, and Padre Island burros became extinct.

The island's vegetation is sparse and simple. It includes beach croton, morning glory, sea oats, sea purslane, dodder, and many grasses. Among the bright wildflowers are red gaillardia and the big yellow primroses called buttercups which quiver in the wind all along the Texas coast. Wild cranberries grow in the marshes near the Laguna Madre. There were once scattered groves of live oaks, some dwarfed, some normal. But the oaks are dying out rapidly.

Inland from the dunes are the grass flats and ponds which have made cattle ranching possible on the island. It began in the days of Father Nicholas and is still going on.

All the problems of mainland ranching, plus some peculiar to Padre Island, have plagued the ranchers here. In years when the fresh-water ponds went dry, the cattle stood for hours each day in the Gulf, absorbing water through their hides to keep alive. Instinct told them not to drink it. Their hides filtered the salt out of the water so that it didn't kill them. In the days of the open range, they say, the toughest and most self-reliant of all longhorns were those raised on Padre Island.

Car campers on the island usually bring drinking water with them. Backpackers can dig two or three feet in the sand, well above sea level, and find fresh water. (It needs purifying, though.) It is there because a mass of fresh water, held in sand, will "float" on the denser salt water beneath—somewhat as a block of wood floats, with part of the mass above sea level.

When the wind is high, and it often is, the hiker's choice is to camp on the beach and be wet with spray, or camp in the dunes where blowing sand gets into eyes, ears, sleeping bags, and food. Bacon and eggs crunchy with sand are not good. It is wise to take at least some foods that can be eaten fast from their containers, with no cooking.

Sand fills the air up to ten feet above the ground. If you let go of a map, a handkerchief, or a piece of toilet paper, it soars away over the dunes. But there are also intervals of calm—days of pure sunlight and a smiling sea, when the waves are mere wavelets and every grain of sand stays in place.

Fishing is good either in the Gulf or the Laguna Madre. The lagoon, about five miles wide and six feet deep, has shallows and mud flats where ducks feed in the winter by the tens of thousands. The Intracoastal Waterway runs through it from end to end, and the lagoon is dotted with small islands where shorebirds nest and raise their young.

Several of the islands are bird sanctuaries, watched over by the Audubon Society. When the water is low enough, coyotes wade out to the islands to stuff themselves with birds' eggs. Sometimes they get all the way across, to Padre Island.

Wild mustangs were once numerous on Padre. Wild hogs, armadillos, opossums, pocket gophers, and kangaroo rats have lived there, and some of these species still do. There are horned toads, rattlesnakes, and lizards. If a hurricane wipes out snakes or mice from one stretch of the island, the survivors in another part eventually repopulate the empty section.

The southern end of Padre is almost due south of the northern end. In between, the island curves like a hunting bow aimed west, following a similar curve in the mainland coastline. Both ends of Padre have motels, restaurants, and housing developments. The center section, about eighty miles of it, is the Padre Island National Seashore. Here, in the immensity of dunes and grass flats, on the beach that disappears into infinity in both directions, a sense of openness remains. The beach is a highway for balloon-tired vehicles. But if you move away from it, into the dunes or grasslands, the world is empty and belongs to you.

Sunrise on Matagorda Island south of Port O'Connor.
(The Gulf Coast)

RIGHT: Barrier island dunes advancing into coastal bluestem and flowers on Mustang Island east of Corpus Christi. (The Gulf Coast)

Live oaks on Dagger Point, Aransas National Wildlife Refuge. (The Gulf Coast)

Padre Island seashore south of Corpus Christi
near Malachite Beach. (The Gulf Coast)

A coquina shell beach on Padre Island south
of Corpus Christi. (The Gulf Coast)

Saltwort on mudflats north of Rockport. (The Gulf Coast)

LEFT: Salt grass and a brackish pond on Matagorda Island
south of Port O'Connor. (The Gulf Coast)

RIGHT: Anacahuita and wild grasses northwest of Rio Grande City.
(The Rio Grande Plain)

A fresh-water marsh in the Aransas National Wildlife Refuge.
(The Gulf Coast)

Cactus and mesquite brush south of Falcon.
(The Rio Grande Plain)

Ebony seed pods and leaves by the Rio Grande
north of Salineno. (The Rio Grande Plain)

Ceniza sage flowering at Paisano north of Liveoak County.
(The Rio Grande Plain)

Spanish moss in the Santa Ana National Wildlife Refuge.
(The Rio Grande Plain)

Retama and thorn bushes east of Zapata. (The Rio Grande Plain)

Some boulders in the Rio Grande southeast of Fronton. (The Rio Grande Plain)

CONCLUSION: "NO DEPOSIT, NO RETURN"

The notion that the state of Texas is poor is not widespread, but it is true: we are poor compared with the wealth that might have been ours if we hadn't plundered the land.

Subtract the cubic miles of topsoil that have slid into the Gulf. Subtract Galveston Bay, once two hundred square miles of gamebirds and seafood, now a smelly half-dead sea of sewage and oil. Subtract all the damage that mesquite and cedar have done—occupying millions of acres, sucking up fertility and water that might have grown something useful. Subtract the huge, easy harvests of unpolluted oysters and shrimp we used to get all along the coast. Subtract the astronomical cost of root-plowing brush in the Rio Grande Plain. Subtract, each year, the tens of thousands of head of additional cattle that our grasslands would have supported if we hadn't overgrazed them. Subtract all the hundreds of springs and small streams that have gone dry as the water table dropped, and subtract all the life that those streams supported. Subtract whatever value there was a century ago in the fact that almost every creek in Texas was good to drink; now none is. And so on.

Much of our wealth, the showiest part of it, is one-shot wealth—oil, gas, coal, and other minerals which make a few people rich and are gone—well, maybe not forever but for quite a while, a few million years, until nature in her deliberate way gets around to putting them back.

Don't dip into capital! That has been the businessman's first commandment since capitalism began. But we Texans have not just dipped into our natural capital, we have squandered it—forests, grass, water, soil, oil. Not only is Texas poor compared with what might have been, it is getting poorer all the time—being used up, worn out.

Laws of nature can't be broken without consequences. The Law of Gravity lets us know at once that defiance is useless. Unfortunately the punishment for other efforts to transgress is not so immediate. Mistreated land wears out gradually, unnoticed, the way clock hands move, the way men grow old. And because we don't see it happening, we let it happen.

To us, poor shabby Texas still looks pretty good, chiefly because we

[241]

The Rio Grande below the Falcon Dam.
(The Rio Grande Plain)

can see that a lot of profit is still there, and still being squeezed out. But read any of the books written by travelers in Texas in the 1840s and '50s and you'll find them almost ecstatic over the depth of the grass, the abundance of flowers and birds, the swarms of game. Matched against what it was in those days, Texas is now halfway to the barrenness of the moon.

Granted, we could not have kept it just as it was in those days. The state can't hold eleven million people and remain wilderness. The black bears and the jaguars and lots of virgin land had to go. But it didn't *all* have to go. Life would be more interesting if, somewhere along the Rio Grande, we'd kept a wilderness area with jaguars in it; if, a few miles west of Fort Worth, a piece of the Cross Timbers still had black bears eating wild dewberries and grapes. Certain animals that we actually do put up with in our cities—thirty million rats—are quite a bit more destructive, even of human life, than the occasional big cat or bear would be, straying into town.

We Texans are rigorously proud of the Dallas Cowboys, the Alamo, the Astrodome. And we believe we are proud of Texas itself, but our feeling seems to be for the word, the idea, not for the actual dirt. That piece of earth where your beer can lands *is* Texas. The Houston frog, Capote Falls, the Big Thicket, the spring at San Marcos—these are more deeply of this country than the Alamo and ought to be cherished accordingly.

"No Deposit, No Return," says the bottle, and this bland masking of the facts helps us to consume with peace of mind. An honest statement would go something like this: You have to buy this bottle from us, but we won't buy it back from you; your only choice is to add it to the national trash pile.

Various other slogans and attitudes, if we continue to accept them unquestioningly, will lead us right up to the edge of the abyss. El Paso, a city, and the Staked Plain, a region, will soon face a water crunch. El Paso may well wither into history's biggest ghost town. Many ranchers on the Edwards Plateau are kept from bankruptcy only by royalties from wells of natural gas. When the gas is gone from below and the remaining grass from above, the Edwards Plateau will be a burnt-out case.

"No Deposit, No Return" can have another meaning. It's the one the French peasant has in mind when he hauls cartloads of manure, steaming on December mornings, from his barnyard to his fields. It's this: You have to respect the land you live on, you have to deal with it intelligently and give it what it needs, or it will play out on you. In that sense, "No Deposit, No Return" is not a slogan for a bottle, it's the handwriting on the wall.

CHAPTER NOTES

1 | THE TRANS-PECOS

1. William L. Bray, *Distribution and Adaptation of the Vegetation of Texas* (Austin: The University of Texas, 1906).
2. Ellen Quillin, *Texas Cacti: A Popular and Scientific Account* (San Antonio: Texas Academy of Science, 1930).
3. W. Hubert Earle, *Cacti of the Southwest*. Desert Botanical Garden of Arizona, Science Bulletin No. 4 (1970).
4. The Texas Society of Professional Engineers, *Water, A Plain Statement* (Austin, 1954).
5. Ross A. Maxwell, *The Big Bend of the Rio Grande* (Austin: The University of Texas, 1968).
6. Walter B. McDougall and Omer E. Sperry, *Plants of Big Bend National Park* (Washington: The National Park Service, 1951).
7. David Riskind, "A Vegetation Survey of the Lower Canyons of the Rio Grande." A report prepared for the Texas Parks & Wildlife Department (1973).
8. A description of the natural bathtub given in 1901 still fits it exactly. See Robert T. Hill, "Running the Canyons of the Rio Grande," *The Century Magazine*, Vol. 61 (1901).
9. William H. Echols, *Camel Expedition Through the Big Bend Country*. A Senate Document of the 36th Congress (October, 1860).

2 | THE EDWARDS PLATEAU

1. William Bray, *Vegetation of the Sotol Country in Texas* (Austin: The University of Texas, 1905).
2. W. W. Newcomb, Jr., *The Rock Art of Texas Indians*. Paintings by Forrest Kirkland (Austin: The University of Texas Press, 1967).
3. William Edward Dunn, "The Apache Mission on the San Sabá River," *Southwestern Historical Quarterly*, Vol. 17 (April, 1914).
4. Walter P. Taylor, "Food Habits and Notes on Life History of the Ring-Tailed Cat in Texas," *Journal of Mammalology*, Vol. 35, No. 1 (February, 1954).
5. James G. Teer, *Texas Deer Herd Management: Problems and Principles*. Texas Parks & Wildlife Department, Bulletin No. 44.
6. William Bray, *The Timber of the Edwards Plateau*. U.S. Department of Agriculture. Bureau of Forestry Bulletin No. 49 (Washington: Government Printing Office, 1904).
7. Fritz Arnold Toepperwein, *Charcoal and Charcoal Burners* (Boerne, Texas: The Highland Press, 1950).
8. Walter J. Cartwright, "The Cedar Chopper," *Southwestern Historical Quarterly*, Vol. 70 (October, 1966).

9. U.S. Army Corps of Engineers, "Survey Report on the Edwards Underground Reservoir," (Fort Worth, 1964).
10. Ernest L. Lundelius, Jr., and Bob H. Slaughter, *Natural History of Texas Caves* (Dallas: The Gulf Natural History Co., 1971).
11. "A City Bat Roost," *The Literary Digest* (April 17, 1915).
12. *The Caves of Texas.* Bulletin 10 of the National Speleological Society (April 1948).

3 | THE LLANO UPLIFT

1. William A. Matthews, III, *The Geologic Story of Longhorn Cavern* (Austin: Bureau of Economic Geology, The University of Texas, n.d.).
2. J. W. Thomas, R. M. Robinson, and R. G. Marburger, *Studies in Hypogonadism in White-Tailed Deer.* Technical Series No. 5, Texas Parks & Wildlife Department (Austin, 1970).
3. Eula Whitehouse, "The Ecology of Enchanted Rock." An unpublished thesis submitted at the University of Texas (1931).

4 | THE STAKED PLAIN

1. E. H. Sellards, W. S. Adkins, and F. B. Plummer, *The Geology of Texas,* Vol. I (Austin: The University of Texas, 1966).
2. Arthur G. Day, *Coronado's Quest: The Discovery of the Southwestern States* (Berkeley and Los Angeles: The University of California Press, 1940).
3. Josiah Gregg, *Commerce of the Prairies* (Norman: University of Oklahoma Press, 1954).
4. Fred Rathjen, "The Physiography of the Texas Panhandle," *Southwestern Historical Quarterly,* Vol. 64 (January, 1961).
5. J. Evetts Haley, *The XIT Ranch of Texas* (Norman: University of Oklahoma Press, 1954).
6. Cordia Sloan Duke and Joe B. Frantz, *6,000 Miles of Fence* (Austin: The University of Texas Press, 1961).
7. William A. Matthews, III, *The Geologic Story of Palo Duro Canyon* (Austin: Bureau of Economic Geology, University of Texas, n.d.)
8. J. Evetts Haley, *Charles Goodnight, Cowman and Plainsman* (Norman: University of Oklahoma Press, 1949).
9. Vernon Bailey, *Biological Survey of Texas* (Washington: U.S. Government Printing Office, 1905).
10. David F. Costello, *World of the Porcupine* (Philadelphia and New York: J. B. Lippincott, 1966).

5 | THE PRAIRIES AND CROSS TIMBERS

1. Wayne Gard, *The Chisholm Trail* (Norman: University of Olkahoma Press, 1954).
2. D. E. McArthur, "The Cattle Industry of Texas," an unpublished manuscript quoted by Walter Prescott Webb in *The Great Plains* (New York: Grosset & Dunlap, 1957).
3. Randolph B. Marcy, *Thirty Years of Army Life on the Border* (New York: Harper & Brothers, 1874).
4. Tom McHugh, *Time of the Buffalo* (New York: Knopf, 1972).
5. Francis Haines, *The Buffalo* (New York: T. Y. Crowell, 1970).
6. Carolyn Thomas Foreman, *The Cross Timbers* (Muskogee, Okla., 1947).

7. Randolph B. Marcy, *Thirty Years of Army Life on the Border* (New York: Harper & Brothers, 1874).

8. E. R. Kalmbach, *The Armadillo: Its Relation to Agriculture and Game* (Austin: Texas Game, Fish, and Oyster Commission in Coöperation with the U.S. Fish & Wildlife Service, 1943).

9. J. K. Greer, *Grand Prairie* (Dallas: Tardy Publishing Co., 1935).

10. Robert T. Hill, *Geography and Geology of the Black and Grand Prairies.* U.S. Geological Survey Annual Report, 1899–1900 (Washington: U.S. Government Printing Office, 1901).

11. O. B. Collins and David H. Riskind, "The Blackland Prairie of Texas—Community Types and Conservation Needs." An unpublished report prepared for the Texas Parks & Wildlife Department (n.d.).

12. Wann Langston, Jr., *The Onion Creek Mososaur.* Museum Notes No. 10, The Texas Memorial Museum (Austin, n.d.).

13. Agnes Chase, *First Book of Grasses* (San Antonio: W. A. Silveus, 1937).

14. H. L. Bentley, *Cattle Ranges of the Southwest.* U.S. Department of Agriculture, Farmers' Bulletin No. 72 (Washington, 1898).

6 | THE EAST TEXAS FORESTS

1. W. W. Newcomb, Jr., *The Indians of Texas* (Austin: The University of Texas Press, 1961).

2. Pete A. Gunther, *The Big Thicket, A Challenge for Conservation* (Austin: Jenkins Publishing Co., 1972).

3. William Bray, *Distribution and Adaptation of the Vegetation of Texas* (Austin: The University of Texas, 1906).

4. H. B. Parks and V. L. Cory, *The Fauna and Flora of the Big Thicket Area* (College Station, Texas: Texas Agricultural Experiment Station, 1938).

5. C. A. McLeod, *The Big Thicket of East Texas* (Huntsville, Texas: Sam Houston Press, 1967).

6. Ilo Hiller, "Caddo Lake State Scenic Park," *Texas Parks & Wildlife Magazine* (March, 1973).

7. Carl G. Hartman, *Possums* (Austin: The University of Texas Press, 1952).

8. Eula Whitehouse, "Annual Phlox Species," *The American Midland Naturalist*, Vol. 34, No. 2 (September, 1945).

9. Ross A. Maxwell, *Geologic and Historic Guide to the State Parks of Texas* (Austin: Bureau of Economic Geology, The University of Texas, n.d.).

7 | THE GULF COAST

1. *The Handbook of Texas*, Vol. 1 (Austin: The Texas State Historical Association, 1952).

2. W. W. Newcomb, Jr., *The Indians of Texas* (Austin: The University of Texas Press, 1961).

3. Bureau of Sport Fisheries and Wildlife, *Whooping Cranes* (Washington: U.S. Department of the Interior, n.d.).

4. Bureau of Sport Fisheries and Wildlife, *Whooping Cranes: The Captive Flock* (Washington: U.S. Department of the Interior, n.d.).

5. Glynn A. Riley and Roy T. McBride, *A Survey of the Red Wolf (Canis Rufus)* (Washington: U.S. Department of the Interior, Bureau of Sport Fisheries and Wildlife, 1972).

6. Wilfred T. Neill, *The Last of the Ruling Reptiles* (New York: Columbia University Press, 1971).

7. A special paperback volume is sold locally along the coast: James A. Lane, *A Birder's Guide to the Texas Coast.*

8. William Beebee, *Galapagos, World's End* (New York and London: G. P. Putnam's Sons, 1924).

9. Henry John Oosting, *The Study of Plant Communities* (San Francisco: W. H. Freeman, 1948).

10. *Tree Regions of Texas.* Circular 75 of the Texas Forest Service (College Station, Texas: Texas A. & M. University, n.d.).

11. Paul S. Galtsoff, *Gulf of Mexico: Origin, Waters, and Marine Life.* Bulletin 89 of the U.S. Fish and Wildlife Service (Washington, 1954).

12. *Food and Game Fishes of the Texas Coast.* Texas Parks & Wildlife Department, Bulletin 33, Series IV (Austin, n.d.).

8 | THE RIO GRANDE PLAIN

1. J. Frank Dobie, "The First Cattle in Texas and the Southwest, Progenitors of the Texas Longhorns," *Southwestern Historical Quarterly*, Vol. 42, No. 3 (January, 1939).

2. Bureau of Sport Fisheries and Wildlife, *Laguna Atascosa National Wildlife Refuge: Master Plan* (Washington: U.S. Department of the Interior, n.d.).

3. Lawrence F. Hill, *José de Escandón and the Founding of Nuevo Santander* (Columbus: Ohio State University Press, 1926).

4. J. Frank Dobie, *A Vaquero of the Brush Country* (Dallas: The Southwest Press, 1929).

5. Jack M. Inglis, *A History of Vegetation on the Rio Grande Plain.* Texas Parks & Wildlife Department, Bulletin 45 (Austin, n.d.).

6. J. Frank Dobie, *The Roadrunner in Fact and Folklore* (Austin: The Texas Folklore Society, 1939).

7. Howard B. Passey, *Grassland Restoration, Part IV: Grassland Management* (Temple, Texas: U.S. Department of Agriculture, Soil Conservation Service, 1966).

8. Thadis W. Box, *Plant Communities of the Welder Wildlife Refuge.* Contribution No. 5, Series B, Welder Wildlife Foundation (Sinton, Texas, 1966).

9. William Mahan, *Padre Island, Treasure Kingdom of the World* (Waco: The Texian Press, 1965).

A LIST OF BOOKS AND MAPS

For less than forty dollars you can assemble a good collection of field guides and hand-books on the natural phenomena of Texas. A few dollars more will buy good maps. People accustomed only to the kind you get free in gas stations are often delighted to find how beautiful and satisfying skillfully made maps are, and how they can tell in a flash what pages of prose cannot. Finally, there are a few books that every Texan, as a matter of self-respect ought to own and to read more than once. I have listed below some items in all of these groups.

BIRDS. Texas has its own bird book, *A Field Guide to the Birds of Texas,* by Roger Tory Peterson. Mr. Peterson is a famous ornithologist, a former director of the National Audubon Society. The Texas Parks and Wildlife Department asked him to produce the book, and the state's most skilled observers of birds helped him. The result is first-rate. A larger, more beautiful, and far more expensive book is *The Bird Life of Texas,* by Harry C. Oberholser, edited by Edgar B. Kincaid, Jr., and published in two big volumes by the University of Texas Press. Its paintings by Louis Agassiz Fuertes are splendid but not numerous—540 species of birds, 36 paintings of them. Full notes, careful distribution maps, many personal observations and anecdotes.

MAMMALS. William B. Davis's *The Mammals of Texas,* a paperback publication of the Texas Parks and Wildlife Department, is homely, inexpensive, thorough, accurate, and use-ful. Comparing a few of its entries with the corresponding ones in a standard field guide to North American mammals, I find that Mr. Davis comes off best, largely, of course, because he deals only with Texas mammals and has more space and some personal observations to give each one. Photographs, crude-looking distribution maps. The book is available at some state parks and some offices of the Soil Conservation Service, or at the Texas Parks and Wildlife Department in Austin.

WILDFLOWERS. The perfect wildflower book—comprehensive, handsomely illustrated in color—would cost too much and weigh too much, and thus fail of perfection on those counts. No illustrated book has all Texas flowers in it. Your best bet is to examine all the wildflower books in a big library, and go out and buy copies of those you like best. You might consider *Roadside Flowers of Texas,* published by the University of Texas Press, which has good paintings by Mary M. Wills and a good text by Howard S. Irwin. Or *Texas Flowers in Natural Colors* by Eula Whitehouse. Miss Whitehouse's notes are loving and authoritative, but alas! she was no painter.

TREES. A good, inexpensive paperback is *Forest Trees of Texas,* which is Bulletin 20 of the Texas Forest Service, a part of Texas A. & M. University. It is illustrated by small, clear black-and-white drawings which contain exactly the details you need in identification. Its drawback is that only about 140 species are included.

Far more comprehensive and far more costly is *Trees, Shrubs, and Woody Vines of the Southwest,* by Robert A. Vines, a publication of the University of Texas Press. Its drawings are excellent. Its text, stiffly repeating a formula from page to page, reads in places like a computer printout. For Mr. Vines, the Southwest includes East Texas; all of the Piney Woods pines, hollies, etc., are included.

GEOLOGY. Texas geology is such a vast and technical subject that there is no book about it for amateurs, and there may never be one. *The Geology of Texas,* by Sellards, Adkins, and Plummer, is a thousand-page paperback bulletin of the University of Texas at Austin. It is a reference book; only those with a course or two in geology and a passionate interest in the subject are likely to find it useful. The more casual reader can find books about a single region—the Staked Plains, the Cross Timbers, etc. They are of varying quality.

MAPS. The one I like best to travel with is the *Geological Highway Map of Texas,* compiled by Philip Oetking and published by the Dallas Geological Society. In bold colors it sets off the various geological systems, so that you can see the exact extent of the Callahan Divide or the Llana Uplift, know almost to the foot where your highway leaves one physiographic region and enters another. This is true for everything inland from the Balcones Escarpment; the Coastal Plain's geology does not automatically provide these distinctions. The back and margins of the map are filled with material that amounts to an introduction to geology.

The *General Soil Map of Texas,* published by Texas A. & M. University, is big and bright but highly technical. The language of soil science (scores of words like fluvaquent, haplaquoll) is not attractive to laymen. But in the corners of the huge sheet are two small maps of Texas which show *all* the physiographic regions, including those of the Coastal Plain, and the countries they cover.

The Texas Highway Department publishes road maps of every county in the state, all but a few on large individual sheets. They show every creek and gully and individual farmhouse, and contain more information about road surfaces and bridge types than anyone but an engineer could possibly want. But it is fun and sometimes useful to study one of these maps of any county that especially interest you.

The Texas coastline in considerable detail, with scores of tiny islands in the lagoons and bays, is given on a single map (or chart, probably, since water occupies more space on it than land does), U.S. Coast and Geodetic Survey No. 1117. Far more detailed charts (of Corpus Christi Bay, for example) are also available for sections of the entire coast.

If any book about Texas is a classic, it's *Goodbye to a River* by John Graves, a calm, humorous, reflective account of the author's last canoe trip, before the dams went in, down a part of the Brazos he had loved all his life. We have all crossed the Brazos on various Highway Department bridges without giving the river a glance or a thought. Those who have read *Goodbye to a River* no longer do that. We look over the railing hoping to glimpse a little something of what John Graves found down there. But from highway bridges it can't be seen.

The Great Plains, by Walter Prescott Webb. A few chapters of this book (copyright 1931) are as out-of-date as cars of that year. The rest are as good as new. Mr. Webb plods along, flat-footed, prosaic, intelligent, and thorough, dealing with Indian sign language, wild horses, windmills, Plains plants and animals, the development of the six-shooter, and barbed-wire fencing. His chapter on the Cattle Kingdom makes the book worth buying.

Adventures with a Texas Naturalist, by Roy Bedichek. Mr. Bedichek's leisurely, loving, well-read way of observing the world is a good one to imitate, or try to. And he is dismayingly well-informed. Try comparing your knowledge of the golden eagle, or the Davis Mountains, or cliff swallows, with his. His other book, *Karankaway Country,* is equally good.

The Mustangs, by J. Frank Dobie. Also *The Longhorns, Rattlesnakes,* and *The Voice of the Coyote,* to name works that deal primarily with animals. Mr. Dobie's subjects are nature, ranching, folklore, and Texas history, and he tends to mix them all together in every book. It is always a pleasant mixture.

INDEX